The Structure of Spinoza's World

The Structure of Spinoza's World

EMANUELE COSTA

OXFORD
UNIVERSITY PRESS

Oxford University Press is a department of the University of Oxford.
It furthers the University's objective of excellence in research, scholarship,
and education by publishing worldwide. Oxford is a registered trade mark of
Oxford University Press in the UK and in certain other countries.

Published in the United States of America by Oxford University Press
198 Madison Avenue, New York, NY 10016, United States of America.

© Oxford University Press 2025

All rights reserved. No part of this publication may be reproduced, stored in a retrieval system, transmitted, used for text and data mining, or used for training artificial intelligence, in any form or by any means, without the prior permission in writing of Oxford University Press, or as expressly permitted by law, by license or under terms agreed with the appropriate reprographics rights organization. Inquiries concerning reproduction outside the scope of the above should be sent to the Rights Department, Oxford University Press, at the address above.

You must not circulate this work in any other form
and you must impose this same condition on any acquirer

CIP data is on file at the Library of Congress

ISBN 9780197758069

DOI: 10.1093/9780197758090.001.0001

Printed by Integrated Books International, United States of America

Contents

Introduction	1
I.1 What's in a World?	1
I.2 Metaphysical Monism and Interpretative Pluralism	6
I.3 Structures and Relations	10
I.4 A Summary of the Chapters	13

1. **The Bare Bones of the World: Causation, Limitation, Inherence, Conception** — 17
   1.1 Method and Methodology — 17
   1.2 A Metaphysical Ride — 19
   1.3 Immanent Causation, Panentheism, and Limitation — 26
   1.4 From Pluralist Structure to Causal Independence — 33
   1.5 From Causal Independence to *Causa Sui* — 40
   1.6 A Structure of One: Monism — 46
   1.7 *Naturare* — 53

2. **The Winding Paths of Substance: Expression, Involvement, and Aspectual Distinction** — 61
   2.1 Ontological Expression — 61
   2.2 Expressionism and Explanation — 66
   2.3 The Attributal Deadlock — 72
   2.4 Aspects, Distinctions, and the Realm of *Quatenus* — 79
   2.5 Enter Finitude — 93
   2.6 Attributes at Work (Spinoza's Parallelism) — 99
   2.7 White Modes — 104
   2.8 The Decalogue of Expression — 108

3. **Unfolding Time: Eternity, Duration, and the Essences of Things** — 113
   3.1 Time as a Construct — 113
   3.2 Modal Time — 116
   3.3 The Aspects of Essences — 121

3.4	The Onto-Temporal Grid	130
3.5	An Essence in Time	139
3.6	The Fleeting Laws of Time	145

4. **To Build a World: Individuals, Composition, and the Universe as a Whole** — 149
  - 4.1 Questioning Individuality — 149
  - 4.2 Knowing Individuality — 153
  - 4.3 The Definition of Individuality — 156
  - 4.4 Shifting Structures — 164
  - 4.5 The Face of the Whole Universe — 171
  - 4.6 The Puzzles of Infinite Individuals — 177

5. **The Human Point of View: Action, Passion, Striving, Affects** — 185
  - 5.1 Reducing Action — 187
  - 5.2 God as *Agens* and *Patiens* — 191
  - 5.3 Striving for Action — 197
  - 5.4 The Con-Struction of Affects — 203
  - 5.5 Acting Freely — 209
  - 5.6 The Eternal Bento — 214

Acknowledgments — 221
Bibliography — 223
Index of Terms — 233
Index of References — 237

Introduction

I.1 What's in a World?

The title of this book is a provocation. In fact, it is a double provocation.

First, it opens with the word "structure." In the scholarly studies surrounding Spinoza's philosophy, few notions are more overlooked than the concept of structure. In the last twenty years, a relatively short span considering the centuries that separate today's scholars from Spinoza, there has been an intense flourishing of studies on the concept of relation in Spinoza's thought—and even more, of *specific* relations such as conception, causation, expression, and inherence. However, these studies present a built-in bias. In fact, studies such as these analyze relations making use of a traditional approach. They assume the existence of entities (*relata*) that are intertwined and connected through relations as a second-order predicate. The approach I intend to flesh out in this book is radically opposite. It takes relations as the primary object of interest in Spinoza's metaphysics, and it constructs the *relata*, the objects or entities of Spinoza's ontology, as resulting from these relations. Due to linguistic and theoretical biases, however, it is rather difficult to conceive of relations independently from their *relata*. For this reason, in this study I shall prefer the use of the term *structure*. Intuitively, it is easier for us to represent a structure existing independently of the bolts, joints, and phenomena that make its existence available to our experience.

An alternative name for this concept would be *network*. A net exists priorly, and (in a way) independently from the knots that

The Structure of Spinoza's World. Emanuele Costa, Oxford University Press.
© Oxford University Press 2025. DOI: 10.1093/9780197758090.003.0001

realize its purpose—namely, to capture anything that has a certain size and shape, the object of the catch predetermined by the structure of the net (i.e., the distance between its threads). Far from applying uniquely to Spinoza's philosophy, this approach participates in the global philosophical shift away from so-called objectual or object-oriented ontology. Several authors and contemporary researchers, belonging to the analytic school as well as the continental, have urged the world of philosophy to take seriously the ontology of relations and structures. Their aim is to elaborate a paradigm capable of capturing their depth without reducing them to second-order properties.[1]

The second provocation contained in the title of this book is the term "world." Understanding what Spinoza could mean with such a term is a complicated assignment, one that has puzzled scholars for centuries.[2] Idealists (especially German and British idealists, but contemporary scholars too) have interpreted Spinoza's world to be identifiable with Spinoza's God in a biunivocal fashion. God—*Natura naturans*—is everything that exists, and common-sense objects (chairs, calculators, apricots, cats, and human beings) are manifestations or expressions of this unitary God. Thus, the "world" is reducible to *Natura naturans* and its expressions. By contrast, materialist interpreters have argued that modes—Spinoza's term for common-sense objects—are primarily real, and that the *sum* of all such existing objects constitutes the existence of the one substance. In other words, those interpreters argue that Spinoza's world constitutes Spinoza's God. Once again, we find here a biunivocal correspondence between God and the world, although the priority order is reversed. The striking similarities between these two opposite approaches should not surprise us, especially once we consider that the most emblematic formula of Spinoza's philosophy suggests just such biunivocal identification: *Deus, sive Natura* (God, that is to say, Nature).

---

[1] I discuss this at greater length in Section I.3 of this introduction.
[2] An interesting uptake of this question is discussed in Melamed, "Spinoza, Tschirnhaus et Leibniz: Qu'est un monde?," 85–95.

However, as several scholars have already noted, this simplistic reduction of Spinoza's differentiation between God (source of all being) and Nature betrays the spirit and the letter of Spinoza's metaphysics. As I shall demonstrate, Spinoza clearly distinguishes between Nature intended as the active God (*Natura naturans*) and a parallel Nature, structurally linked to the former, which encompasses the passivity of finite beings (*Natura naturata*). The two "natures" exist at once, albeit in radically different "time" paradigms. In fact, while *Natura naturans* exists in the realm of eternity, the objects constituting *Natura naturata* exhaust their life cycle in the realm of duration. An entire chapter of this book shall be dedicated to making proper sense of this distinction—one of the most crucial junctions of Spinoza's philosophy. Therefore, the extension of the term "world," as I will intend it, explores the structural link between these two aspects of Spinoza's Nature, which gives rise to the universe as we know it.

What is the utility of this approach? Why do we need a structuralist, or relational, approach to Spinoza's metaphysics? The question is a fair one. Considering the plethora of accurate and comprehensive reconstructions of Spinoza's metaphysical thought that the scholarly community has produced in recent years, the need for yet another study aimed at such reconstruction might seem excessively theoretical. Yet, as I have already shown in these brief lines, by describing the opposition between materialistic and idealistic interpretation of Spinoza, the temptation of overreading Spinoza is almost endemic. These two main tendencies show an attraction toward a certain post-Cartesian (or perhaps Hobbesian) view of extension as the main feature of being; or—and here comes the idealistic strand—a Leibnizian and Hegelian reading of Spinoza as a philosopher of thought, primarily concerned with the connection between epistemic and ontological properties of being. Both these approaches certainly have their merits, and they have immensely enriched the scholarly discussion surrounding Spinoza. However, my argumentation in this volume aims at restituting

Spinoza to his unique status in the history of Western philosophy as the true "savage anomaly" in the Early Modern *continuum*.

Spinoza's uncompromising philosophy of being is the boldest attempt in the Early Modern era to create a system capable of capturing the full depths of *both* extension and thought, finitude and infinity, time and eternity. The aim of this book is therefore to maintain such equidistance, avoiding the twin pitfalls of idealism and materialism, and to remark Spinoza's theoretical distance from his contemporaries.

Aside from these important historical goals, there is ulterior and pressing motive for us to reconsider Spinoza's metaphysics of structure. Contemporary philosophers are currently expressing the need for metaphysical accounts capable of going beyond the boundaries set by traditional metaphysics of objects. That is to say, we are observing and recognizing the necessity of metaphysical frameworks endowed with the ability of surveying the deep structure of reality, beyond its ephemeral and epiphenomenal appearance through "objects" and "things." This metaphysical necessity is becoming apparent in research outputs produced by the most diverse programs. Such programs include the "ontic structural realist" school—which advocates for the apparently scandalous slogan that "every *thing* must go," in favor of a more direct approach to the structure highlighted by contemporary quantum physics; Kris McDaniel's "Theory of Ordinary Physical Objects," which focuses on the importance of nonmonadic tropes for our understanding of objects as mereological bundles; and the "new materialist" current, which recognizes the emergence of objects as the biased byproduct of the human gaze observing underlying structures of power and action.

In this volume, I show how Spinoza's rigorous and fearless metaphysical approach can—and should—help us to make sense of these focal shifts, challenging our presuppositions regarding the framework of "reality" and ultimately advocating a more radical approach. This final metaphysical step shall aim at uncovering the hidden structure of the world, which is logically and metaphysically prior to the entities that we commonly capture through talk of "objects."

The fact that Spinoza's metaphysics is inescapably drawn to structures, or relations, is evident even in the reading of one of the sharpest and most obstinate defenders of the primacy of substance operating in the contemporary landscape, Michael Della Rocca. In the course of an argument aimed at delegitimizing the independence (and perhaps the very existence) of relations, Della Rocca claims that for Spinoza, modes are by their very nature dependent on another (we will see in detail what a mode is, and how this dependence works, in Chapter 1). Yet, Della Rocca affirms, "this relation of dependence is not a mere logical consequence of the mode's essence or nature; it is partially constitutive of that nature."[3] This is a telling hint. Even when disparaged, relations find a way to steal the limelight and occupy center stage in Spinoza's metaphysics. Every attempt to begin from the objective reality of substance and modes—"objects"—ends up calling on explanatory relations to fulfil the role of sufficient reasons. However, their usual secondary role prevents them from absolving this task fully, leaving too many questions unanswered.

My work in this book represents an attempt to turn the tables on such approaches. I privilege the structure and relations at work in Spinoza's ontology over the objects and *entia* (beings) that exist within it.[4] However, I happily recognize that this interpretative stance is not entirely new, although it has not been fully fleshed out in the literature regarding Spinoza's metaphysics. One way to describe this debate is by opposing what is (perhaps idiosyncratically) named "relational ontology" to a more common "ontology of relations." In the latter, the analysis of relations "forms part of

---

[3] Della Rocca, *The Parmenidean Ascent*, 66.
[4] The internal distinction between structures and relations will become clear in Section I.3 of this introduction.

a more general ontology that determines in advance the nature of the specific ontology of relations."[5] Against this stance, several philosophers (many of which openly inspired by Spinoza's philosophy) have begun to develop a genuinely "relational ontology," which sees relationality as an original and nonderivative presence in metaphysics.[6] In other words, relational ontology develops when the "traditional hierarchy of substance and relation is inverted"; only once this crucial step is taken, we might begin to focus primarily on relations and to create the structured space that allows us to insert objects in a more organic scheme.[7]

However, it is my firm conviction that the adoption of relational ontology as an interpretative lens when studying Spinoza is not a mere ideological stance. As I demonstrate below, utilizing this framework to read Spinoza's metaphysics provides a genuine interpretative gain, clarifying some of his most perplexing texts and uncovering some of the hidden tenets that guide the developments of his thought. The prejudice that pushes us to prefer objects to structures might be a feature of the imagination, after all.

I.2 Metaphysical Monism and Interpretative Pluralism

Spinoza's metaphysics is perhaps the most organized, parsimonious, and organic metaphysical system produced in the Early Modern period. Increasingly, Anglo-American scholarship is recognizing how this complex system is based on a few basilar principles, which function as foundations for a plethora of metaphysical corollaries and deductions.[8] While this interpretative attitude

---

[5] Durie, "Immanence and Difference: Toward a Relational Ontology," 161.
[6] Benjamin, *Towards a Relational Ontology*, 2; see also Gasché, *Of Minimal Things*, 105–108.
[7] Morfino, "Spinoza: An Ontology of Relation?," 110.
[8] Recent examples include but are not limited to: Della Rocca's *Representation and the Mind-Body Problem*, his own *Spinoza*, Nadler's *Spinoza's Ethics*, Melamed's *Spinoza's*

is certainly justified by Spinoza's own interest toward a schematic presentation of his metaphysics, some attempts aimed at reducing *all* of his metaphysics to the *lowest* number of principles do not entirely do justice to the richness and diversity that Spinoza's thought is capable of capturing. In this volume, I will advocate for an interpretative approach that recognizes the existence of *several* metaphysical keystones within Spinoza's thought.

In short, I shall argue against an approach that we may define "interpretative reductionism," seeking to reduce Spinoza's metaphysics to just one, just two, or just *the fewest* principles. Instead, I shall defend the thesis that Spinoza's philosophy presents a plurality of metaphysical principles, which are rationally irreducible. In other words, my approach is captured by the following "slogan": Spinoza's substantial monism must be defended through interpretative *pluralism*.

There are two reasons for this pluralism: one is historical and the other is interpretative. First—and foremost, since this work aims to reconstruct Spinoza's metaphysical structure in its own right—interpretative pluralism is motivated by the absence of an explicit attempt, on Spinoza's part, to reduce metaphysics to *the lowest possible number* of principles. There is, of course, a general attitude against the unwarranted multiplication of beings in Spinoza's philosophy—motivated by his metaphysical *naturalism* (i.e., the belief that every existing being is subject to the same rules or laws of nature). Nonetheless, we would search in vain through Spinoza's works for an explicit statement claiming that laws of nature can and must be reduced to the simplest (and fewest) principles. Spinoza is indeed a naturalist and a rationalist (i.e., he believes in the Principle of Sufficient Reason [PSR], according to which everything—including laws—must have a cause that suffices

---

Metaphysics, Lin's *Being and Reason* (and their respective investigations into the PSR), Schneider's "Spinoza's PSR as a Principle of Clear and Distinct Representation," and Newlands' *Reconceiving Spinoza*.

to explain their existence). Yet, everything that can be defended through the PSR, no matter how numerous it may be, has citizenship in Spinoza's philosophy. Ontological parsimony—if we may so call the identity of distinct attributes in one and the same substance and the identity of distinct modes across attributes—does not apply to structures and in particular to dependence relations.[9] In other words, Spinoza is not a reductionist. As I will show in this book, the reductionist tendency of Spinoza's philosophy is, in large part, an interpretative fiction, created by Anglo-American scholars during the last century.

The second reason is an interpretative one. By providing a reconstruction of Spinoza's metaphysics that takes relations as the starting point, I show how it is possible to avoid interpretative pitfalls and overcorrections. The classic flowchart of Spinoza's metaphysics—comprising substance, attributes, infinite modes, and finite modes—can be redrawn, avoiding the Hegelian accusation of having "merely established [beings] in this way as conceptions."[10] As Hegel suggests, the most productive way of reconstructing Spinoza's metaphysics entails a "deduction" of the above categories from the relations that produce them.

To be clear, this book does not constitute an attempt at "hegelizing" Spinoza. Such anachronistic and "backwards" interpretations fall far from their mark insofar as they project an entirely alien spirit into the work of a previous philosopher. Spinoza's metaphysical deduction is not motivated by the flow of substance in terms of self-negation and self-reconciliation, as we can ascertain not just from his published works but also from his ample correspondence. Instead, as I will argue in the coming chapters, Spinoza maintains a naturalistic attitude toward ontology, positioning himself as a student of Nature, and reconstructing the a priori necessary paths that being must follow in the deployment of its essence

[9] Cf. Newlands, *Reconceiving Spinoza*, 16–18.
[10] Hegel, *Lectures on the History of Philosophy*, 3:260.

and existence. Forever consistent with his skeptical attitude toward miracles, Spinoza finds it absurd that God, the one substance, would go against the laws of nature. For the same reason, only partially aligning with coeval rationalists such as Descartes and Malebranche, Spinoza thinks that God's power—which is identical to his will—is bound not just by laws of logics but also by laws of nature. Yet, faithful to a metaphysical tenet that has been described as the "Principle of Plenitude," Spinoza argues that God is expressed through all the possible (i.e., noncontradictory) channels.[11] Conversely, the impossible channels are just that—impossible.

Thus, the *Ethics* can be read as a metaphysical journey exploring the outlands between necessary and impossible. The present book represents an attempt to reconstruct this journey and the paths that lead Spinoza onto his exploration. Once again, however, let me remind the reader that the number of these paths is greater than one: there is not one way to follow Spinoza's footsteps. For this reason, the present book aspires to provide a tool that can be useful in a multiplicity of ways. The reader will be able to follow what I consider the main route of the unfolding of Spinoza's premises, starting with canonical structures such as causation, conception, and inherence; and continuing with expression, eternity, and affect. However, I urge the reader who disagrees with me on the "proper order of philosophizing" (to use a Spinozian *dictum*) to pick her own favored order. The book will be structured in modular chapters, so that each one only moderately relies on the previous ones. The winding paths of Spinoza's metaphysics will eventually converge, but it is far from my intentions to dogmatically select a starting point beyond what is indicated to us by Spinoza's own geometrical method and writing style.

---

[11] Newlands, *Reconceiving Spinoza*, 18–28. Cf. also Lovejoy, *The Great Chain of Being*, 144–182.

I.3 Structures and Relations

In his juvenile works, such as the *Cogitata Metaphysica* (*CM*) and the *Treatise on the Emendation of the Intellect* (*TIE*), Spinoza expresses very stern judgments regarding relations. In these works, relations are often mentioned as *entia rationis* (beings of reason) in a context that bears a clearly disparaging tone.[12] For this reason, excellent commentators have usually disregarded talk of relations from the ontological point of view, deeming them unfit for the metaphysical standard set by the substance and its modes. A recent study by Zach Gartenberg rightly points out that relations, for the young Spinoza at least, appear as "purely heuristic representations that govern the mind's comprehension of empirical reality."[13] Spinoza's relations might even turn out to be Kantian pure forms, inescapable yet merely projected unto the world.

This approach is entirely legitimate. After all, Spinoza clearly affirms that "except for substances and modes, there is nothing" (E1p15d). This is also the golden standard of knowledge for Spinoza, since any "actual intellect, whether finite or infinite, must comprehend God's attributes and God's affections, and nothing else" (E1p30). Therefore, little if any space is left for relations to ontologically subsist on their own, and Spinoza is bound by his apparent commitment to considering relations—such as Socrates is *taller than* Plato—just mere beings of reason. Thus, we are tempted to assume, Spinoza aligns with Leibniz in wanting to eliminate all sorts of "extrinsic denominations," which would identify a given being through its exogenous predicates. Predicates that do not pertain to the nature or essence of a given thing cannot be contained

---

[12] However, it must be noted that in these works, Spinoza mostly refers to logical and linguistic relations such as negation (cf. *CM* I, 1 | G I/234/28; *Letter 19* | G IV/92/20); time, measure, number, etc. (see Chapter 3). Alternatively, he uses this language to refer to "appreciative," perspectival notions such as good and evil. The few occasions on which he explicitly refers to what I call "structure" in terms of *entia rationis* shall be thoroughly analyzed in the pertinent chapters.

[13] Gartenberg, "Spinoza on Relations," 182.

in that thing's proper definition. By contrast, predicates that are attributed to a given thing in virtue of its relationship with another subject must be reduced to the essential (and monadic) properties of the thing, just as Leibniz intended.

Yet, this approach is also dangerous. Spinoza's inescapable use of structural notions in each of his definitions (especially the core ones, one might say) is just as clear as his apparent rejection of relations from the ontological horizon of being. I shall expand on this point in each of the chapters of this book, illustrating how Spinoza refers to relational concepts every time he defines one of the key elements of his metaphysics. For now, it will suffice to refer the reader to Spinoza's core definitions of substance (which "is in itself and must be conceived through itself"), attribute (that which "the intellect conceives as constituting an essence of the substance"), and mode (that which "is in another through which it must also be conceived"). As it is plain to see, Spinoza from the very beginning introduces structural notions such as causation, inherence, conception, and constitution as the raw materials necessary for the construction of the most important elements of his ontology. If, as Spinoza maintains, a definition includes only the concepts that are involved in the essence of the *definiendum*, then it is hard to explain how relations are to be excluded from such essence.

The solution that I am proposing in this book is to renounce this issue altogether. Instead of focusing on the establishment of the ontological status of relations a priori, I offer the reader a functional alternative. I will discuss relations *in themselves*, without assuming their ontological status, and describe how they are instrumental to the construction and connection of every other metaphysical element of Spinoza's world. For this reason, as we have seen in Section I.1 of this introduction, the present work must be understood as an attempt at a genuine relational ontology, which considers relations as the "first word" in philosophy. Thus, I will strive to eliminate as much as possible the term "relation" from what follows—I shall prefer the term "structure," which does *not* include second-order predicates such as *taller than x, shorter than y, further from z*. To be sure, this kind of predicate is *not* what I have in mind when I refer to structure.

Moreover, this attitude toward relational ontology is not to be understood as birthed exclusively by analytical philosophy or by an analytical approach to the history of philosophy (whatever relevance we should assign to such labels). In fact, one of my main inspirations toward the substitution of relational notions with structural notions is a champion of the continental reading of Spinoza, Louis Althusser. In his *Reading Capital*, Althusser describes a species of causation, which he dubs "structural," as that in which "the effects are not outside the structure, are not a pre-existing object, element or space in which the structure arrives to *imprint its mark*: on the contrary, it implies that the structure is immanent in its effects."[14] As Owen Hulatt has already pointed out in his wonderful study, this reading is extremely helpful in interpreting Spinoza.[15] Althusser's structural causation implies a feedback mechanism capable of altering the whole structure with each instantiation of causation, which perfectly aligns with Spinoza's intentions regarding *Natura naturata*, as I will show in Chapter 4. "In order to comprehend the production of effect B," says Althusser, "it is not enough to consider cause A (immediately preceding, or visibly related with effect B) in an isolated manner, but cause A instead as an element of a structure in which it assumes a place, therefore as subject to relations, specific structural relations, that define the structure in question."[16] The blueprint designed for causation here, I believe, can be applied throughout Spinoza's metaphysics. It represents a most helpful tool to conceptualize the role and ontological status of Spinoza's structural notions. However, Althusser's approach is somewhat limited insofar as it takes a materialist stance

---

[14] Althusser, *Reading Capital*, 186. Emphasis in the original.
[15] Hulatt, "Structural Causality in Spinoza's *Ethics*."
[16] Althusser, "On Genesis," 2.

as inescapable when interpreting Spinoza. Althusser assumes (as a true son of Marx) a grounding priority of the causal over the conceptual. By contrast, I will argue that this reductionism to causation—whether motivated by analytical worries of parsimony or by a Marxism-inspired materialist structuralism—is simply extraneous to Spinoza's intentions.

I will thus reject reductionism; in the interest of historical accuracy, however, I will not defend an unregulated proliferation of structures. While Spinoza *is* a pluralist in terms of what types of relations must be included in the metaphysical structure of the world, he is still fairly parsimonious in this regard. The number of structures included in this ontological picture is relatively small, and it encompasses a group ranging around ten categories (pardon the Aristotelian temptation): causation, inherence, limitation, conception, expression, aspectual distinction, eternity, duration, action, and passion. Of course, this list suffers from the same defect as most lists: it is not completely exhaustive, and at the same time it may be too inclusive.[17] Yet, it remains a useful roadmap to keep us on the right track while examining the structure of Spinoza's world.

I.4 A Summary of the Chapters

It is arguably impossible to achieve a complete reconstruction of Spinoza's extensive, multifaceted metaphysics in a single book-length study. It is even harder to attempt to reach an account comprehensive of his whole philosophy. However, studying Spinoza's thought through the lens of the structuralist interpretation I suggest will allow us to survey most of the metaphysical themes of his

---

[17] For example, one could want to reduce passion to negative action or both to perspectival outlooks on causation. I am partially sympathetic to such attempts, which I will indulge in Chapter 5.

work and to plunge deeply in some of the most interesting ethical and epistemological issues directly deriving from them.

In the first chapter, I will analyze what I describe as "the first order" of metaphysical structure in Spinoza's philosophy, comprising the most fundamental relations that ground the world of substance and modes. These relations include causation, inherence, and conception (the triad that is quickly becoming a "canonical" description of Spinoza's metaphysics, thanks to Della Rocca and several other experts, including Yitzhak Melamed and Samuel Newlands). However, for reasons that will be clear by the end of Chapter 1, I shall describe limitation as an equally fundamental structure, which grounds the very ontological difference responsible for the distinction of modes from the substance.

In Chapter 2, I will expand my description of Spinoza's metaphysics by introducing two more relations, which are of capital importance toward the understanding of Spinoza's philosophy: expression and aspectual distinction. These two relations walk the thin line between metaphysics and epistemology, generating the diversified universe that we experience.

Chapter 3 is dedicated to a delicate but all-important progression, which allows Spinoza to build a genuinely omnipotent metaphysical system, capable of comprehending the infinite multitude of beings that populate his world. The relations on which this system hinges are the differentiation of eternity and duration, which frame Spinoza's deep engagement with modal notions (despite their natural understanding as "temporal" structures).

Chapter 4 will take on the apparently paradoxical challenge of reimagining individuality on the basis of structural notions. Once we take away the delusions and imaginative idols of object-first ontology, we find ourselves in need of a profound refurbishing of our concept of item, individual, or *id*. To this end, I undertake an analysis of Spinoza's wonderfully complex mereology. As I will argue, he provides only a derivative notion of individuals. Instead, he privileges metaphysical structures such as composition, wholehood, and parthood, which he takes to be the most primitive and foundational elements in the ontology of modes.

Finally, in Chapter 5, I will attempt the ambitious feat of putting all the above relations to work. I will abandon the "pure" world of ontology to delve into more "embodied" branches of Spinoza's philosophy such as psychology and anthropology. I shall use my interpretative lens to suggest a more refined image of action and passion, the key structural network in Spinoza's philosophy of finite beings. This network is cashed out by Spinoza in a multiplicity of ways—I shall focus mainly on the affective structure deriving from it, which is specific to an epistemological (and arguably rationalistic) attempt to describe the complete set of beings that exist and have cognition of the world. This attempt peaks, according to Spinoza, in the attainment of the third kind of knowledge, which shall be the final theme explored in this book. The third kind of knowledge is not just an epistemic goal but also an affective transformation, as testified by its alternative descriptions as "intellectual love of God" and "beatitude." Thus, the epistemological peak of cognition coincides with a knowledge of the structures that cause, ground, and allow for the conception of beings, individuated as finite or infinite, eternal or durational, extended or thinking, active or passive. All these ontological features, for Spinoza, derive from a fundamental order that is rationally accessible but that cannot be understood through an objectual lens. Instead, as I will conclude, the pathway to universal knowledge is paved with structures.

1
The Bare Bones of the World
Causation, Limitation, Inherence, Conception

> *As the geometer intently seeks*
> *to square the circle, but he cannot reach,*
> *through thought on thought, the principle he needs,*
> *so I searched that strange sight: I wished to see*
> *the way in which our human effigy*
> *suited the circle and found place in it—*
> *and my own wings were far too weak for that.*[1]

1.1 Method and Methodology

Spinoza's masterpiece, the *Ethics*, is a difficult text to read and interpret. Part of this difficulty derives from the genre chosen by the author. Spinoza composed the *Ethics* in geometrical order, allegedly inspired by the clarity of Euclid's *Elements* and Descartes's *Responses* to the Second Objections. The *more geometrico* philosophical style entails setting definitions for one's key elements, declaring one's axioms and postulates, and then arguing for propositions by way of a priori demonstrations. The attractiveness of this method of inquiry and exposition is undoubtable. It presents all the appearance

---

[1] Dante Alighieri, Divina Commedia, Paradiso, Canto XXXIII. Trans. A. Mandelbaum.

of exact scientific rigor, and it shows one's philosophical reasoning in a summarized and organized manner. However, the downside of this style is its low readability. Spinoza's readers are caught in a tornado of argumentation, seemingly irrefutable, and it is easy to be swept toward agreeing with his conclusions, or to reject them in block, assuming a fundamentally defensive stance. It is much more difficult to pull apart his claims and establish the exact meaning of each term, proposition, or theory, due to the complicated structure of his arguments.

In a *more geometrico* philosophical work, the order of the claims is perhaps just as important as the arguments establishing them. Geometrical reasoning is anti-egalitarian by nature, insofar as it establishes the foundations for later arguments through the initial definitions and axioms. Therefore, I will pay close attention to the order of Spinoza's arguments, seeking to reconstruct an intellectually sound picture of his ontology. I shall thus adopt the "naïve reader" point of view recently defined by Martin Lin. He means this term as suggestive of an examination of the text from "the perspective of a reader who has no knowledge of how this material will be used by Spinoza later in the *Ethics*."[2] This approach is useful not just for expositional purposes but also because it restitutes to us a coherent picture of the way the geometrical method would *supposedly* work. The conditional is necessary, since there will be instances where Spinoza's meaning in an earlier proposition, definition, or axiom will be unintelligible without reference to later texts. For the most part, however, I will attempt to follow the "naïve" method.

In this chapter, I shall focus on three relations or structures that famously lay the foundation for Spinoza's metaphysical edifice: causation, inherence, and conception. To these three "modern-day classics" of analysis I will add a fourth, which I believe has been too hastily dismissed by recent interpreters: limitation.

---

[2] Lin, *Being and Reason*, 26.

1.2 A Metaphysical Ride

The first part of the *Ethics* is dedicated to discussing the notion of God. However, it is not God—or Nature, or substance—that serves as the initial definition of Spinoza's metaphysical journey. In fact, God does not appear until the sixth definition. Instead, it is *causa sui*, or cause of itself, the first concept that Spinoza goes on to define. It is noteworthy that in the very first page of his major metaphysical work, Spinoza does not begin by discussing his notion of substance (i.e., an object) but establishes a fundamental structure: self-causation. This fact, due to the fundamental top-down orientation of the geometrical method, suggests an interpretation of his philosophy that is less radically object-oriented and more focused on structure.[3] Spinoza's first definition reads:

> By cause of itself I understand <u>that</u> whose essence involves existence, or that whose nature cannot be conceived except as existing—*Per causa sui intelligo <u>id</u>, cujus essentia involvit existentiam, sive id, cujus natura non potest concipi, nisi existens.* (E1d1; my emphasis)

The "protagonist" of this causality, which Spinoza only mentions as "that" (*id* in the Latin), is not defined as an object.[4] Instead, it emerges through the presentation of an ontological property: the necessary entailment of existence in its essence. The foundational property of self-causation is thus identified as a two-place logical predicate (i.e., a relation: x causes y), in which the two places are occupied by the same noun. In a partially formalized language, this

---

[3] Contra this, commentators usually read Spinoza as rejecting any attempt "to ground his monistic ontology of substance" (Gartenberg, "Spinozistic Expression," 3). In this chapter, I offer reasons to take seriously an exploration of the path of structural grounding, even in the case of the one and only substance.

[4] In this volume, I will often follow Spinoza's example and adopt the term *id* as a placeholder to avoid suggesting any bias toward an object-based ontology.

definition could be presented as follows: x is cause of itself, if and only if x is caused by x by virtue of the entailment of existence in its essence. The *Ethics* opens with the definition of the structure of self-causation, explained through the reflexivity of the entailment of some *id*'s existence in its own essence.

This kind of structure might be suggestive of a model of "essential causation."[5] According to this model, x causes y (where y does not necessarily differ from x) if y's existence is entailed by x's essence. This seems to be a very bold thesis, and indeed I have my doubts that Spinoza would have argued for such a position. In fact, as I will show briefly, Spinoza's substance (the universal cause) is both essentially and existentially prior to its effects. However, if y is the effect of x, and x <u>essentially</u> causes y, then it would be fair to ask if x can exist without causing y. The answer could very well be in the negative. Thus, the very existence of x is subject to the instantiation of y. Under the model of essential causation, the cause actualizes its essence if and only if it has some effects. This conclusion, while maybe correct on Spinoza's terms, is highly counterintuitive. Common sense suggests that causes must be logically—if not temporally—prior to their effects.

What about the opposite thesis? It could be argued that x causes y if x's existence implies y's essence. There are reasons to believe that a dispositive such as this—which I would call "existential causation" —is at work in Spinoza's metaphysics. Several interpreters of the Neo-Platonist persuasion have argued for a similar thesis. After all, reading Spinoza along these lines has the privilege of safeguarding the priority of the cause while, at the same time, grounding the essence of effects in the existence of the cause. However, existential causation can hardly account for self-causation. Indeed, if x is the existential cause of y, then y cannot

---

[5] This term has been suggested by some recent scholars—most importantly, Viljanen in his *Spinoza's Geometry of Power*. However, he uses the term to cover a model of causation that I think is best described by the name "existential causation."

be instantiated prior to x. This would incur in a notorious vicious circle, according to which an *ens* (being) cannot exist prior to its essence, but its essence must be instantiated by the existence. This is the very reason that pushed Aristotelians to position the prime mover beyond all movement. Spinoza will employ a similar strategy by introducing eternity, as I will show in Chapter 3. For now, it will suffice to have dispelled the twin hypotheses of essential *and* existential causation.

Let us go back to the *Ethics*. As we have said, according to Spinoza, causation is a structure that can be reflexive. Keep in mind that Spinoza defines causation as a reflexive relation *even before* describing it as a nonreflexive, transitive relation. As we will see, the latter relation is the foundational system that ground all the finite universe. But for the latter to exist, self-causation must be defined first. In other words, while the causal structure that allows E1d1's unnamed *id* to function as transient cause of the world of finite individuals is nonreflexive, Spinoza begins the *Ethics* by focusing on immanent, reflexive causation.

The initial insistence on self-causation (and the way Spinoza defines it) provides us with the clues to partially solve the mystery. In fact, Spinoza does not just portray self-causation as the relation whereby the essence of x entails its existence. E1d1 also states that its "nature cannot be conceived except as existing." One immediate way to cash in this relation is by concluding that causation and conception are coextensive. Another option, however, is to read this sentence as affirming that the nature of x (where "nature" is a term that we can take as a synonym for essence)[6] requires x to exist. Therefore, x's essence cannot be instantiated in absence of x's existence. Conceptual priority appears to run in the opposite direction, when compared to causal priority. Again, however, we encounter the common-sense objection stating that to conceive an effect prior to its cause is an absurdity.

---

[6] Lin, *Being and Reason*, 13.

The reason why I think this should not trouble us (at least here) is the following: Spinoza does not intend the causal and conceptual models exemplified by E1d1 as universal models. He is referring to a sui generis case, the case of self-causation. This case, as we shall see in what follows, remains unique in Spinoza's metaphysics.[7] However, teasing out the refined threads that weave the texture of the definition that marks the beginning of the *Ethics* has allowed us to insinuate the doubt that conception and causation are not necessarily intertwined, and that they might not be coextensive.

Let us now proceed to discuss Spinoza's second definition, highlighting once more its structuralist tendencies. E1d2 reads:

> That thing is said to be finite in its own kind that can be limited by another of the same nature. For example, a body is called finite because we always conceive another that is greater. Thus, a thought is limited by another thought. But a body is not limited by a thought, nor a thought by a body—*Ea res dicitur in suo genere finita, quæ alia ejusdem naturæ terminari potest. Ex. gr. corpus dicitur finitum, quia aliud semper majus concipimus. Sic cogitatio alia cogitatione terminatur. At corpus non terminatur cogitatione, nec cogitatio corpore.* (E1d2)

Again, in this case we can observe how Spinoza defines one of the most fundamental notions of his ontology—the notion of "finite thing"—through a structural conception, which gives priority to dyadic properties over monadic ones from the logical point of view. For Spinoza, being finite equates to being limited. As in the first definition, a key concept of Spinoza's metaphysics is defined through a two-place predicate (a relation): x is a finite thing, insofar as x is possibly limited by y. The nature of this limitation is clearly relative to a structure, even more so when we consider Spinoza's specification: x is limited by y if and only if y belongs to the same

---

[7] Despite the objections that I challenge in Section 4.6.

kind of being—a body or a thought.[8] I will expand on this specific claim in the context of Chapter 2, where I address the structures of conception and expression in Spinoza's thought.[9] For now, I am content to highlight how E1d2 depends on the co-belonging of x and y (the limited and the limiter) to the same kind (or realm) of being. Finitude, then, is a structural property that depends on two criteria: x is a finite object if and only if x and y both belong to the same kind *and* y can possibly act on x to limit x.

Only by the time we reach the third definition of the *Ethics* we encounter what is widely considered the leading actor, Spinoza's substance. Like the two definitions above, E1d3 highlights structural properties of the *definiendum*.

> By substance I understand what is in itself and is conceived through itself, i.e., that whose concept does not require the concept of another thing, from which it must be formed—*Per substantiam intelligo id, quod in se est, et per se concipitur: hoc est id, cujus conceptus non indiget conceptu alterius rei, a quo formari debeat.* (E1d3)

As it was the case for E1d1, Spinoza leaves blank the objectual content of the definition (*id*—"that") to focus on the structural properties that allow us to identify the substance. E1d3 establishes the meaning of "substance" through a pair of reflexive relations: x is a substance if and only if x inheres in x *and* is conceived through x. An early problem in the interpretation of Spinoza's ontology is how to read the binary option offered by the text. Leibniz, for example, objected that he could not make sense of the definition. It

---

[8] Or a mode of the infinite unknown attributes. Spinoza in E1d2 has not yet made a case for the infinity of God's essence, so he clearly relies on Cartesian dualism to provide quickly cashable examples. This could also provide us with an important hint toward the intended readership of the *Ethics*, but this may be beside the point here.

[9] I will also discuss how this structure impacts on Spinoza's notions of composition and individuality in Chapter 4.

was impossible for him, he declared, to discern whether the two conditions posited by Spinoza (existence and conceivability) would have to be satisfied conjunctively or disjunctively.[10] Must a substance in Spinoza's sense be in itself *and* be conceived through itself; or rather must it be in itself *or* be conceived through itself?[11]

The same problem appears while observing Spinoza's fifth definition, which aims to characterize the use of the word "mode."

> By mode I understand the affections of a substance, or that which is in another through which it is also conceived—*Per modum intelligo substantiæ affectiones, sive id, quod in alio est, per quod etiam concipitur.* (E1d5)

Just like in his definition of substance, Spinoza here offers two parallel and binary relations as criteria of identification for the item he calls "mode." Per E1d5, x is a mode if and only if x inheres in y (where y must necessarily not be identical with x) *and* is conceived through y. But once again, we might ask with Leibniz: are the two criteria to be read conjunctively? Must they both be satisfied for x to be a mode, or in the previous case, a substance?

These problems appear to be partially solved by tracking down Spinoza's references. In a recent study, Carriero makes an interesting argument through the identification of the corresponding definitions in several key passages of Aristotle, Aquinas, Ockham, and Descartes.[12] His conclusion is straightforward. "The two clauses in Spinoza's definitions of modes reflect the Aristotelian

---

[10] See Leibniz, *Textes inédits*, 278. See also Leibniz, G I:139.

[11] Leibniz—who had received a copy of Spinoza's *Opera Posthuma* shortly after its publication—had at least another reason for questioning the definition of substance. He found the *definiens* to be obscure, as it results from the reading note that accompanies E1d3: "For what is it to exist in se?" (G I:139). For a more detailed account on Leibniz's criticisms of Spinoza, see Hart, "Leibniz on Spinoza's Concept of Substance," 73–86. See also Antognazza, *Leibniz: An Intellectual Biography*, 177–178.

[12] Cf. Carriero, "On the Relationship between Mode and Substance in Spinoza's Metaphysics," 246–250.

theses that substances are prior to accidents in being and in definition."[13] This helps us establish that the two criteria must indeed be considered conjunctively. For Spinoza, then, conception and inherence might just proceed on parallel tracks. Furthermore, Carriero shows that the conjunction between inherence and causation (which we shall tackle in a moment) is not a novelty of the *Ethics*. In fact, this binary requirement is common among Spinoza's predecessors, as "in the medieval Aristotelian tradition... something's being a property of a substance and its being efficiently caused by that substance" are not incompatible.[14]

However, as I suggested above, solving this problem through a historical account is only a partial answer. A more complete interpretation must account for the mutual interactions that involve the four kinds of relation that we have identified so far: causation, limitation, inherence, and conception. Let us sum up these reciprocal features, as we have uncovered them so far:

a. x is cause of itself, if its essence causally entails its existence.
b. x is cause of itself, if its essence *and* its existence conceptually imply each other.
c. x is finite if it might be limited by another item, y, which *must* belong to the same realm of being.
d. x is a substance if it inheres in itself *and* is conceptually dependent on itself.
e. x is a mode if it inheres in another (y) *and* is conceptually dependent on y.

In just four definitions, Spinoza has taken us on a long metaphysical ride. Note that in this context, I have not included E1d4 in the discussion of Spinoza's most fundamental metaphysical properties. The reason for this exclusion is that the semantic richness of E1a4

---

[13] Ibid., 250.
[14] Ibid., 259.

requires us to guarantee a more intensive analysis, which can only be provided through deep consideration of Spinoza's concept of expression. I will dedicate the entirety of Chapter 2 to such analysis. This concludes my initial sketch of the structural network Spinoza builds in the definitions of the first part of the *Ethics*. In the next section, we shall consider how these structures relate to each other, and in what manner they are irreducible to each other.

1.3 Immanent Causation, Panentheism, and Limitation

In the previous section, I have highlighted why the attempt to account for Spinoza's structural relations by reducing them to each other (e.g., by reducing conception and inherence to causation; or by reducing causation and inherence to conception) is doomed to fail. Not only—as we will see in the following chapters—do they have a different extension (that is to say, they apply to different domains or items); more importantly, their internal properties also differ.

In self-causation, the structure of causality offers prima facie a reflexive façade, which turns into one-way implication if we separate existence and essence as Spinoza apparently does. Essence causally entails existence and not the other way around. The structure of conceptual implication, instead, is truly biconditional and reflexive: essence and existence conceptually entail each other, and thus the *id* which is the "object" of this structure can be properly named *causa sui*.

Additionally, Spinoza's need for a specification on the matter of self-causation hints at one of the deepest divides in his metaphysics. Namely, the fact that (efficient) causation can be either transitive or immanent. This radical distinction is incepted in Spinoza's works from an early stage. In the *Short Treatise*, which is considered by scholars the first experimental attempt at developing a consistent metaphysics on Spinoza's part, God's causation is described as follows: "He is an immanent and not a transitive cause, since he does everything in himself, and not outside himself (because outside him there is nothing)."[15] From this text, we learn that to be an immanent cause is to have the effect fall within oneself; conversely, being a transitive cause means having the effect fall outside oneself.[16] Thus, immanent causation can be described as causation joined by inherence of the effect in the cause, while transitive causation is efficient causation absent inherence.

Does this mean that any occurrence of immanent causation is ipso facto also an occurrence of self-causation? This is an interesting question, which lies at the very heart of the important debate seeking to identify Spinoza as a pantheist or as a panentheist. In the first case, since everything "is" God, immanent causation and reflexive causation would be one and the same thing. In the latter case, since everything is merely "in" God, we can conceive of a distinction (and we shall see in the next chapter how this is not a merely rational distinction) between self-causation and causation joined by inherence.

Some evidence toward the solution of this puzzle comes from another section of the *Short Treatise* to which Spinoza awkwardly assigns the title "On God's Predestination." In this section, Spinoza employs is usual logical style to distinguish whether a thing is self-caused or caused by another: "We must seek this cause, then, either in the thing or outside it ... if existence belongs to the nature of the thing, then certainly we must not seek the cause outside it. But if existence does not belong to the nature of the thing, then we must always seek its cause outside it."[17] On the face of it, this passage does not seem particularly original: it only establishes the axiomatic self-causation of God. However, on closer look, it reveals

---

[15] *Short Treatise [KV]* I.3.2 | G I/35/19–20.
[16] On this topic, see Zylstra, "Spinoza on Action and Immanent Causation," 38–42.
[17] *KV* I.6.4 | G I/42/1–7.

that things whose essence does not entail existence must have their causes *outside* of themselves. This apparently innocent clause effectively excludes the possibility of reciprocal pantheism in Spinoza's metaphysics. God must be *external* to the things he causes. Therefore, while singular things can inhere in God, the reciprocal proposition can never be true. Consequently, panentheism is the only alternative available to Spinoza. Individual things are in God, but God is not *in* them. Thus, as we have argued above, immanent causation and reflexive causation are distinguished in important respects: not all immanent causation is reflexive, while (by definition) all reflexive causation is immanent. The *id* which E1d1 identifies as *causa sui* is thus an exceptional, if all-important, case of reflexive immanent causation.[18]

On the opposite side of Spinoza's ontological spectrum, the structure of limitation effectively introduces plurality in his metaphysical framework. A limited *id* cannot be limited by itself—thus, limitation is irreflexive by nature. Spinoza explicitly inserts the notion of "another" in this context, as well as the notion of a plurality of segregated realms of being (which will soon become the attributes). Despite the Spinozist maxim claiming that "all determination is negation," the *Ethics* offers a key role for limitation—albeit restricted to the case of finite beings.[19] Spinoza, in this context, would ideally oppose Hegel's antithetical structure since self-negation is metaphysically impossible.

We can also force Spinoza's apparent hand to show how limitation is a symmetric structure. In fact, if x is limited by y, then by this very fact y is limited by x. If a body is limited by another—for example, a table occupying the space in which I wish to position my

---

[18] I expand on this divide between immanent and transitive causation in the concluding section of this chapter, where I discuss Spinoza's ultimate structure: *naturare*.

[19] Cf. *Letter 50* | G IV/240b/34. On the (doubtful) legitimacy of the attribution of this maxim to Spinoza in the contemporary sense of the terms "negation" and "determination," see the two important studies produced by Stern ("The Adventures of a Doctrine") and Melamed ("Determination, Negation, and Self-Negation").

new armchair—then the table is clearly limited by the armchair in the same way. Furthermore, it seems that limitation is in some sense transitive. Spinoza states that "we always conceive *another* [body] that is greater" (emphasis is mine). In other words, to be the kind of being that limits another, a thing becomes subject to further limitation: just like my armchair is limited by my table, my table is also limited by that chest of drawers that has been in my office for longer than anyone can remember. If x is limited by y, then y is conceivably limited by z. The internal properties of limitation, then, set this structure apart from the ones analyzed above, allowing Spinoza to introduce a genuine plurality of beings in his metaphysical system. It also makes limitation irreducible to causation—since the latter can be reflexive, while the former is irreflexive by nature.

What about the overlapping of inherence and conception, which as we have seen appear conjunctively in the definition of *both* substance and modes (E1d3 and E1d5 respectively)? The intuition for the reader of the *Ethics* could very well be that, since what is conceived through x is also inherent in x, then conception and inherence collapse on each other. In other words, Spinoza should employ Ockham's Razor, the metaphysical principle according to which entities should not be multiplied without necessity. Thus, he should prune his metaphysics free of one or the other. First, let me warn the reader that I am not entirely convinced of the appropriateness of adopting Ockham's Razor when dealing with structures. After all, this principle was developed with the specific goal of restricting ontological expenditure within the domain of beings (*entia*). Given the relative youth of structural ontology, it has not yet been proved that structures and beings are equally affected by this principle. Yet, since this reconstruction of Spinoza's metaphysics along structural lines is scary enough without the scandalous move of throwing the venerable Razor to the wind, I will not challenge it here. Let us proceed as if there were a genuine demand for ontological parsimony, even in dealing with structures, and see where that lands us.

The possibility of reducing Spinoza's inherence to conception (and vice versa) has been famously advocated by Della Rocca; but this hypothesis has recently come under attack from a multiplicity of fronts, both metaphysical and historical.[20] Della Rocca's exceptional studies have been instrumental in bringing the study of Spinoza's relations to the forefront of the scholarship. I do believe that he takes the reasoning a step too far, beyond what Spinoza would have wanted—and what his texts can prove. However, a more complete assessment of these reasonings is beyond the scope of this chapter. Here, I would like to limit myself to a skeletal argument proving that the two relations of inherence and conception can be (sometimes) uncoupled for Spinoza. In particular, I would like to beg the reader's pardon as I abandon my naïve reader pose for a moment and jump ahead in the *Ethics*. As we will briefly see, the principled stance demanding the reduction of all structures cannot accommodate all of Spinoza's uses in the rest of the text. For the record, I do not think that this accommodation is necessary, or even desirable, for Spinoza. Much of the fascination with his metaphysics comes from its irreducible multiplicity of structures, only apparently tamed by their regular concurrence.

Let us first focus on E1p10s, a crucial text in many respects (as we shall see in the next chapter). In this passage, Spinoza argues that the attributes of substance, the features that allow its conceivability and constitute its essence, must be conceived through themselves. I will not dwell here on the metaphysical status of these "attributes" and the ways in which Spinoza innovatively adopts them to "fill out" his ontological world. That is the task of Chapter 2. Instead, allow me to quote a line from E1p10s:

---

[20] The clearest source for Della Rocca's original claim is perhaps his *Spinoza* (41–47). Some convincing counterarguments to this thesis have since appeared in Melamed (*Spinoza's Metaphysics*, 91–95), Newlands (*Reconceiving Spinoza*, 70–89), and Schmaltz (*The Metaphysics of the Material World*, 199–212).

it is of the nature of a substance that each of its attributes is <u>conceived through itself</u>, since all the attributes it has have always <u>been in it</u> together (*est de natura substantiæ, ut unumquodque ejus attributorum <u>per se</u> <u>concipiatur</u>; quandoquidem omnia, quæ habet, attributa simul <u>in ipsa</u> <u>semper fuerunt</u>*). [Emphasis is mine].

Attributes, as we can plainly observe, are conceived per se. Yet they are *in* the substance, as Spinoza nonchalantly affirms.[21] It is not entirely clear how an attribute can inhere in the substance since it constitutes its essence. Yet, the above text is proof at the very least that conception showcases reflexive properties in a case when inherence does not. On the face of it, we have here a case where *x* inheres in *y* but is conceived through *x*. This strikes me as an important counterexample to the reductionist thesis that *all* occurrences of inherence and conception are congruent for Spinoza, and that we are allowed to collapse these two structures on each other without any interpretative loss. As we will see in the next chapter, this discrepancy between conceptual content and inherential grounding generates a potent ripple in Spinoza's metaphysics, which can only be addressed using hyperintensional logic. But I am getting ahead of myself: back to disproving the reducibility of structures.

A potentially more disruptive case is showcased by E4p2.[22] Here, Spinoza utilizes his dormient structure—limitation—to claim that "we are acted on, insofar as we are a part of Nature, which cannot be conceived through itself, without the others [parts]." The deep metaphysical significance of this tenet will become our main object in Chapter 5. However, we can already see how Spinoza seems to invoke conceptual dependence in a case of "being acted on," which

---

[21] As Della Rocca pointed out to me, this might constitute a conflict with E1p29s. The contradiction rests on the leeway (in my case, very little) that we allow Spinoza in enunciating is ontological commitments in the scholia.
[22] Spinoza consistently employs versions of this argument throughout *Ethics* IV and V. I only cite E4p2 as the first and (perhaps) simplest example.

represents an instance of limitation. As we have seen above, limitation is radically distinct from inherence. To unearth my previous example: my table can hardly be said to inhere in my chair, and since their limitation is mutual, if we wanted to claim that inherence and conception are congruent, we would also have to figure out how to conceptualize mutual inherence (which must also be reflexive).[23] In E4p2, if we can take Spinoza at his word, we have a case in which x is conceived through y, yet it does not (and cannot) inhere in y insofar as x and y are involved in a mutual relation of limitation. This radical irreducibility of limitation might perhaps explain its consistent exclusion from the classic "triad" of structures formed by inherence, conception, and causation. However, its insertion in E1d2 (right after *causa sui!*) speaks volumes about Spinoza's confidence in its crucial role.

Of course, this might all be anecdotal evidence when confronted with a principled reading. One can sincerely believe that Spinoza must offer a reduction of all structures. This belief might be encouraged by the fact that he offers a reduction of all substance, and that he does in fact support substantial monism (through a particularly strong reading of his Principle of Sufficient Reason [PSR]).[24] Nonetheless, as I have shown in the sections above, it is far from clear that Spinoza believes that structures and beings behave in one and the same way. According to the evidence I have brought, the structures incepted by Spinoza at the beginning of

---

[23] Although both Schmaltz and Melamed have claimed the existence of similar problems within Della Rocca's reductionism, I am not aware of either's use of E4p2 in developing their counterexamples.

[24] Garrett ("Spinoza's *Conatus* Argument," 155) and Della Rocca (*Spinoza*, 69) support precisely this argumentation, invoking a "partial" inherence to save the reductionist interpretation and accommodate the second piece of textual evidence presented above. However, as I will show in Chapters 4 and 5, there are less counterintuitive pathways to achieve mutual limitation and conceptual co-implication. While less counterintuitive arguments should not be preferred *because* of their being less counterintuitive, I do believe that (all textual support being equal) we are allowed to include a view that is less demanding and that this does not affect our seriousness as historians of philosophy. Moreover, as I have shown, there are several textual problems that require the structural reductionist to invoke ad hoc solutions.

the *Ethics* are mutually irreducible since they do not share their definitory properties nor their applicatory domain. Moreover, it is far from clear that Spinoza is a reductional monist with respect to structures. In the next three sections, I explore the asymmetry between structural pluralism and substantial monism, which is perhaps the most recognizable feature of Spinoza's metaphysics. My aim will be to account for Spinoza's monism of substance *through* (and not just despite) his pluralism of structure. If I am successful in this attempt, I will have provided one more reason to abandon the reductionist project with respect to structures.

1.4 From Pluralist Structure to Causal Independence

If you asked your average college student what they know about Spinoza, the answer is likely to resemble some form of the following: "Ah yes, it's that madman who thinks that all is one, and everything is God!" In other words, Spinoza's single most famous thesis is his substantial monism. As I have affirmed in the introduction, there is good reason for this state of affairs. Spinoza time and again returns to the central notion of substance as one and indivisible, against Descartes—and honestly speaking, against common sense. Affirming the unicity of substance, and its overlapping with the realm of existence, appears (at the very least) one of the chief purposes of Spinoza's *Ethics*.

In the following sections, I will reconstruct Spinoza's argument for substantial monism, examining the philosophical process that leads him to conclude that there exists but one substance. This is not, by any means, a novel exercise in the literature. During the three and a half centuries that have passed since the posthumous publication of the *Ethics* (and even before, as we will briefly see) readers have closely scrutinized Spinoza's argument for substantial monism, with varying degrees of good faith. In fact, borrowing a term from Berkeleyan lingo, we could almost affirm that this is Spinoza's "Master Argument." What will be new about my attempt in these pages will be the goal of the analysis, which will focus—as I have promised—on the structural features unveiled by the argument. In other words, my analysis shows that Spinoza's monism of substance does not obtain *in virtue of* the kind of object that substance is. Instead, Spinoza's substantial monism obtains *in virtue of* the structures that justify the existence of substance as such. Monism is thus grounded in structure and is not grounded (or it is only secondarily grounded) in objectual metaphysics.

One more caveat for my conscientious reader. Spinoza's argument for substantial monism, as he offered it, makes heavy use of the notion of attribute. As I have indicated before, a full analysis of the concept of attribute will be one of the main subjects of the next chapter. For now, it will be sufficient to translate "attribute" with the locution "realm of being," indicating the set of all the objects that share an identifying property (e.g., extension, thought, etc.). This philistine simplification will help us to streamline our argument, showing more clearly how Spinoza's skeletal demonstration for monism is supposed to function.

Let us begin from the end. The key proposition in which Spinoza affirms his substantial monism is E1p14. "Except God, no substance can be or be conceived (*Præter Deum nulla dari, neque concipi potest substantia*)."[25] Spinoza doubles down on this thesis in the first corollary to this proposition, where he affirms that "God is unique, i.e., in Nature there is only one substance, and that it is absolutely infinite" (E1p14c1). What kind of proof does Spinoza bring for such a strong thesis? In E1p14d, he relies on the fact that God is an absolutely infinite substance. This is implicitly granted by E1d6, where God is described as "a being absolutely infinite, i.e., a substance consisting of an infinity of attributes." "Absolutely infinite" is an idiosyncratic notion in Spinoza's metaphysics, which

---

[25] I will analyze this proposition and its detailed argument in Section 1.6 below.

indicates the joint impossibility of limitation *and* possession of all attributes. In this section, I focus on how he applies this notion to obtain the causal independence of substances, which is a key step in his path to substantial monism. In the next two sections, we will complete the journey to monism after a momentary detour in the territory of parallel argumentation.

Now, we should ask ourselves: is Spinoza entitled to the expensive metaphysical move delineated above, whereby he seemingly introduces a new feature of being—absolute infinity—with the apparently sole purpose of justifying monism? I think that he is, despite some reservations about the apparently abrupt way he achieves this introduction. In fact, absolute infinity is based on the impossibility for substances to share attributes, which Spinoza affirms in E1p5.[26] As we will see in the next section, the combination of E1p5 and E1d6 takes away some of the uneasiness resulting from Spinoza's unorthodox introduction of absolute infinity across attributes. Attributes demarcate different realms of being, as we have affirmed before. Belonging to a realm of being potentially exposes substance to limitation, per E1d2. In fact, for two beings *a* and *b* to exist within the same domain means that *a* and *b* can potentially limit each other, if they come within the range of each other. Yet, Spinoza wants to withdraw substances from this process of mutual limitation. He achieves this by affirming that two given *id*s are identical if and only if they share the same attribute and the same affections, or properties.[27]

Here comes the interesting part, for the structure-obsessed metaphysician. Spinoza claims that one and only one *id* can exist in

---

[26] E1p5: "In nature there cannot be two or more substances of the same nature or attribute."

[27] Cf. E1p4: "Two or more distinct things are distinguished from one another, either by a difference in the attributes of the substances or by a difference in their affections." This can be read as a formulation of the Principle of the Identity of Indiscernibles: *a* and *b* differ if and only if they differ either in attribute or in affection. By contrast, if *a*'s attributes and affections are identical to *b*'s attributes and affections, then *a* and *b* will also be identical.

each attribute (without the two being identical with one another). Thus, he must prove that two *ids* (1) cannot share attributes and (2) cannot share affections or modifications. This seems a bit of an overkill, considering that Spinoza is only allegedly interested in (1). This first half of the demonstration is easily obtained from the very terms of the problem: if they do not share attributes, *a* and *b* are not identical. Thus, they must be distinguished by means of their affections or modifications. How does Spinoza obtain (2)? He claims that substances are prior in nature to their affections. Thus, every affection must be conceived through its substance and inherits a conceptual "mark" that distinguishes it from all the other affections, which depend on other substances. For example, say that m1 is an affection or modification of substance s1; even though m1 is virtually identical to its brother m2, the latter is an affection or modification of substance s2. In the example, m1 and m2 share everything: the same duration, the same chemical composition, the same haircut. Yet, the fact that they are modification of distinct substances ipso facto establishes their mutual distinction. Our two siblings, m1 and m2, are distinguished insofar as they must be conceived through their respective substances.[28] Thus, their distinction could never explain the distinction of s1 and s2, since this distinction would be established by means of a circular reasoning. Notice that at no point in this reasoning I (or Spinoza) have invoked any structure except conception.[29] On conception alone, he has obtained that substances cannot be distinguished by means of their attributes or by means of their modifications.

---

[28] In virtue of the respective definitions of substance and mode, E1d3 and E1d5.

[29] The independent appeal to conception in this circumstance has understandably caused Newlands to conclude that Spinoza believes in a form of "Conceptual Dependence Monism," whereby conceptual relations are the only kind of relations Spinoza needs to get his metaphysics off the ground (see his *Reconceiving Spinoza*, 60–64; and his "Another Kind of Spinozistic Monism," especially 474–478). However, I am not convinced that Spinoza can do without the full array of structures that he puts in place to ground his metaphysics, as I aim to show in the remainder of this chapter.

Since they cannot be distinguished, the two *ids* considered here must be one and the same substance, from the point of view of numerical identity. If Della Rocca and Newlands were right, however, Spinoza could stop here, since he has already grounded, using only conception, the unicity of substance (or the unicity of an *n* number or numerically identical substances, if you do not believe in the Identity of Indiscernibles). Yet, Spinoza immediately disproves the reducibility of structures, since in E1p6 he proceeds to claim that "one substance cannot be produced by another substance." If there were any doubts regarding the fact that this proposition refers to causation, they are quickly dispelled in the demonstration, where Spinoza clarifies that he means to prove that "one cannot be the cause of the other." If conception and causation were mutually reducible, this proposition would not be needed since its object would have already been posited by E1d3.[30] The definition of substance, as we recall, claims that each substance is inherent in itself and must be conceived through itself.

Instead, Spinoza insists that the fact that substances cannot have anything in common—no attributes and no modes, as we have just seen—also means that they cannot cause each other (*una alterius causa esse nequit*). Thus, the conjunction of conception and causation is yet to be proven. Moreover, Spinoza goes on to show the irreducibility of these two structures in the process of demonstrating the causal independence of substances in E1p6c, which argues that "a substance cannot be produced by anything else."

How does he obtain this conclusion? First, a warning: Spinoza's demonstration for E1p6c is a deeply convoluted text. If you are resistant to seventeenth century phrasing, you might want to skip to the paragraph below, where I provide a streamlined summary of the argument. Without further ado, let us dive in the text:

---

[30] As Della Rocca has kindly pointed out to me, Spinoza here might be just drawing out an implication of E1d3 in which case limitation and conception would not be metaphysically separable. However, within my framework, saying that conception is fundamental for an epistemic access to limitation is not enough to claim that limitation is metaphysically reducible to conception.

From this it follows that a substance cannot be produced by anything else. For in nature there is nothing except substances and their affections, as is evident from E1a1, E1d3, and E1d5. But it cannot be produced by a substance (by E1p6). Therefore, substance absolutely cannot be produced by anything else, q.e.d.

Alternatively: This is demonstrated even more easily from the absurdity of its contradictory. For if a substance could be produced by something else, the cognition of it would have to depend on the cognition of its cause (by E1a4). And so (by E1d3) it would not be a substance.

What are the components of this demonstration? E1p5 is the proposition that we have just read, which excludes that substances can belong to the same realm of being (i.e., they share no attribute). E1p6, as we just saw, establishes the causal disjunction of substances, as a consequence of E1p5. E1p2 is the logical prerequisite of this thesis, since it claims that substances that do not share attributes have nothing in common.[31] E1p3 is a text that we have not considered yet but a crucial one in Spinoza's architecture of causation. It affirms that causation can only exist between *id*s that have something in common. In turn, this thesis is based on Spinoza's so-called causal axiom (E1a4), which claims that "The cognition of an effect depends on, and involves, the cognition of its cause."[32] However, if you do not assume straightaway that Spinoza's relations are reducible to each other, there is something weird going on in this passage.

Stretching the terms (just a bit) to allow that cognition is in this context replaceable with conception, we have *two* parallel, valid,

---

[31] E1p2 is correctly based on E1d3 alone, that is, on the self-conception and self-inherence of substances.
[32] Translation modified. The Latin reads: "*Effectus cognitio a cognitione causæ dependet, et eandem involvit.*" E1a4 is one of the most fascinating theses of Spinoza, and it has rightly received much attention in the literature. For some highlights of this literature, see Wilson, "Spinoza's Causal Axiom"; and Morrison, "Restricting Spinoza's Causal Axiom."

THE BARE BONES OF THE WORLD 39

and conclusive arguments for the causal independence of substance. In fact, Spinoza presents them as *alternative* arguments. Both provide an independent demonstration for E1p6c.

The first argument is based on commonality (i.e., potential limitation, per E1d2), with an important appearance by conception and inherence, and it comprises six steps:

1. Effects must have something in common with their causes (E1p3).
2. Substances with different attributes have nothing in common with one another (E1p2).
3. There cannot be more than one substance per attribute (E1p5).
4. Thus, substances cannot cause each other (E1p6).[33]
5. But in nature, there are only substances and their affections (E1a1, E1d3, E1d5).
6. Therefore, substance cannot be caused by anything else (E1p6c).

The second argument is based on conception, and it runs as follows:

1. Effects must be conceived through their causes (E1a4).
2. Each substance is conceived through itself (E1d3).
3. Substances cannot be conceived through one another (by the converse of E1d3).
4. Thus, substances cannot cause each other.[34]

Spinoza reaches identical conclusions in each of the two arguments. Interestingly, each argument relies on a different structure—conception for the second, limitation and commonality for the

[33] Cf. E1p6d*Aliter*.
[34] Cf. E1p6d.

first. In each, the impossibility of external causation only comes in as a *result* of (respectively) self-conception and impossibility of external limitation. Why would Spinoza provide two independent and nonintersecting arguments, if he believed that conception (or another structure) could function as a reductionist panacea? The fact that distinct arguments can be provided by using distinct structures represents proof that Spinoza does not believe in the reducibility of these structures.

It is possible that I am reading too much into Spinoza's supererogatory friendliness. After all, he might not be flirting with structural pluralism when he decides to provide two independent lines of argumentation for the same exact conclusion. Yet, if he is convinced of the mutual reducibility of fundamental metaphysical structures, it must be admitted that this forwardness in offering two distinct arguments for the same conclusion is at least worth of suspicion. If he is instead convinced that metaphysical structures are distinct, it is possible that God/substance is a unique case in which the structures of conception, causation, and inherence *coincide*. If the latter case is true, as I suspect, then it makes perfect sense that Spinoza would go out of his way to prove that the causal independence of substance(s) is not proved *exclusively* by means of its (theirs) conceptual independence.

If what I have argued in this section is right, then the paramount example of this structural coincidence is *causa sui*, the reflexive species of causation where the caused and the causer are identical. In the next section, I adopt this background conviction as a useful lens to read and interpret Spinoza's final step toward substantial monism.

1.5 From Causal Independence to *Causa Sui*

When we left Spinoza in the previous section, he had just reached the conclusion that substances are causally independent of each other. Of course, this is not enough to prove substantial monism. As Garrett and others have pointed out, the argument from causal independence might potentially prove the existence of any number of substances, as long as they possess independent causal justification.[35] In other words, to quote the immortal Dr. Egon Spengler, "Don't cross the streams. It would be bad."

So how does Spinoza attempt to secure the unicity of God's existence as substance? As I have mentioned in the previous section, he recurs to the notion of "absolute infinity," which is paramount to his attempt of subtracting God/substance from the arena of limitation. After demonstrating that a substance cannot be caused by another substance (due to its causal independence), Spinoza makes a radical move. Since substances cannot cause each other, what can they be caused by? One option to briefly consider is that they could be caused by their attributes or their modifications. However, Spinoza quickly dismisses this option since he claims, in E1p6c, that the chain of inherence cannot be reversed. Here, we see how in addition to limitation and causation, he calls in play yet another structure (inherence) to demonstrate the causal independence of substance from another angle. I base this claim on the text of E1p6c:

> From this it follows that a substance cannot be produced by anything <u>else</u>. For in nature there is nothing except substances and their affections, as is evident from E1a1, E1d3, and E1d5. But it cannot be produced by a substance (by E1p6). Therefore, substance absolutely cannot be produced by anything <u>else</u> [*ergo substantia absolute ab alio produci non potest*]. Q.e.d.

So, we conclude that substances cannot be produced by other substances, or by attributes, or by modifications. As it should be evident from my emphasis in the text above, however, Spinoza

---

[35] For the original argument, see Garrett's seminal article "Spinoza's 'Ontological' Argument." For Della Rocca's interesting take on it, see his *Spinoza*, 52–58.

leaves himself a backdoor into the causal process of substances. By claiming that substance cannot be caused by anything *else*, he is implying that they can be caused by something that is identical to them. In other words, he is intentionally opening the door to self-causation, as we will see in a moment.

Before going through that door, let us pause for a moment. The conclusive line of E1p6c gives us another piece of information, one that I feel has been overlooked despite the close scholarly attention dedicated to these pages of the *Ethics*. Let us read it again: "substance <u>absolutely</u> cannot be produced by anything else, q.e.d." What is interesting is that Spinoza apparently did *not* set out to demonstrate this thesis. The *demonstrandum* of E1p6c reads simply "from this it follows that a substance cannot be produced by anything else." During the process of demonstration, Spinoza smuggles in the adverb "absolutely" [*absolute*]. Even though this might look unwarranted, if we consider the meaning assigned to this term, we can conclude that Spinoza did nothing wrong. After all, "absolute" causation means causation "separated from anything else," which is exactly what Spinoza intends to obtain with this corollary. However, it is curious that the characterization "absolute" should appear in this text, even more so considering that (as I have mentioned in the previous section) this adverb also characterizes the infinity of substance, the very feature that guarantees Spinoza's monism.

This absolute absence of external causation emboldens Spinoza to make the final jump. Since it cannot be caused by anything *else*, substance can only be caused by itself.[36] It must be *causa sui*. By definition (E1d1), *causa sui* is that whose essence implies existence, that is, that which must exist. Substance, then, must exist; or as Spinoza puts it, "it pertains to the nature of a substance to exist" (E1p7). This argument appears simple; in fact, here Spinoza is just drawing together the conclusions of the more controversial

---

[36] E1p7d: "A substance cannot be produced by anything else (by E1p6c); therefore, it will be the cause of itself."

arguments he has disseminated in the earlier pages of the *Ethics*. Doubts can certainly be raised about the consistency and validity of this argument—as it will happen with the argument demonstrating God's necessary existence, in E1p11d. Nonetheless, as this argument does not add anything to the discussion on structures that permeates this first part of the *Ethics*, I am willing to take Spinoza on his word and accept the validity of this argument.[37]

More controversy, I believe, should be raised by the next proposition, which reads "every substance is necessarily infinite" (E1p8). Spinoza proves this thesis by appealing to the notion of limitation, as I will show through a reconstruction of the demonstration.[38] Substance must exist, as we just saw. It can either exist as limited or as unlimited. If it exists limitedly, then (tautologically) it would be subject to limitation. But to be subject to limitation, per E1d2, implies sharing one's attribute with some other *id*. This other *id* could either be a substance or not a substance. If it is a substance, this would violate the claim that only one substance can exist in each realm of being (E1p5). We are thus left with only two alternatives: either we take substance to be unlimited, or we conceive of substances as potentially limited by nonsubstances. Spinoza concludes his demonstration without ruling out the latter case. This is, in my opinion, the largest gap in Spinoza's argumentation throughout *Ethics* I. Of course, to claim that modifications can limit a substance is a highly unorthodox view, and from a dialectical point of view, it is unlikely that any Early Modern antagonist could have taken this stance against E1p8. However, the uneasiness at an unfinished argument in such a delicate passage remains.

---

[37] Highlights from the important literature on this topic include the aforementioned studies by Jarrett and Della Rocca, as well as Melamed's *Spinoza's Metaphysics*, 33–34; and Kulstad, "Spinoza's Demonstration of Monism," 272–277.

[38] "A substance of one attribute does not exist unless it is unique (E1p5), and it pertains to its nature to exist (E1p7). Of its nature, therefore, it will exist either as finite or as infinite. But not as finite. For then (by E1d2) it would have to be limited by something else of the same nature, which would also have to exist necessarily (by P7), and so there would be two substances of the same attribute, which is absurd (by E1p5). Therefore, it exists as infinite, q.e.d."

Spinoza must have felt this uneasiness, too, as he immediately adds a scholium to attempt to close the gap. In the scholium, Spinoza begins by offering a clarification on the notion of finitude (or limitedness), which we had already noted: "Being finite is really, in part, a negation." By contrast, he claims, "being infinite is an absolute affirmation of the existence of some nature, it follows from E1p7 alone that every substance must be infinite" (E1p8s1). In other words, being *causa sui*—which is, after all, what E1p7 demonstrates— would *also* be equivalent to being absolutely infinite. Moreover, in the Dutch version of the *Opera Posthuma*, Spinoza continues: "if we assumed a finite substance, we would, in part, deny existence to its nature, which (by P7) is absurd." Finitude is established as a privation of existence, which cannot be attributed to *causa sui* insofar as *causa sui* is self-affirming existence—and thus, apparently, resistant to limitation.

The impossibility of limiting a self-causing substance is not as trivial a point as Spinoza attempts to imply. He even goes as far as to claim that "this proposition would be an axiom for everyone, and would be numbered among the common notions," if philosophers just "would attend to the nature of substance" (E1p8s2). The nature of substance, as Spinoza defines it in E1d3, is to be in itself and to be conceived through itself. Thus, the nature of substance, in the structural language developed in this chapter, is to be self-conceived and self-inhering. Self-causation and the incompatibility with limitation are absent from the definition (which, as Spinoza would agree, must capture the nature of its *definiendum*). Thus, it is only by means of *enriching* the definition of substance by adding unlimitedness that Spinoza can obtain absolute infinity. This aligns with Spinoza's claim that God's essence is affirmative and has nothing "imperfect or limited."[39] The joint intervention

---

[39] *KV* I, 2 | G/I/20. On this topic, see Hübner, "Spinoza on Negation, Mind-Dependence and the Reality of the Finite," who traces the development of affirmative definitions in Spinoza's early works.

of the structures developed throughout *Ethics* I is the only mechanism that can grant Spinoza the absolute infinity that he wants to award to substance.

Fortunately for Spinoza, there is nothing counterintuitive or even disturbing in this association. Readers who were prepared to accept that *causa sui* is self-inhering and self-conceived are unlikely to challenge its absolute infinity. This is one of the main reasons, I believe, why Spinoza can achieve his most desired objective, the unification of structures. To be sure, he wastes no time and immediately puts the readers' trust to good use, claiming in rapid succession that "the more reality or being each thing has, the more attributes belong to it" (E1p9), and that "God, or a substance consisting of infinite attributes ... necessarily exists" (E1p11). These two claims are logical consequences of the association between self-causing, self-inhering, self-conceived substance (to which we will henceforth refer as *causa sui*) and absolute infinity. As we have seen, the leap of faith that Spinoza asked of us in E1p8s2 required granting that nonsubstances cannot limit substances. Attributes, then, cannot limit substances, and the self-affirmation of substance overcomes what we may imagine as "attributal boundaries" to achieve an even wider conceptualization of absolute infinity.[40]

In this sense, E1p11 achieves little more than assigning the name of "God" to this absolutely infinite entity, which we have constructed through the union of distinct structures. If God is a substance, then it is *causa sui*. If *causa sui* entails absolute infinity, then God cannot be limited by anything else, including attributes. If God is *causa sui*, he also has necessary existence. All the structural chickens of Spinoza's *Ethics* have come home to roost: the

---

[40] A large portion of Chapter 2 will be dedicated to the sense in which attributes can constitute these so-called attributal boundaries and the structural mechanisms that allow Spinoza to preserve them while developing his metaphysics.

union is complete. Moreover, this argument can rely on E1d6, which (as my reader will recall), affirms that God is "a being absolutely infinite, i.e., a substance consisting of an infinity of attributes." It is interesting to note, once again, how Spinoza does not take this argument for granted, invoking the analytical truth of God's resistance to limitation. He chooses instead the roundabout course of proving God's identity to substance, and the necessary existence of both, before claiming their congruence. This course, to my mind, is justified by the fact that Spinoza is aware of his reliance on a plurality of metaphysical structures. In accordance with his abidance to the PSR, he thus provides sufficient reason for their compatibility by employing them all—in their distinct roles—in his argument for the necessary existence of God as an absolutely infinite substance. This interpretation also provides us with some insight on Spinoza's apparently supererogatory demonstration of E1d6—or at least, of the existence of an *id* corresponding to that definition. Given that the definition and the argument rely on distinct structures (conception, limitation, and causation), their synergy is not taken for granted. By contrast, Spinoza establishes the coming together of such metaphysical structures as the result of the amplest demonstrative arc of *Ethics* I. The arc, however, is not completed with the establishment of the necessary existence of *causa sui*. Spinoza continues to push on the path of structural pluralism, to achieve the only apparently paradoxical conclusion that only one such item can exist.

1.6 A Structure of One: Monism

In this section, we complete our long journey toward monism. As I have mentioned before, this is perhaps the most recognizable feature in Spinoza's metaphysics. Showing the capacity to account for substantial monism will provide credibility for my structural pluralism and help me in the efforts of establishing its compatibility with more familiar versions of Spinoza's philosophy.

In the previous section, we have observed how Spinoza obtains the notion of *causa sui* as an absolutely infinite being (which possesses all attributes) only if he incorporates in its definition the structure of limitation (or rather, the absence of it). The necessary existence of such being is almost analytic and inexpensively acquired by Spinoza. However, once he has obtained the necessary existence of God as absolutely infinite *causa sui*, the final step cannot be far away. The crucial proposition is E1p14: "Except God, no substance can be or be conceived." From the phrasing, we can see that this proposition relies on the very definition of substance, E1d3, to establish the domain in which Spinoza's monism must be understood. The proposition appeals to the independent existence and conception of substance as the benchmark employed to adjudicate God's lonely role as the only substance allowed in Spinoza's metaphysics.

By following Spinoza's argument in the demonstration[41] to E1p14, we can identify which structures he employs to achieve his grand finale. Here, as he did in E1p6, he also provides two distinct arguments. The main difference between E1p6d and E1p14d is that in the latter, Spinoza is explicit about why two steps are needed in the proof. The first step in the argumentation demonstrates that only God can be (or exist); the second demonstrates that only God can be conceived. Thus, from the beginning Spinoza distinguishes between existence and conception, an important hint at the fact that he is once again relying on multiple structures to achieve his metaphysical goals. The arguments can be reconstructed as follows.[42]

1. God is absolutely infinite; i.e., God possesses all attributes (E1d6).

---

[41] I quote the full demonstration above: see Section 1.4.
[42] For an alternative reconstruction, see Kulstad, "Spinoza's Demonstration of Monism," 264–266.

2. God necessarily exists (E1p11).
3. No two substances of the same attribute can exist (E1p5).
4. If *a*, a substance distinct from God, existed, it would have to share one of God's attributes.
5. In virtue of (3), (4) is impossible.
6. Only God exists, or only *a* exists. Thus, in virtue of (2), *a* cannot exists.
7. Only God exists (QED).

This concludes the first part of the demonstration. The second part assumes (7) as a premise, and it argues that

8. *Ex hypothesis*, *a* is a substance.
9. As a substance, *a* cannot be conceived except as existing.
10. Yet, in virtue of (6) and (7) above, *a* cannot be conceived as existing.
11. Any substance *a* (nonidentical to God) cannot be conceived (QED).

As a first-time reader of the *Ethics*, many years ago, I must confess that this demonstration was one of the hardest to accept. In particular, the step marked as (9) in the above reconstruction was the main obstacle to my assent, mostly because it reads as a dogmatic introduction of a brute fact. Substances cannot be conceived except as existing. How does Spinoza prove this fundamental tenet? And what does it mean to conceive something as existing or nonexisting? In his recent book, Lin seems to share similar worries, indirectly claiming that this demonstration amounts to nothing more than a (mistaken) ontological argument.[43] I agree with Lin that the connection between conceiving an essence and the turning of that essence into existence plays a major role here. Therefore, the accusation is that of "an illicit logical leap from the mental world of

---

[43] Cf. Lin, *Being and Reason*, 61.

concepts to the real world of things," a charge leveled against most ontological arguments.[44]

Spinoza's insistence on the fact that substances cannot be conceived except as existing effectively exposes him to criticisms based on the blueprint of the refusal of any ontological argument. Such criticisms depend directly on the a priori argument for God's necessary existence offered by Spinoza in E1p11. Moreover, they supposedly highlight how Spinoza's argument for monism depends entirely on the structure of conception, supporting Newlands's reductionist approach, which claims that all relations of dependence amount to manifestations of conceptual dependence.[45] This would be a searing defeat for my pluralistic approach. We would have just escaped the frying pan of Della Rocca's rationalist reductionism, only to fall into the fire of conceptual reductionism.

The question becomes doubly urgent: can we understand Spinoza's argument in E1p14d as nondogmatic? And can we do so in a way that maintains Spinoza's rich plurality of structures? I contend that we can (and we must). The key point in Spinoza's second argument (numbered as 9 in the reconstruction above) is the *content* of conception, that is, that which makes substance unconceivable except as existing. In fact, as most criticisms to the ontological argument underline, being conceived as existing is not a sufficient condition for any old thing's existence.[46] Spinoza must make his case that it is the content of the essence of substance that entails its existence, to rule out its conceivability as nonexisting. This is, to my mind, the deep fact about Spinoza's metaphysics

---

[44] Indeed, this quote comes from Lawrence's article, "Descartes' Ontological Argument," where it is used to describe the dialectic between Anselm's and Descartes's versions of the a priori argument for the existence of God. Another brilliant narration of this tension is traced by Scribano, *L'esistenza di Dio*, 39–64.

[45] Newlands calls this interpretative doctrine "Conceptual Dependence Monism" (cf. *Reconceiving Spinoza*, 65) and argues that it is conception that grounds E1p14d as an argument applicable exclusively to the being *conceived* as *ens perfectissimum* (cf. ibid., 37).

[46] I am here thinking of the infamous parodic objections to the ontological argument, such as Gaunilo's perfect island, Caterus's lion, and Kant's hundred thalers.

that Rebecca Goldstein highlights when she affirms that Spinoza collapses "the ontological into the logical," and that he must thus argue that "all facts come with an accounting so complete as to rule out the very possibility that they might not have been facts."[47] The inconceivability and nonexistence of a given *id* must equally be explained, especially if that *id* is a (potential) substance threatening God's status as the only substance.

Fortunately for Spinoza, his metaphysics does in fact offer an account of why such a substance (e.g., *a*) is unconceivable as nonexisting (and conversely, why God must be the only substance that exists *and* is conceived). As we saw in the previous sections, however, Spinoza must conflate his argument from limitation and his argument from causation to reach the conclusion that substance cannot be conceived except as existing. This conflation of a multiplicity of structures speaks against most explanatory reductionisms, including Della Rocca's rationalist reductionism, Newlands's conceptual monism, or even Di Poppa's alternative proposal for causal reductionism.[48] So, how does the conflation work?

The object of our argument is *a*, an aspiring up-and-coming substance that wants to challenge God's unique role as the only conceivable substance. For *a* to be conceived, *a* must first be conceived as a substance. But to be conceived as a substance means two things, as we have seen in our analysis of E1p6d: first, substances cannot be limited; second, substances must be *causa sui*. But if *a* were in fact cause of itself, as Spinoza claims in E1p8, then it would be infinite because no other substance (say *b*, or God himself) could intervene to stop its infinite development through an infinity of attributes. To do so, *b* (or God) would first need to share an attribute with *a*, in

---

[47] Goldstein, "Explanatory Completeness and Spinoza's Monism," 285. I think this also entails that Spinoza must provide a "two-way" version of the PSR, which demands reasons for the existence of existing things *and* for the nonexistence of nonexisting things. As far as I can tell, this is the most extensive coverage of any Early Modern version of the PSR.
[48] Cf. Di Poppa, "Spinoza on Causation and Power," 306–317.

order to have causal efficacy on *a*. But this is impossible because substances cannot share attributes. Thus, the causal self-origin of *a* and its refractoriness to limitation make it the case that if *a* existed, then it would also be absolutely infinite, eventually clashing against God in an attributal arms race. Therefore, *a* cannot exist. But why can it not be even conceived? This further step in Spinoza's argument calls back into action the definition that opened the *Ethics*, E1d1. In fact, to conceive something as nonexisting means to deny that it is *causa sui*, since E1d1 reads "by cause of itself I understand that whose essence involves existence, or that whose nature cannot be conceived except as existing." In other words, to conceive of something is to give it an essence, and the essences of *ids* that are identified as *causa sui* demand those *ids*' existence.

Interestingly, the two formulations proposed by Spinoza in E1d1 and in E1p14d present the same phrasing but have different objects, since the latter is concerned with "substance" *simpliciter*, while the former concerns only *causa sui*. Even though Spinoza has made it clear that God's substantiality and God's self-causation are coextensive, there is no guarantee that this would work for all substances, from a purely theoretical point of view. Therefore, we must insert two more premises in the second step of Spinoza's demonstration of E1p14. These two premises provide the content needed to make his "ontological argument" valid for all conceivable substances and thus to achieve his desired inconceivability of nonexisting substances. Let me reconstruct the argument for Spinoza's second step one more time, marking those extra premises as (8*) and (8**) to preserve (9)'s status as the crux of the problem.

8. *Ex hypothesis*, *a* is a substance.
8*. Substances are *causa sui*, and they are absolutely infinite.
8**. If something is a substance, then (in virtue of 8*), its essence entails existence.
9. As a substance, *a* cannot be conceived except as existing (in virtue of 8**).

10. Yet, in virtue of (6) and (7) above, *a* cannot be conceived as existing.
11. Any substance *a* (nonidentical to God) cannot be conceived (QED).

Thus, Spinoza's proof for the inconceivability of nonexisting substances only works if we also assume that causation and limitation play a role in the demonstration, alongside conception. The structural pluralism that imbues the first part of the *Ethics* steps up once more to guarantee that Spinoza can stabilize his delicate metaphysical system. We can then conclude that Spinoza's substantial monism is established by means of a concurrence of structures (namely limitation, causation, and conception), which actively determine the metaphysical limits and properties of the *id*s resulting from the interaction of such structures. Once again, let me remind the reader that for my structuralist pluralist thesis to obtain, I do not require any structure to appear in isolation from the other main Spinozist structures. In fact, all that is needed for the preservation of the pluralism I am claiming is the following: that a given structure play *some significant metaphysical role as truthmaker or sufficient reason* for one of Spinoza's arguments to be sound and valid, a role that *cannot be fulfilled* by another, distinct structure.[49]

The missing structure is inherence, which is yet to be inserted in this framework. Spinoza readily does so in E1p15, where he affirms that "Whatever is, is in God, and nothing can be or be conceived without God." The argument, here, proceeds by exclusion. Since God is the one and only substance existing and conceivable, then anything else that we may conceive cannot be a substance. Thus, it must be either an attribute or a mode of God. The possibility of an inhering between substance and attributes will be explored in the

---

[49] I thank Michael Della Rocca and Sam Newlands for inviting me to make this point explicit.

next chapter, but for now, Spinoza holds that "except for substances and modes, there is nothing" (E1p15d). Thus, we find that inherence is the grounding of all modes.[50] Any modes conceivable must be conceived within God, and any modes that are causally determined must be causally determined by God. The twin relations of causation and conception, defined in their reciprocal relationship by E1d3 and E1d5, are grounded by E1p15 in Spinoza's inherence monism.

We have now reached the end of a long demonstrative arc, which has won Spinoza his desired substantial monism. The cost of this purchase was perhaps not as modest as it first seemed, since it required him to maintain a delicate equilibrium between distinct structures, and an equally sophisticated balance among the relations that link the objects resulting from such structures. But the cost is paid, and Spinoza's metaphysical palace is built. From what he has told us so far, it contains God and all his infinite attributes. However, we must not forget that the goal of our interpretative enterprise is to seek shelter for Spinoza's concept of the world as well. In the last section of this chapter, I shall explain how Spinoza can fulfill his promise and fit both God and the world within one and the same monism.

1.7 *Naturare*

Throughout *Ethics* I, Spinoza displays an impressive range of structural notions. As I have shown in the previous sections of this chapter, such metaphysical structures are all employed (and oftentimes combined) to construct Spinoza's ontological system. In this

---

[50] For an illuminating analysis of this thesis, see Hulatt, "Structural Causality in Spinoza's *Ethics*," 4.

system, God occupies the place of honor as the only existing and conceivable substance.

Thus, Spinoza's metaphysical system is a substantial monism; and as we have seen in Section 1.2, finite individuals such as pens, tulips, elephants, and human beings are comprehended within this system as modifications, or modes, of God. Jonathan Schaffer affirms that Spinoza's system exemplifies "priority monism," whereby "exactly one basic concrete object exists—there may be many other concrete objects, but these only exist derivatively."[51] I agree with this reading, at least prima facie. However, investigating the exact nature of this "derivative" connection between Spinoza's substance and its modes is vital for establishing whether my structural account of Spinoza's metaphysics is sustainable and whether Spinoza's metaphysics as a whole is a credible account of the phenomenological landscape. In this section, I will lay the foundations of this investigation, which will be completed in the following chapters by examining how finite individuals exhibit distinct properties that are ascribable to different attributes, how they possess a duration, and how the structure of their individuality is subject to continuous changes due to the compositional nature of Spinoza's ontology of singular things (*res singulares*).

Before moving to such wide-ranging explorations, however, I focus in this section on how modes—generally speaking—are connected to substance. This dependence structure is named by Spinoza toward the end of *Ethics* I as "*naturare*" (literally "naturing"), a term that perfectly conveys the kind of essential and existential dependence that he has in mind. The term is introduced at the end of (yes, another) demonstrative arc, which establishes God's unicity as a "free cause" (E1p17c2), and the necessary expansion of God's causality to include all modes as effects

---

[51] Schaffer, "Monism" (2018 edition).

of God's essential causation.[52] For this reason, given the overlap of God's causal determination with the inherence and conception of modes through God (E1p15), we can conclude with Spinoza that "God is the efficient cause, not only of the existence of things, but also of their essence" (E1p25). Modes—even those conceived as nonexisting, since they are not substances—depend on God for their essential determination, since (in virtue of E1d5) their essential being depends on God as inhering subject *and* as conceptual grounding.

It is in this rich metaphysical soil that Spinoza decides to plant a new and original structure, *naturare*, with the purpose of representing this causal and essential dependence of modes. The passage is rather long, but it is worth to quote it in its entirety to appreciate Spinoza's insistence on structural pluralism.

> By *Natura naturans* we must understand what is in itself and is conceived through itself, or such attributes of substance that express an eternal and infinite essence, i.e. (by E1p14c1 and E1p17c2), God, insofar as he is considered as a free cause. But by *Natura naturata* I understand whatever follows from the necessity of God's nature, or from any of God's attributes, i.e., all the modes of God's attributes insofar as they are considered as things which are in God, and can neither be, nor be conceived without God. (E1p29s)

In this text, *Natura naturans* is defined both in terms of its scope and in terms of its structural properties. Scopewise, *Natura naturans* includes the essential aspect[53] of substance in an unlimited and

---

[52] I have argued elsewhere that Spinoza's criteria for essential determination might result in a seemingly paradoxical conception of the essence of finite modes; see my "Spinoza's Metaphysics of Freedom and Its Essential Paradox."

[53] For an extensive explanation of what I mean by "aspect," see Section 2.4 below. See also Melamed, *Spinoza's Metaphysics*, 17–18. Melamed (correctly to my eyes) establishes that *Natura naturans* and God only overlap under a specific understanding of God— what I call here the "differentiated" essential understanding of God.

differentiated sense (the infinite attributes). With regards to properties, *Natura naturans* is identified as the *id* that embodies the undifferentiated essence of substance, that is, self-conception, self-causation, self-inherence, and (this is the new entry in Spinoza's exclusive list) self-determination. "Self-determination," as Spinoza understands it, is nothing more than the freedom deriving from entirely essential causation.

Let us, then, briefly examine what Spinoza means by freedom. E1d7 establishes the notion of a "free thing" as that which "exists from the necessity of its nature alone and is determined to act by itself alone." By contrast, things are nonfree or "compelled" insofar as they are "determined by another to exist and to operate."[54] I would like to signal here a textual hint that has been (as far as I can tell) neglected by the scholarship. The two definitions contained in E1d7 are not symmetrical. While free things "exist" and "act" (*existit* and *agendum*), compelled things only "exist" and "operate" (*existendum* and *operandum*). This discrepancy is much more than a *lapsus*, for Spinoza. We will observe in detail how important it really is in the initial sections of my Chapter 5, dedicated to Spinoza's philosophy of action. For now, let us accept Spinoza's definition at face value and return to the idea of self-determination. "Freedom," in the acceptation designed by Spinoza, possesses two requisites:

F1. x is free if it exists from the necessity of its nature;
F2. x is free if it is determined to act by itself (i.e., by its own nature).

As we should know by now, F1 immediately restricts the entry to the "free things club" to substances only. Since only substances are causes of themselves, only substances exist from the necessity

---

[54] Translation modified. The Latin reads "*ab alio determinatur ad existendum, et operandum*"; whatever the merits of Curley's translation of *operandum* as "producing an effect," it shows a considerable bias toward object-oriented ontology that is not present in the Latin original.

of their own nature—any other *id* existing in the universe is causally determined to exist by some substance (and as we have seen, ultimately there is only one: God).[55] The second requirement F2 is apparently just as intuitive: nothing else (*alio*) can act on God; therefore, God will not be determined to act by anything else. F2, however, has deeper effects on Spinoza's metaphysics. If things are free only insofar as they are *exclusively* determined to action through their own essence, this effectively imports God's agency into every action undertaken by things that are not substances. To the dismay of Malebranche and other "moderate" occasionalists, not even minds are spared from this agential assimilation.[56] Since minds are modifications of God just as much as bodies are, and since God—an absolutely infinite being—does not recognize any attributal limitations to his action, the essences of minds are ipso facto not free nor it is free from any of their modifications (the ideas).[57] To steal Francesca Di Poppa's beautiful phrase, "an ontological gap is posited between the essence of a thing and its causal activity" through Spinoza's metaphysics of freedom.[58] This ontological gap effectively hinders the possibility that anything caused (in its essence) can act freely, since to act freely means to act out of one's essence.

Hence, a joint reading of E1d7 and E1p29s results in determinism.[59] By *naturing* his modifications (i.e., causing their nature), God also determines the lack of freedom of their actions. We will see in Chapter 5 the deep effects that this tenet has on human action, as well as the way in which it complicates our optimism for

---

[55] Cf. E1p16c1: "God is the efficient cause of all things which can fall under an infinite intellect."

[56] On this topic (and the correlation between Cartesian philosophy of mind and occasionalism), see Platt's exceptional monograph, *One True Cause*, especially 27–33.

[57] Spinoza's correspondents and friends also noticed this significant implication of Spinoza's doctrine of freedom: see, for example, Blijenberg's *Letter 20* | G/IV/7–9.

[58] Di Poppa, "Spinoza and Process Ontology," 276.

[59] Spinoza's theory of freedom as independent essential causation entails at the very least determinism, if not necessitarianism. On this interesting distinction, see Newlands, "Spinoza's Modal Metaphysics," §2.

beatitude. Anything outside of God is determined by God, both in its essence and in its existence. Thus, nothing except God is free, and even God is only free in the sense of being self-determined, self-caused in his existence and action through his essence.[60]

By way of conclusion, let us sketch a summative explanation of the role of *naturare* in Spinoza's metaphysics. *Naturare* is a second-order structure, in the sense that it depends on more fundamental structures. We can affirm that x is "natured" by y if and only if y is the cause of x's existence, *and* the substrate of x's conception, *and* the subject of x's inherence. *Naturare* unifies the distinct structures that we have observed during this chapter, and it does so by providing a culmination for Spinoza's argument in *Ethics* I.[61]

In an important sense, *naturare* is a structure diametrically opposed to *causa sui*. While the latter establishes reflexive causation, reflexive conception, and reflexive inherence, *naturare* determines an irreflexive dependence on conceptual, inhering, and causal terms. The natured is structurally dependent in each and every way upon the *naturans*. Logical inherence and conceptual containment function as borders, demarcating the distinction between *naturans* and *naturata*. Meanwhile, essential causation assumes the role of fuel in this model, providing inexhaustible carburant to the process of production of essences and existences. Thus, we can claim that "naturing" is a result of the *joint* presence of most of Spinoza's main metaphysical structures, with the notable exception of limitation.[62]

---

[60] Cf. Viljanen, *Spinoza's Geometry of Power*, 45–46; and Arola, "Under the Aspect of Eternity," 142–147.

[61] Samuel Newlands kindly invited me to produce an explanation for the arising of second-order structures from first-order structures. I take the former to be grounded on the latter in a relevant metaphysical sense, akin to the one fleshed out by Jonathan Schaffer in his "What Grounds What" under the rubric of "supervenience." I take *naturare* to be a supervenient structure, which is dependent for its realization on other, more fundamental structures such as the ones illustrated so far in this chapter. However, my suggestion is that *naturare* adds important semantic insight to Spinoza's metaphysical project, and that for this reason it is worth discussing on its own, without by this denying that it is fundamentally supervenient on other structures.

[62] As I have shown above, this joint presence does not ipso facto call for the mutual reduction of Spinoza's metaphysical structures (cf. Section 1.3).

This absence could—in principle—merely be the result of the fact that the present occurrence of *naturare* fortuitously happens to feature God (an unlimited being) in the role of "natur-er." I will return to the possibility of limited "naturing" in Chapter 5, when I shall examine how finite modes determine their own effects, how the natured become naturers.

Before reaching that point, however, we have a long road ahead of us. One of the key consequences of Spinoza's model of *naturing*, as I sketched it in these brief lines, is that "from the necessity of the divine nature there must follow infinitely many things in infinitely many modes."[63] In other words, God's nature is unlimited. Therefore, his action must be unlimited as well, both in depth and in breadth. The impossibility of capturing God's infinite essence under any of the infinite attributes generates several interpretative puzzles, and I still owe the reader a thorough exposition of Spinoza's concept of attribute. Fulfilling such promise (and solving the riddles deriving from it) will be my goal in the next chapter. Not all evil comes to harm, though. In the process of facing these difficulties, we will also enjoy the opportunity of exploring Spinoza's most harmonious and beautiful structure: expression.

---

[63] E1p16.

2
The Winding Paths of Substance
Expression, Involvement, and Aspectual Distinction

Since all that beat about in Nature's range,
Or veer or vanish; why should'st thou remain
The only constant in a world of change,
O yearning Thought! that liv'st but in the brain?
Call to the Hours, that in the distance play,
The faery people of the future day—
Fond Thought! not one of all that shining swarm
Will breathe on thee with life-enkindling breath,
Till when, like strangers shelt'ring from a storm,
Hope and Despair meet in the porch of Death![1]

2.1 Ontological Expression

In the previous chapter, we have repeatedly touched on the topic of attributes. In the context of Spinoza's metaphysics of structure, attributes occupy a place of utmost importance since they designate the realms of being and action in which the only substance—God—can exert its essential existence and causation.

This chapter will be devoted to explaining the ontological status and metaphysical role of the attributes, by focusing on what is

---

[1] S.T. Coleridge, *Constancy to an Ideal Object*.

perhaps the single most convoluted structure of Spinoza's metaphysics: expression. As such, it is sure to test the patience of my reader, as we will need to follow Spinoza in the darkest alleys of his metaphysical city. The questions that we will investigate are the following: starting from a monistic standpoint, where only one substance exists, how can we fill out the world? How does *content* arise? What framework is necessary to understand the multiplicity and variedness of the world, if the ultimate justification lies in a monolithic God?[2]

As I have anticipated, the crucial notion in this endeavor is that of expression. Spinoza introduces this powerful tool as early as definition 6 of the first part of the *Ethics*, where he explicitly defines what he means by "God," as we have seen in the previous chapter.

> By God I understand a being absolutely infinite, i.e., a substance consisting of an infinity of attributes, of which each one <u>expresses</u> an eternal and infinite essence—*Per Deum intelligo ens absolute infinitum, hoc est, substantiam constantem infinitis attributis, quorum unumquodque æternam, et infinitam essentiam exprimit.* (E1d6; my emphasis)

Spinoza ushers in expression as the structure guaranteeing the realization of God's infinite essence. As we have seen in the previous chapter, this structure is neutral, in the sense that it does not need to go outside of itself to be realized. Being stranger to all limitations, *causa sui* could prima facie exist in a vacuum of self-causation, neutral to all determinations. *Causa sui* is self-sufficient, and its essence is "naked" existence, existence beyond all specifications. Thus, the realization of substance across distinct and determined realms of

---

[2] A similar criticism is offered by Gasché, who employs Heidegger to represent monistic substance as the adversary of relation: "Visibly, relation has with respect to substance, and its unity, a multiplying power. It secures the difference of things, their singularity" (*Of Minimal Things*, 10).

being might turn out to be an illusion. However, *pace* Hegel, I do not think that this is what Spinoza has in mind.[3]

The fact that Spinoza's substance cannot be contained by any of its attributes shall not be understood as an instance of negative theology. The impossibility of properly covering all of God's features does not generate, in Spinoza's mind, a reverential silence that does not dare to predicate any attribute of God. Spinoza's answer is the very opposite: *all* attributes must be recruited to give justice to God's range of being, and their number is infinite. We can attempt to understand this stance by using a familiar example. If a concept is too great to be expressed in words, we may be tempted to abandon the endeavor; Spinoza's boldness, as it were, does not allow this. Instead, he enlists all languages on Earth, and all words in each language, to simultaneously and infinitely express the infinity that constitutes God's essence and definition.

God's expression through the attributes follows a similar pattern. The absolute infinity described in E1d6 demands that an infinite number of attributes simultaneously and infinitely provide content, in order to satisfy God's eternal lust for being.

How are we to understand, then, the meaning of expression? Spinoza, uncharacteristically for his geometrical method, does not define this notion in an adequate, exhaustive manner. As a consequence, scholars of the past four centuries have carefully chiseled around the resources that Spinoza does provide in a veritable effort of conceptual reverse-engineering. One of the most competent and courageous attempts in this enterprise is Gilles Deleuze's book, translated in English with the title of *Expressionism in Philosophy*. Given its protean richness, I will take his work as a useful initial reference to develop my interpretation of this key concept. Deleuze's intent is to provide a framework for understanding Spinoza's conception of expression, while also maintaining a rigorous attention to the texts. In Deleuze's interpretation, expression comes in two

---

[3] See, for example, Newlands, "Hegel's Idealist Reading of Spinoza," 105.

stages. The first level concerns the way attributes express the essence of substance, as dictated by E1d6. The second level focuses instead on the expression of the attributes themselves, insofar it explains the origin (*causa sive ratio*) of the finite individuals that populate Spinoza's world. E1p25c stands out as the key text in this regard, since it reads: "Particular things are nothing but affections of God's attributes, or modes by which God's attributes are <u>expressed</u> in a certain and determinate way" (my emphasis).

Thus, the two levels of expression are nested within one another. The first level gives content to God's essence through the attributes, and the second level modifies the attributes to give them content through modes, that is, finite individuals. Each of the two levels can also be constructed as a "triad," to use Deleuze's term: the first triad includes substance, attributes, and essence in a structure where "substance expresses itself, attributes are expressions, and essence is expressed."[4] The second triad involves attributes, affections, and modes: in this case, attributes express themselves, modes are expressions, and affections are expressed. As it is plain to see, the triadic strategy employed here possesses two main advantages. First, it is modular, insofar as it can be repeatedly applied to both the main cases of ontological expression. And second, it is relational, in a way that safeguards Spinoza's utilization of a relational predicate to describe the rise of plurality from singularity. To make matters clearer, let us observe the graphic representation below (Figure 2.1).

The two triads of ontological expression connect *Natura naturans*, which is constituted by God and his attributes, to modes and affections, which form *Natura naturata*. In two short steps, Spinoza seems to have bridged the distance between infinite and finite, between free and determined. How is this possible?

If you asked a Spinozist scholar which items are contained in Spinoza's ontology, the answer would resemble some version of

[4] Deleuze, *Expressionism in Philosophy*, 27.

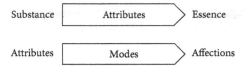

Figure 2.1 The triads of expression

the following list: substance, attributes, modes.[5] This is a fairly contained ontological expenditure, which involves just three kinds of alleged "objects." The triadic structure of expression transforms these items, commonly understood through an objectual paradigm (in the first case, attributes; in the second case, modes) into functional structures. Notice that under the lens of expression, two out of the three key objectual elements of Spinoza's ontology are translated into their structural counterparts. As we have already established in the previous chapter, substance is defined as a structural being from the start, since it was introduced in Spinoza's ontology under the reflexive and relational mantle of *causa sui*.

Thus, thanks to the concept of expression, we can affirm to have completed the initial stage of the translation of Spinoza's main ontological elements into structural notions. Of course, this metaphysical translation is nothing but a mere skeleton; it tells us *which* elements we must interpret through the notion of expression. Yet, it tells us virtually nothing about *what* expression is, or *where* (and how) it is supposed to do work within Spinoza's metaphysics. Answering these two questions and providing my reader

---

[5] Some scholars might wish to cast attributes out of this list, for reasons that are entirely understandable; attributes might be interpreted as features of the substance that require an intellect to interact with them (the so-called *subjectivist* interpretation of Spinoza's attributes). I will discuss this interpretation, and its relative solidity, in Section 2.3 below. Other scholars might wish to add a distinction between infinite modes and finite modes, which are interrelated through either an emanative structure or a parthood relation. I am entirely sympathetic to this reading, but I would still like to point out how the main ontological species "mode" remains unaltered by this distinction. A mode still *is* an affection of God's attributes, whether finite or infinite, and it therefore expresses God's attributes according to E1p25c.

with meaningful explanations of their metaphysical fallout is the task I undertake in the following paragraphs.

2.2 Expressionism and Explanation

The word "expressionism" has sometimes been used to describe Spinoza's metaphysics. This terminology might sound unappealing or even downright scary. Indeed, what does it mean to affirm that a metaphysical theory is "expressionistic"? How are we supposed to cash out this adjective in the rigorous language of Spinoza's philosophy? The task of this section will be to debunk this concept, in order to put it to serious interpretative work and to develop an expressionistic lens to approach Spinoza's metaphysics.

The Latin term *expressio* is not formally defined by Spinoza in any of his works, as I have noted before. Nonetheless, we can attempt to formulate a makeshift definition through a careful observation of the use that Spinoza makes of this notion. This task will require a thorough observation of the most significant texts containing expression in Spinoza's *Ethics*. We have already encountered two of the main uses: namely, the way in which attributes express the essence of substance, and the way in which modes express the affections of the attributes.[6]

Let us now focus on the first instance, which describes the relationship between the attributes, the substance, and its essence. What does it mean for something to *express* an essence? Spinoza offers an important clarification of this notion in the second scholium to E1p8. There, he affirms that "the true definition of each thing neither involves nor expresses anything except the nature of the thing defined (*veram uniuscujusque rei definitionem nihil involvere, neque exprimere præter rei definitæ naturam*)."[7] The first

---

[6] As a reminder, these two structural applications of expression are introduced by Spinoza respectively in E1d6 and E1p25c.
[7] G II/50/24.

thing to note, here, is that the relation of expression is equated to the notion of involvement. This is an important and controversial issue, to which I shall dedicate ample space in the next section of this chapter. For now, let us just note that intuitively, involvement represents the flip side of expression. Something can only express what is involved in it. In addition to this introduction of involvement as a correlate to expression, however, E1p8s provides us with another important feature of expression: namely, that definitions can express the nature of things.

The correlation between expression and definitions highlights how expression operates at the featural level of things. A natural interpretation of Spinoza's thesis in E1p8s would claim that the definition of x expresses φ if and only if φ is involved in the essence of x. While a thorough examination of Spinoza's doctrine of definitions would be beyond the scopes of this chapter, some clarificatory words are certainly in order if we are to ascertain the meaning of this thesis. In 1663, during an epistolary exchange with his pupil Simon De Vries, Spinoza carefully explains his views regarding definitions.[8]

> A definition either explains a thing as it is [NS: in itself] outside the intellect—and then it ought to be true and to differ from a proposition or axiom only in that <u>a definition is concerned solely with the essences of things or of their affections</u>, whereas an axiom or a proposition extends more widely, to eternal truths as well—or else it explains a thing as we conceive it or can conceive it—and then it also differs from an axiom and a proposition in that it need only be conceived, without any further condition,

---

[8] Spinoza's views in *Letter 9* are constructed as a polemical response to the views on definitions expressed by the popular divulgator of Euclid's geometry, Giovanni Alfonso Borelli, who De Vries had quoted in his solicitation to Spinoza. For a brilliant discussion of Borelli's theoretical work and his distance from Spinoza's own views, see Brandau, *Spinoza on Definition and Essence*, 29–38.

and need not, like an axiom [NS: and a proposition] be conceived as true. So a bad definition is one that is not conceived.[9]

In this text, Spinoza's aim is to differentiate the role of definitions from that assigned to axioms and propositions. While the latter extends to include a claim to eternal truths, in the emphasized portion of the text we can see how the scope of definitions is limited to the essence of things and the essence of the affections of things (*circa rerum, rerumque affectionum essentias versatur*). However, Spinoza's remark at the end of this passage is quite puzzling. Aside from the difference regarding their respective scopes, definitions and axioms are distinguished because the former needs *only* to be conceived, while the latter may *just* be conceived. The final sentence reinforces this concept, by affirming that a definition "fails" only when it is *not* conceived.

What can this mean? To find a solution we can fortunately look to one of the rare examples that Spinoza provides in his *corpus*. Suppose that I am asked to provide a definition of Solomon's Temple, he says. To this question, I can either respond with a true definition—one that describes the essence of the thing and its properties as they are *outside of the intellect*—or with some description of a temple that I have in my mind. If I respond with the description of my own temple, Spinoza is glad to affirm, I would certainly be able to go out, buy land and stones and all the required materials, and start construction. I would even end up with an actual temple, and no one "in his right mind [would] tell me that I have drawn a bad conclusion because I have perhaps used a false definition."[10] Alas, there is a caveat. Although my description of the temple I have designed is most useful, insofar as it can help me build a real, stone-walled temple, it happens to fall short of being a *true* definition. As you will recall, I was asked to provide a

---

[9] *Letter 9* | G IV/43/29–36. Emphasis is mine.
[10] *Letter 9* | G IV/43/24–25.

definition of Solomon's Temple, not a new (and perhaps even fancier) one. Consequently, the definition I offered (despite its practical usefulness) did simply not respond to the request because it did not match its "determinate object." Thus, according to Spinoza, "I ought to give him a true description of the temple [NS: as it was] unless I want to talk nonsense to him."[11] A definition that does not match its determinate object, as it is outside the intellect, is thus dismissed as nonsense. Moreover, this determinate object must be either a thing or a property of a thing, and it must be conceived. The latter requirement is supposed to maintain the relationship between the intellect and the reality that exists outside of the intellect.

Now that we know what a definition contains, and that we know that its scope is limited to things and their properties, we can move to the next step in understanding Spinoza's expressionist endgame. In the passage quoted from *Letter 9*, he gives us another important piece of information. A definition, he affirms, "explains a thing" (*explicat rem*). We seem to be in the presence of another item of philosophical jargon: what is explanation? Why does it pop up now? In the *Ethics*, Spinoza does not pay particular attention to the notion of explanation, at least under this name.[12] Two key occurrences of the term, however, inextricably tie it to expression: first, E1p14d, where attributes are described as expressing the essence of substance; and second, E1p20d, where attributes are associated with the affirmation of existence. Let us examine these two passages in detail.

In E1p14d, Spinoza proves that no substance can exist beyond God. His argument is baffling in its simplicity, and I will devote to it more attention in the following pages. For now, let us focus exclusively on the way in which explanation and expression weigh on God's unicity. To support this crucial tenet of his ontological

---

[11] *Letter 9* | G IV/43/19–21.
[12] Cf. Deleuze, *Spinoza: Practical Philosophy*, 68–69. Deleuze reconstructs the notion of explication as a precedent to expression; contra this interpretation, see Gartenberg, *Spinozistic Expression*, 2n2.

monism, Spinoza shows how God must exhibit all attributes, being absolutely infinite. Thus, he infers, "no attribute which expresses an essence of substance (*quod essentiam substantiæ exprimit*) can be denied" of God. If, for the sake of argument, we admitted that another substance could exist, then that substance "would have to be explained through some attribute of God (*explicari deberet per aliquod attributum Dei*)." The essence of any substance (both God and the other, nonexisting ones) is both expressed and explained through an attribute. Deleuze makes a similar point, although admittedly in an enigmatic form: "what is expressed," he says, "has no existence outside its expression, but is expressed as the essence of what expresses itself."[13] In other words, the substance could not exist without expressing itself through its attributes.[14]

A similar dynamic occurs in E1p20d. Here, Spinoza's goal is to prove the identity of the essence and existence of substance, which is to say, its necessary existence. Given Spinoza's definition of eternity, in order to claim that something necessarily exists, we must claim that it is eternal.[15] Since God's essence and his attributes, as we have seen, are at least coextensive if not identical, then Spinoza rightly claims that "each of [God's] attributes express existence. Therefore, the same attributes of God which (by E1d4) explain God's eternal essence at the same time explain his eternal existence" (emphasis is mine). Let us supersede on the merits of the argument equating eternity to necessary existence, to which I will return in Chapter 3. In the context of our present discussion, we should not ignore Spinoza's allusion to the fact that God's essence is "explained" through attributes. To support this claim, he refers the reader back to E1d4, namely the definition of attribute,

---

[13] Deleuze, *Expressionism in Philosophy*, 43.
[14] I have examined some of the possibly perplexing consequences of this reading in my "Triadic Metaphysics: Spinoza's Expression as Structural Ontology."
[15] Cf. E1d8: "By eternity I understand existence itself, insofar as it is conceived to follow necessarily from the definition alone of the eternal thing."

which is identified as "what the intellect perceives of a substance as constituting its essence." The reversal of this definition, as we have already seen, appears in E1d6, where God is described as "a substance consisting of an infinity of attributes, of which each one expresses an eternal and infinite essence." The similarity between E1d6 and E1p20d is striking, except for one difference: the substitution of "expression" with "explanation."

To employ expression and explanation as synonyms might be, on first sight, just an idiosyncratic usage by Spinoza or even a slip of the pen.[16] Yet, as we have seen in our analysis of E1p8s and *Letter 9*, this use has a significant metaphysical foundation. A definition must "explain a thing," and definitions are supposed to provide us with the essence and affections of that thing. Thus, there is an overlap between explanation and expression, insofar as expression is the relation holding between an essence of the substance and the attributes or features of a substance. The explanatory power of expression, so to speak, is the reason why certain definitions are true and others are not: the features of an essence express (or explain) it because they are involved in it. In conclusion, a definition is true only if it matches a determinate essential object, which the attributes (or, more generally, the features) of a substance express in existential form.

So far, our analysis of the concept of expression has provided us with important clarifications regarding not just expression itself but involvement and explanation, as well. According to Spinoza, an expressive structure must hold between two ontological *id*s, x and y, when y existentially explains the essential contents of x. By contrast, involvement is a structure whereby the existential forms of y are necessarily contained in the essence of x. The structural framework of expression is thus in place. It is now time to start providing semantic content to fill out this framework, beginning from

---

[16] The second option is statistically improbable. Similar occurrences of this use of "explanation" include: E2p5, E2p7s, E2p11, E2p43, E2p44c2d, E3p2d, E3p56d, and E4p4d.

the notion of *attribute*, as it appears to stand at a crucial fork in the road of Spinoza's metaphysics.

2.3 The Attributal Deadlock

In the previous section, we have established how Spinoza conceptualizes attributes as the features of substance, which are able to existentially give content to the infinite essence of God. Yet, the gap from an infinite and undifferentiated substance to describable features is too wide to be filled by the simple concept of expressionist metaphysics as described above.

In fact, the width of this gap appears so insurmountable that it generated one of the biggest deadlocks in Spinoza scholarship: the debate between subjectivists and objectivists. The dilemma is the following: given Spinoza's monism of substance, are attributes real features of substance that possess a relative ontological independence? Or are they, rather, better conceived as epiphenomena, that is, features that the intellect applies to substance to be able to conceive it? The view that attributes are real features of substance and, as such, really existing within substance, has been denominated "objectivism." Conversely, the view that attributes are ideas in the intellect has been named "subjectivism."

Subjectivist interpretations of the ontological nature of attributes understand them as existing only *in intellectu*, that is, in the mind of the perceiver of the essence of substance. The strongest champion of this interpretation is arguably Wolfson, who maintains that the literary and philosophical evidence provided by Spinoza's works points in the direction of subjectivism. Taking Wolfson as the paradigmatic example of subjectivism, however, does not entail that I am claiming that the subjectivist reading peaked at the beginning of the twentieth century, never to be amended and updated. Contemporary readings that align with subjectivism have emerged in the aftermath of the objectivist dominance at the end of the century, thus reigniting the debate and reinforcing the deadlock.

What is, then, the core tenet of subjectivism? "The attributes have no independent existence at all but are identical with the essence of the substance."[17] Therefore, the subjectivist posits, attributes are metaphysically dependent on the mind or intellect that conceives them. I shall refer to this thesis as subjectivist mind-dependence (SMD).

Attributes, according to this position, are not real features of substance; instead, they are what a finite or infinite intellect perceives when it attempts to conceive of substance. To be conceivable, the essence of substance must be "reduced" to perceived attributes.

The philosophical reason for holding this position, according to Wolfson, is Spinoza's claim that God or substance is a being "absolutely simple."[18] Such simplicity excludes any kind of plurality, whether metaphysical, logical, or physical. Wolfson claims that an objectivist position, to the effect that attributes have extra-mental reality, denies that simplicity; and according to Wolfson, such a denial would be incompatible with Spinoza's monism. Therefore, having excluded the possibility of the extra-mental reality of the attributes, the only remaining option is to hold SMD and its fictionalist cognate: *attributes only exist in the mind of a subject.* In support of this option, Wolfson argues that Spinoza only refers to attributes using a terminology related to thought.

> He describes [them], for instance, as that which the intellect perceives (*percipit*) concerning the substance, or as that which expresses (*exprimit*) or explains (*explicat*) the essence of substance, or as that under which God is considered (*consideratur*) or every entity is conceived (*concipi*), or as that which is the same

---

[17] Wolfson, *The Philosophy of Spinoza*, I:146.
[18] Ibid., I:147.

as substance but is called attribute with respect to the intellect (*respectu intellectus*).[19]

The terms "perceive," "express," "explain," "consider," "conceive" all arguably pertain to the intellect and thus to a conceiving subject.[20] This thorough (although not unchallengeable) textual analysis leads Wolfson to the conclusion that Spinoza refers to attributes in subjective terms because they are nothing but a way of conceiving substance.

As Wolfson also notes, SMD entails another thesis. This is the view that "the two attributes [extension and thought] appear to the mind as being distinct from each other. In reality, however, they are one."[21] I shall refer to this as subjectivist real identity (SRI), which can also be stated as follows: the subjectivist interpretation entails that *Spinoza's attributes are really identical but rationally distinct*. SRI can be seen as a further development of SMD. The attributes have a merely mental existence; therefore, their distinction must be limited to a mental operation, too. It is impossible that they are distinct in extra-mental reality.

The main textual evidence for SRI is E1p10s: "although two attributes may be conceived as really distinct (i.e., one may be conceived without the aid of the other), we still cannot infer from that that they constitute two beings, or two different substances." Additional textual evidence can be found in the earlier *Cogitata Metaphysica* (*CM*), where Spinoza explicitly declares that attributes are "distinguished only by a distinction of reason."[22] Furthermore, Wolfson notes that SRI is essential to Spinoza's argument for the indivisibility of substance. The steps of this argument are found in the

---

[19] Ibid., I:152. Wolfson is respectively quoting (in successive order of occurrence of the mentioned terms): E1d4; E1p10s and E32d; *TTP* chapter 13; E2p6, E2p7s and *Letter 64*; E1p10s; *Letter 9*.

[20] The term "express," to my eyes, stands out as not fully homogenous within this series.

[21] Wolfson, *The Philosophy of Spinoza*, I:156.

[22] *CM* I, 3 | G I/240/9.

familiar words of E1p12 and E1p13: "No attribute of a substance can be truly conceived from which it follows that the substance can be divided" and "a substance which is absolutely infinite is indivisible." These propositions, situated within the context of the *Ethics*, allegedly aim at demonstrating how one and only one substance can exist, notwithstanding the subjective plurality of its attributes. Wolfson considers SRI as a necessary step in Spinoza's demonstration of the singularity of substance. In sum, Wolfson's paradigmatic version of subjectivism amounts to two theses:

(SMD) The attributes do not have any extra-mental reality.
(SRI) The attributes are really identical but rationally distinct.

SRI relies on SMD. It is only if two things do not have independent extra-mental reality that the distinction between them must be a purely rational one. If SMD is false, and the attributes have extra-mental reality, then SRI must also be false because of the real distinction between the attributes. A new defense of this interpretation has been put forward by Driggers, who opposes any objectivist interpretations on the basis of the impossibility of a one-to-many identity between the substance and the attributes.[23] Instead, Driggers argues that the attributes representa "cognitive route" for "the finite intellect to come to an idea of God."[24] I will address this more at length in the next section, where I discuss what ground would such intellect have to produce an adequate distinction if its operations were indeed exclusively cognitive.

While subjectivist interpretations take attributes to be mind-dependent entities, objectivist interpretations understand them as being the fundamental features of substance, really existing in it. The substance possesses the properties classified as attributes. For example, the one existing substance is really an extended

---

[23] Driggers, "The Unity of Substance and Attribute in Spinoza," 49.
[24] Ibid., 55.

substance, or the one existing substance is really a thinking substance. According to this view, attributes are not *attributed* to the substance by an intellect. Instead, they possess their own extra-mental reality, although it must be kept in mind that they are still properties. Therefore, the first and most characteristic thesis of the objectivist interpretation is objectivist mind-independence (OMI): *the attributes of substance have extra-mental reality*.

A first argument in favor of OMI appeals to E1d4: "By attribute I understand what the intellect perceives of a substance, as [*tamquam*] constituting its essence." However, an interpretative dilemma arises from the Latin word *tamquam*; this connective can be translated by "as if," suggesting that the sentence is describing mere appearance compared with fact. Such translation would reinforce the subjectivist thesis SMD, and attributes would not have extra-mental reality. However, *tamquam* can also mean "as," and when this translation is adopted, E1d4 would support the objectivist view of attributes.[25] Haserot, one of the main representatives of the objectivist camp, has argued that "Spinoza employs the word [*tamquam*] twenty-nine times in the *Ethics*. In twenty-six of these the word clearly means 'as'. With respect to three [...] the contention might be raised (though with some question) that Spinoza employs the term with counterfactual reference."[26] On the basis of this textual evidence, Haserot concludes that the correct translation of *tamquam* is "as": when the intellect perceives an attribute, it perceives something real, namely the essence of substance.

The objectivist interpretation enables us to develop further philosophical theses, which are entailed by the apparently simple claim that attributes exist outside the intellect. Among them is the claim that, to overturn SMD, we need to reconsider how a finite intellect learns about attributes. While subjectivists maintain that the intellect somehow *invents*, *creates*, or *posits* the attributes

---

[25] Cf. Haserot, "Spinoza's Definition of Attribute," 500.
[26] Ibid., 501. The three "ambiguous" occurrences are E1p33s2, E2p49s, and E5p31s.

when conceiving the substance, objectivism requires (as a corollary to OMI) that the intellect *discovers* the attributes as existing in substance.[27]

Martial Gueroult, one of the most representative members of the objectivist camp, famously argues in favor of OMI by appealing to this latter view. His arguments are better described as a series of objections to the subjectivist thesis SMD, based on the assumption that to hold the latter entails denying that the intellect discovers the attributes. Conversely, the subjectivists stress the creative role played by the intellect when conceiving the attributes. In a recent reconstruction of Gueroult's objections, Shein groups them under the umbrella-term "Illusory Knowledge Objection." The argument underlying each of these objections is that, since subjectivists have to subscribe to the epistemological view that the intellect posits, rather than discovers, the attributes, they have to claim that knowledge of the attributes is in some way illusory. As Shein expresses it, Gueroult's allegation maintains that subjectivists create "a gap between the substance and its attributes. This gap opens up because attributes are contributions of the finite mind, something the finite mind adds to its conception of substance."[28]

Among Gueroult's objections, two are of particular interest for the present debate. The first develops as follows: in claiming that the intellect illusorily adds the attributes to its knowledge of substance, a subjectivist denies that the intellect perceives the substance adequately. According to Gueroult, however, this denial contrasts with Spinoza's epistemological beliefs, especially as they are expressed at E2p44d: "It is of the nature of reason to perceive things truly (by E2p41), namely (by E1a6) as they are in themselves, that is (by E1p29), not as contingent but as necessary."[29]

---

[27] See Wolfson, *The Philosophy of Spinoza*, I: 149–150.
[28] Shein, "The False Dichotomy between Objective and Subjective Interpretations of Spinoza's Theory of Attributes," 508.
[29] See Gueroult, *Spinoza*, I:50–56.

The second objection rests on the allegation that the subjectivist interpretation creates a gap between the substance and its attributes. According to Gueroult, it is impossible to harmonize this "gap" with Spinoza's repeated identification of the substance and its attributes.[30] A clear example of this supposed identification is E1p4d: "there is nothing outside the intellect through which a number of things can be distinguished from one another except substance, or what is the same (by E1d4), their attributes, and their affections." Here, Spinoza clearly identifies substance and its attributes.[31] But this identification conflicts with what Gueroult calls the subjectivist "gap" between attributes and substance.

In sum, the criticism of the subjectivist interpretation put forward by Gueroult focuses on the epistemological side of the problem. He maintains that subjectivists create an unjustified separation between substance and attributes, which makes adequate knowledge of substance impossible.

An objectivist interpretation of the kind Gueroult favors must also entail a second thesis, regarding the separation of attributes. Indeed, if—according to OMI—the attributes of the substance have extra-mental reality, then *attributes must also be really (and not rationally) distinct*. I shall refer to this thesis as objectivist real distinction (ORD). The inference of ORD from OMI holds necessarily: if attributes exist outside of the perceiver's mind, then they have a reality of their own; but if they are distinct, they cannot be distinguished only in the mind (rationally). Therefore, if attributes have extra-mental reality, the distinction between them must have extra-mental reality, too. In synthesis, we can represent the objectivist interpretation of Spinoza's attributes as follows:

---

[30] A similar observation is made by Jarrett, "Some Remarks on the 'Objective' and 'Subjective' Interpretations of the Attributes," 452. Jarrett, nonetheless, is defending this point in order to suggest that the subjectivist option has more textual support than the alternative.

[31] An interesting, if alternative, interpretation of this passage is provided by Trisokkas, "The Two-Sense Reading of Spinoza's Definition of Attribute," 1098–1100.

(OMI) The attributes have extra-mental reality.
(ORD) The attributes are distinct through a real distinction.

However, ORD appears to contrast in a problematic way with Spinoza's monism. If attributes are distinguished through a real distinction, there would be an ontological divide between them, which threatens the unity of the substance. As Lennon puts it, "in denying the simplicity of Spinozian substance, Gueroult risks undoing all that substance is thought to do."[32] In the first part of the *Ethics*, one of Spinoza's main theses—perhaps the main thesis—is the unity of substance. The question therefore arises: how can a real multiplicity of attributes (which are also really distinct) be compatible with the singularity of substance?[33]

2.4 Aspects, Distinctions, and the Realm of *Quatenus*

The deadlock illustrated above delineates the distance between subjectivist and objectivist interpretations of Spinoza's attributes, and by extension, the understanding of Spinoza's concept of expression. Yet, the answer to this stall may be within reach if we consider that Spinoza was the heir to many traditions, including the Scholastic tradition. Scholastic philosophers had elaborated a cornucopian variety of what we may call "hybrid distinctions," which filled the gap between real and rational distinctions.[34] Spinoza, who audited the lectures of one of the main Dutch Scholastics in

---

[32] Lennon, "The Rationalist Conception of Substance," 25.
[33] Recently, an answer to this question (involving Spinoza's substance pluralism) has been proposed by Smith, in his "Spinoza, Gueroult and Substance." Smith defends Gueroult's position by endorsing an understanding of Spinoza's metaphysics that does not entail monism.
[34] Examples of this tradition include Duns Scotus's formal distinction, Suárez's distinction of reasoned reason, Henry of Ghent's intentional distinction, and many more. I explore this topic at length in my "Spinoza and the Hybrid Distinction of Attributes."

Franco Burgersdijk at the university of Leiden, was surely aware of this fertile metaphysical terrain, which was also familiar ground to the Jewish tradition, another of Spinoza's heirlooms.[35]

The key feature of a hybrid distinction lies in its capacity to represent reality, without being invented by the intellect. The relationship between reality and intellect supposed by a hybrid distinction is one of "discovery."[36] The intellect "discovers" in one and the same object a multiplicity of real features, which make that object conceivable through a multiplicity of aspects. The notion of aspect is in turn subject to various interpretations: some philosophers have seen it as a feature of objects that has the capacity to generate in an intellect the occasion for a distinction.[37] Other authors have interpreted aspects as depending on a diversity found *in the essence* of a given thing.[38] Contemporary metaphysicians have also taken an interest in the notion of aspect, which explains a key feature of reality: hyperintensionality.

Something is defined as hyperintensional when it possesses multiple descriptions that are resistant to substitution. For example, take the case of Medea in Euripides's famous tragedy; *qua* mother she wants to protect her children, but insofar as she is enraged at their father Jason, she wants to kill them. This example is taken from Baxter, who is perhaps the most accurate scholar on aspects in contemporary scholarship. As Baxter rightly claims, the difference in species here (Medea *qua* mother, Medea *qua* enraged at Jason) is not a mere distinction of reason. One aspect of Medea's self truly has a desire—protecting her children—which the other aspect

---

[35] For example, divine attributes are intended as aspects of God in the philosophy of Moses Maimonides, one of the main sources of Spinoza.

[36] This important feature of expression is being recognized in philosophical disciplines other than metaphysics—see for example Congdon, *Moral Articulation*, 48.

[37] This is the case of Suárez, who claims that hybrid distinctions "arise not entirely from the sheer operation of the intellect, but from the occasion offered by the thing itself on which the mind is reflecting" (*Disputationes Metaphysicae* 7, I, §4).

[38] This is the interpretation offered by Burgersdijk, who claims that hybrid distinctions arise "when in one and the same thing there is found one and another Quiddity or Definition" (*Monitio Logica*, XXI, a4, §1).

lacks. In other words, Medea here differs from herself. However, such internal difference does not go as far as concluding "that there are distinct parts of the self or distinct, co-habiting selves. Such a conclusion neglects the unitariness [*sic*] of the conscious self."[39] The self-division exemplified here cannot be reduced to a distinction of reason, but it cannot be a real distinction, either.

Real distinctions, which include distinctions of parts as well, presuppose a separability of substances, of *things*, that is simply not available within one individual. Take an alternative example: one could be tempted to say that facets of a dice are irreducible in the same way. They exhibit incompatible properties, such as "displaying two black dots" or "beating the previous throw." However, the difference between an aspectual distinction and a mereological distinction is that the latter presupposes separability. Facets of a die can be separated (more or less easily); the die as an individual would then stop exhibiting incompatible properties; the subject reduplication would dissipate the contradictions generated by the multiplicity of the facets. This is not so with aspectual distinctions; the numerical identity of aspects inhibits their separability. Consequently, aspectual distinctions appear as the ideal candidate to describe the distinction between Spinoza's attributes, since they allow us to fully respect his caveats regarding the indivisibility of substance.[40]

The possible application of some form of aspectual (or "aspectival") distinction in the analysis of God's attributes has been lately defended by philosophers of theology seeking to safeguard God's unicity despite the multiplicity of nonidentical attributes that can be assigned to God.[41] Utilizing hyperintensional aspects

---

[39] Baxter, "Self-Differing, Aspects, and Leibniz's Law," 903.
[40] As a reminder, E1p12 and E1p13 read respectively: "No attribute of a substance can be truly conceived from which it follows that the substance can be divided" and "A substance which is absolutely infinite is indivisible."
[41] See, for example, Sijuwade's recent essay, "Divine Simplicity: The Aspectival Account," that attempts a defense of what I have so far called aspectual distinctions in the context of contemporary theism.

to describe the attributes of substance is not an entirely novel approach in Spinozian scholarship, either. Samuel Newlands has recently proposed a similar approach, which refutes the nonidentity of essence bearers when those essences are not identical. In other words, Newlands proposes that "for Spinoza, one thing can have multiple essences."[42] However, the understandable question that accounts such as these must face still lurks in the shadows: how can we accommodate the demand of Leibniz's law (broadly construed)? How can we preserve the indiscernibility of identicals?

To provide an answer to these questions, we must bring into play one of the most important tools of Spinoza's metaphysics: the *quatenus*. This Latin connective, usually translated with the English locution "insofar as," establishes a thorough conception of hyperintensionality and is the key to open many doors within Spinoza's metaphysical palace.[43] *Quatenus* represents the capacity to synthesize multiple perspectives in one ontological unity. In fact, it demarcates different ways or "respects" in which something can possess a property. This use of *quatenus* as what is technically called a "reduplicative restricted enunciation" appears in several logic manuals of Spinoza's time. In a recent article, Douglas explains how "by adding a restriction to a subject-term, one can form a *new* subject-term whose *suppositum* is something somehow less than the *suppositum* of the original subject (this does not necessarily mean that the new *suppositum* is a *part* of the first)."[44] As a result, "Spinoza can predicate P of God and not-P of God-*quatenus*-he-is-R without formal contradiction, since there is no formal contradiction in predicating contrary things of two distinct subjects," the second subject being formed by the "reduplicative restricted enunciation."[45]

---

[42] Newlands, *Reconceiving Spinoza*, 125. See also ibid., 44, for a justification of the importance of *quatenus* for Spinoza.
[43] Cf. Melamed, *Spinoza's Metaphysics*, 35.
[44] Douglas, "*Quatenus* and Spinoza's Monism," 268. Emphasis in the original.
[45] Ibid.

While this can prima facie appear to be a bit of a semantic trick, the overlaps with contemporary elaborations regarding self-differing and aspectual distinctions are obvious.[46] By introducing distinctions that run orthogonally to the classic mereological distinction of parts and whole, Spinoza—much like contemporary metaphysicians—is able to account for self-differing and multiple, incompatible properties inhering in an apparently united subject. Yet, the significant advantage offered by Spinoza's metaphysical approach is that self-differing and aspectual distinctions are themselves grounded in the expressionistic structure of being.

Thus, we can see how structural features of Spinoza's expressionism can provide a sufficient reason for the exhibition of apparently conflicting properties. Aspectually distinct features—for example, the attribute of thought and the attribute of extension—do *not* express one and the same *aspect* of substance because substance self-differs through the hyperintensionality of its essence. Yet, they *do* express one and the same substance, safeguarding Spinoza's monism and the unity of substance. The breach between objectivist and subjectivist camps can thus be sealed by applying a hyperintensional understanding of aspectual distinctions. The conflict between reality and intellect, which was represented by the opposition between real and rational distinctions, is resolved by an aspect-oriented analysis that can take stock of a multifaceted reality.[47]

---

[46] One difference between Douglas's account and mine is that he explicitly restricts his argument to the domain of logic, whereas I am more concerned with the ontological consequences of Spinoza's respects analysis.

[47] The concepts of "multi-faceted reality" and "respect analysis" have been recently discussed in the field of Spinoza studies by Melamed (cf. especially *Spinoza's Metaphysics*, 35–45). However, one of the most significant differences between my approach and Melamed's is that his version of hybrid (or aspectual) distinctions still requires a significant interaction with an idea (or an intellect) capable of unifying the infinite facets of an object. By contrast, my argument entails that the structural capacities of philosophical expressionism *by themselves* generate an infinity of differing aspects; these aspects are then distinguished, not differentiated, through interaction with intellects and ideas. Hyperintensionality, however, is an *internal* feature of these structures and is not introduced by the interaction with the intellect, finite or infinite as it may be.

This solution accommodates a large portion of the debates regarding Spinoza's account of unity and multiplicity, specifically when it comes to attributes. It is metaphysically sound and even elegant. Moreover, as I have shown before, we possess plenty of historical evidence to demonstrate that Spinoza was aware of solutions resembling hyperintensionality. It is entirely plausible, then, that he was consciously developing his own version of this theory by elaborating the internal differentiation of substance, which results in the expression of attributes.

In the following sections, I shall provide textual evidence for this interpretative claim, while surveying the applications of *quatenus*, aspectual distinctions, and expressionistic structure that Spinoza lies at the foundation of his metaphysics. In particular, I shall focus on questions of logical entailment (how the essence of something is related to its definition) and property preservation (the way in which expression safeguards certain essential properties through its aspectual determination). At the end of this survey, I shall be able to provide a coherent rubric of Spinoza's use of expression and its metaphysical implications.

2.4.1 Eternal Entailment

So, how does Spinoza apply the notion of aspectual distinction and expression in the *Ethics*, and more generally, in his metaphysical system? The first mention of *quatenus*, in E1d8, regards the notion of eternity understood under a modal lens. This topic demands a thorough conceptual analysis, which I will undertake in the next chapter. For now, we can limit ourselves to a superficial observation of the structure of the definition, which reads: "By eternity I understand existence itself, insofar as it is conceived to follow necessarily from the definition alone of the eternal thing [*Per æternitatem intelligo ipsam existentiam, quatenus ex sola rei æternæ definitione necessario sequi concipitur*]." In this definition, Spinoza introduces eternity as an aspect of necessary existence. *Quatenus* is used to establish a connection between the definition of an eternal thing and the eternity that is involved in it. As we have seen in the previous section, involvement is a metaphysical structure that can be elaborated as the converse form of expression. Thus, since necessary existence is involved in the definition of eternity, eternal things express necessary existence.[48]

2.4.2 Carry-over Properties

The following mention of *quatenus* in Spinoza's *Ethics* appears in a crucial text for establishing the ontological status of attributes. In E1p13, Spinoza affirms that "A substance which is absolutely infinite is indivisible"; from this proposition, it also follows that "no substance, and consequently no corporeal substance, insofar as it is a substance, is divisible [*nullam substantiam corpoream, quatenus substantia est, esse divisibilem*]" (E1p13c). The relation between substance and extended substance is established by means of a *quatenus* aspectual distinction, which expresses Spinoza's monistic substance *insofar as* it is extended. Notice that this corollary also teaches us another important feature of Spinoza's expressionism: it has some transitive capacities, since the indivisibility of substance carries over to its extended aspect. Obviously, not all properties can be transitively carried over to expressed aspects; if that were true, then the reduplicative restricted enunciation would be useless because of the indiscernibility of identicals. If an aspect expressed all the same properties as the next aspect, then they would be congruent and identical, and they would not differ. Instead, self-differing ensures that only some features are maintained, insofar as they are *propria* flowing directly from the essence of the *id*

---

[48] In the next chapter, I shall provide a more extensive argumentation for this important innovation elaborated by Spinoza.

expressed. Since in E1p13c Spinoza is discussing the indivisibility of substance, let us take it as a paradigmatic example. Indivisibility is a property that follows directly from the essence of substance; consequently, all aspects of substance should inherit this property. By contrast, it does not follow from the essence of substance for all its aspects to specifically possess extension.[49] For this reason, the aspectual facet of extended substance is subject to a kind of self-differing that distinguishes it from thinking substance.

Spinoza employs the respect analysis enabled by aspectual distinction at its full capabilities in the scholium to this proposition. The example provided shows how the nontransitivity of nonessential features includes mereological properties. "We conceive that water is divided and its parts separated from one another—insofar as it is water, but not insofar as it is corporeal substance." Moreover, this pattern is replicated in Spinoza's analysis of fundamental properties such as generation, duration, and eternity: "water, insofar as it is water, is generated and corrupted, but insofar as it is substance, it is neither generated nor corrupted."[50] The respect analysis of water, in this example, pushes Spinoza's metaphysics to its very limits. Indeed, it seems that one and the same thing, thanks to Spinoza's aspectual distinction, is both substance and nonsubstance. In fact, only substance can be incorruptible, nongenerated (i.e., eternal), and indivisible. On the other hand, substance could never be separated and broken into parts. Even if we take hyperintensionality seriously, the essential divide between the two aspects presented in this example could well appear too wide to be bridged.

---

[49] I am not proposing, here, some sort of non-attributal understanding of substance, of the kind historically offered by Bennett (*A Study of Spinoza's Ethics*, 144–146). By contrast, I am defending a view under which Spinoza's substance must have all attributes at once. Each, however, is individually expressed. This kind of ramified expression accounts for the aspectual differences that attributes present *insofar as* they differ from each other, despite their isomorphism. For a detailed defense of this account, see Melamed, *Spinoza's Metaphysics*, 82–86.

[50] Both excerpts are from E1p13s | G II/60/2–4.

The solution to this apparent contradiction is provided throughout the remainder of Part I of the *Ethics*, and it constitutes the coronation of Spinoza's expressionistic paradigm.

2.4.3 Expressing God's Mind

After establishing his respect analysis in the opening passages of the *Ethics*, Spinoza adopts it as his preferred method of establishing the identity of God's will and intellect, a thesis necessary to secure his necessitarianism.[51] E1p17 states that "God acts from the laws of his nature alone and is compelled by no one." For Spinoza, this absolute freedom is engendered by God's standing as the one and only substance. In order to be compelled (*coactus*) to act, God would need to be acted on by an external cause. Yet, this is impossible since "apart from God there can be no substance by which [the divine nature] would be acted on. All things, I say, are in God, and all things that happen, happen only through the laws of God's infinite nature."[52] In this text, Spinoza directly involves the essence of substance in every event.

God's unbound power results in the shaping of the universe as we know it. However, as most readers accustomed with Spinoza's philosophy will certainly recognize, his understanding of absolute metaphysical freedom is quite far from our contemporary understanding of freedom as a cognate of "free will." For Spinoza, something is "free" when it is not acted upon, and when its action springs from its own essence. Therefore, free does not mean "which has the power to act otherwise." Rather, Spinoza compares free action to necessary consequences.[53] God's actions follow from his infinite

---

[51] Spinoza's early works are already imbued with this thesis, which he largely elaborates as a response to both Jewish and Christian Aristotelians. See my "Spinoza and Scholastic Philosophy."

[52] E1p15s | G II/60/9–12.

[53] I explore this at larger length in my "Spinoza's Metaphysics of Freedom and Its Essential Paradox."

nature "in the same way as from the nature of a triangle it follows, from eternity and to eternity, that its three angles are equal to two right angles."[54] Stating that God could have acted in a different way from what he has acted would mean to threaten the perfection of either his intellect or his power.[55] On the contrary, Spinoza's view maintains God's omnipotence by claiming that God's intellect, his power, and his will are one and the same. The overlapping of these features of God means that there is no distinction between what God understands as necessarily flowing from his nature, what he enacts as a necessary *proprium* of his nature, and what he wills. In this sense, God's power and God's intellect coincide with his essence (as, indeed, Spinoza concludes in E1p34). The essence of God—just like the essence of the triangle—is expressed by his *propria*, which are caused by his power.

However, Spinoza soon begins to show uneasiness with the phrase "God's intellect." The reason for this discomfort is the analogy that the use of this term would create with finite intellects: "if will and intellect do pertain to the eternal essence of God, we must of course understand by each of these attributes something different from what men commonly understand."[56] Spinoza, a long-standing enemy of analogous reasoning, cannot accept a commonality of definition between God's intellect and what we refer to as "intellect" for humans.[57] The main reason he

---

[54] E1p17c2s | G II/62/18–19.

[55] "My opponents," Spinoza says, "seem to deny God's omnipotence. For they are forced to confess that God understands infinitely many creatable things, which nevertheless he will never be able to create. For otherwise, if he created everything he understood [NS: to be creatable] he would (according to them) exhaust his omnipotence and render himself imperfect. Therefore, to maintain that God is perfect, they are driven to maintain at the same time that he cannot bring about everything to which his power extends" (E1p17c2s | G II/62/23–29).

[56] E1p17c2s | G II/62/32–34). Spinoza, here, uses *attribute* in a general and not technical fashion—reminiscent of earlier works such as the *Short Treatise*. The mature Spinoza would realistically deny that will and intellect are attributes—in his idiosyncratic sense—since they are both infinite modes of thought.

[57] A thorough analysis of Spinoza's (and early modern) rejection of analogy is provided by Schmaltz, "The Disappearance of Analogy in Descartes, Spinoza, and Regis."

provides for this stern refusal is the temporal priority order that the functions of intellect and understanding, in themselves, suggest. Humans utilize their intellect to understand events and structures that temporally precede or coincide with their own duration. God, of course, is prior to everything else in essence and existence, and the function described by the name "intellect" is therefore heterogeneous in its application to God and finite beings.

To account for the way in which God's intellect is contained in God's essence, Spinoza recurs once more to aspectual distinction. "God's intellect," he affirms, "insofar as it is conceived to constitute God's essence, is really the cause both of the essence and of the existence of things (*Dei intellectus, quatenus Dei essentiam constituere concipitur, est revera causa rerum, tam earum essentiæ, quam earum existentiæ*)." Of course, due to his theory of parallelism (which we will examine in detail in Section 2.6), Spinoza would never admit that a thing that does not belong to the attribute of thought—for example, a body—could be caused by an intellect. In this sense, this passage expands on the heterogeneity of human intellects and God's intellect—which is just another name for God's power. The *quatenus* serves the double purpose of highlighting this distance and, at the same time, establishing an aspectual distinction amongst God's will, God's intellect, and God's power. Certainly, God's essence *insofar as* it is power does not understand things. Yet, *insofar as* it is intellect it does. The distinction among properties that are expressed by different facets of one and the same thing (what we have so far called hyperintensionality) allows Spinoza to bridge the distinction between discrete aspects while still maintaining that they do not share all their properties *in their own respects*.

2.4.4 Infinite Modes

The next step in Spinoza's expressionistic path is perhaps the most convoluted passage in his metaphysics. The attentive reader will already have noticed what is missing from my reconstruction of the ontological dynamics of *Ethics* I: the connection between the infinity of substance and the finitude of modes, which Hegel had desperately sought. Spinoza activates this connection through the introduction of what are commonly identified in the literature as *infinite modes*. These represent a new element in his ontology, a genuine novelty that finds virtually no precedent in the history of metaphysics.[58]

Spinoza introduces infinite modes to provide an explanation for the emergence of finite beings within an ontological landscape that, so far, had only seen the undeniable dominance of the infinite.[59] The reason for this consistent absence of structures that allow for finitude (with the notable exception of limitation, as we have seen in the previous chapter) is offered by Spinoza in E1p21, which claims that "All the things which follow from the absolute nature of any of God's attributes have always had to exist and be infinite, or are, through the same attribute, eternal and infinite." In other words, Spinoza posits here a particular understanding of the principle according to which "nothing can come from nothing" (*ex nihilo nihil fit*). Taken in its literal meaning, this principle would only prohibit the introduction of being in an ontological environment devoid of it. Yet Spinoza clearly adopts a notably robust reading of this principle, in accordance with his doctrine of homogeneous causality, which claims that "if things have nothing in common with one another, one of them cannot be the cause of the other" (E1p3),

---

[58] Cf. Melamed, *Spinoza's Metaphysics*, 113.
[59] Although infinite modes (both finite and infinite) have certainly not received an abundance of attention in secondary literature, there has been a recent growth in studies dedicated to this issue. Paramount examples are Melamed's analysis in *Spinoza's Metaphysics*, 113–136, as well as Schmaltz, "Spinoza's Mediate Infinite Mode"; Friedman, "How the Finite Follows from the Infinite in Spinoza's Metaphysical System"; and Primus, "Spinoza's 'Infinite Modes' Reconsidered." Each of these studies provides a more comprehensive analysis of the concepts that I mention in this section, since my examination of infinite modes is here limited to their involvement in the expression of certain essential properties of the substance.

and, by extension, that a cause and its effect must have something in common. As a result, the homogeneity between God's attributes and everything that follows from them demands that their effects mush share the characteristics of these facets of God's essence, that is, they must be infinite and eternal.

In other words, eternity and infinity are the kind of property that possess "carry-over privileges" (at least at this stage). This impression is reinforced by the following proposition, where Spinoza clarifies that "Whatever follows from some attribute of God insofar as it is modified by a modification which, through the same attribute, exists necessarily and is infinite, must also exist necessarily and be infinite" (E1p22). While in the previous proposition we saw attributes being *immediately* modified by modes, in E1p22 Spinoza argues that those modes (which follow from an attribute) must be modifiable as well, in order to express their essences. This gives rise to a rank of entities called *mediate* infinite modes in the literature. Spinoza's focus in these propositions is the preservation of certain essential properties. The expression of attributes through immediate infinite modes and the expression of these modes through their own modes (mediate infinite modes) maintain eternity and infinity as constant properties.[60]

The final proposition of the triad dedicated to infinite modes, E1p23, states the converse: every infinite mode must follow either directly from an attribute or indirectly through an immediate infinite mode. In the demonstration, Spinoza introduces his expressionistic structure to motivate the provenance of the necessity and infinity showcased by infinite modes. They derive, Spinoza affirms, from the fact that infinite modes "must necessarily be inferred, or perceived through some attribute of God, <u>insofar as</u> that attribute is conceived <u>to express</u> <u>infinity and necessity</u> of existence"

---

[60] The apparent slip of the pen that leads Spinoza to switch "eternity" with "necessary existence" in this and other passages, in fact, has a nontrivial metaphysical explanation, which I will explore in the following chapter.

(i.e., the essence of substance).[61] The expressing role assigned to the infinite modes parallels their retaining the essential properties of substance: infinity and necessity.[62] As we saw in our depiction of the two expressionistic triads described by Deleuze (see above, Figure 2.1), the attributes function as connective between the two triads by guaranteeing the explication of the properties involved in the essence of substance through their own modifications—the infinite modes.[63] Thus, a crucial function of expression as a structure is the transferring of essential properties from a substance to its *propria* or necessary modifications.

We are now in the position to take stock of what we have learned from this brief survey of Spinoza's use of the term *quatenus*, and its correlated aspectual distinction, in *Ethics* I. Aspectual distinctions are introduced to guarantee the possibility of expressing apparently incompatible features of an infinite being (i.e., all the attributes of substance). Yet, they turn out to be an extremely powerful structure. Through them, Spinoza explains involvement as the correlation between two parallel structures: the containment of a predicate in the definition of a thing x, and the expression of the correlated property in the essence of x.

Moreover, the unique features of aspectual distinctions provide for Spinoza the possibility of discriminating between properties that are preserved through different degrees of causal expression and properties that are not. As we shall see in the next section, this tool assumes a vital role in the introduction of finite beings in Spinoza's metaphysics.

---

[61] E1p23d | G II/67/1–4; emphasis is mine.
[62] This reasoning is put under considerable stress by Spinoza's mereological theory: I assess the consistency of his theory of infinite modes and his declared doctrine of individuation in Section 4.6 below.
[63] See Figure 2.2 below.

2.5 Enter Finitude

One legitimate question, in line with Spinoza's abidance with the Principle of Sufficient Reason, might still be asked: *why* are eternity and infinity the two properties that Spinoza identifies as constant? And since we are applying an aspectual distinction, which claims that attributes have infinite effects *insofar as* they express the essence of substance, this reading of the *Ethics* might reasonably leave our reader unsatisfied. What is the other horn of this distinction? What other properties are we neglecting here?

The answer to these questions is provided in two parallel texts. The first one is a letter that Spinoza sent in the April of 1663 to Lodewijk Meyer, his editor and friend. The second is a rather long demonstration, which Spinoza uses as a crowbar to pry open the gap between different aspect of causality toward the end of *Ethics* I.

Let us begin with the letter. This text, also known as the *Letter on the Infinite*, establishes the important distinction "between what is infinite as a consequence of its own nature, or in virtue of its definition, and what has no bounds, not indeed in virtue of its essence, but in virtue of its cause."[64] By remarking this distinction, Spinoza suggests that *propria*, although they inherit some properties that belong to the essence of their cause, do not retain it fully.

To make this issue clearer, let me offer an example—more analogic than Spinoza would wish, alas, since it involves *entia* that do not inhere in each other. Take a can of red paint, which possesses the essential property of being red. If I paint a door with this paint, the door inherits the property of being red from its cause (the paint). Yet, no one would affirm that the door is red "in virtue of its essence"; the redness of the door is a consequence of the redness of the paint ("in virtue of its cause"). Now, this example

---

[64] *Letter 12* | G IV/53/3–6. Translation modified: Spinoza's meaning, with the adverb "*vi*," is logically equivalent to the locution "in virtue of" as it is intended in the contemporary metaphysical landscape. By means of this locution, Spinoza intends to provide the *grounding* of a given thing's infinity.

clearly has limits since the redness of the door is not bound by necessity to the redness of a particular can of paint, and the can does not immanently cause the door. Thus, the door's redness is not a *proprium* of the paint's redness. However, the example can help us shed light on how some essential properties retain transferability (which I have called "carry-over privileges" above) if they are essential and if they express a thing's definition; and yet, this transferability is lost once the property is transferred over to something that does not possess it essentially.

However, Spinoza immediately remarks that there are properties that do not benefit from such a privileged status. The two kinds of infinity mentioned above can also be explained as a "kind of Infinite [that] cannot be divided into any parts, or cannot have any parts, and [a] kind of Infinite [that] can, on the other hand, be divided into parts without contradiction."[65] The answer to the question that opened this section is thus readily provided. Mereological simplicity (i.e., indivisibility) is not the kind of property that survives expressionistic causation. But why? Mereological simplicity is, after all, one of the essential properties of substance. As Spinoza puts it in E1p13, "A substance which is absolutely infinite is indivisible"; from this, as we have described above, subjectivists deduct SRI, claiming that attributes must be only rationally distinct, since a real distinction would introduce substantial pluralism in Spinoza's monist ontology.

Yet, as E1p23d states, these characteristics of substance are only true of the attributes, expressed through infinite modes, insofar as attributes are "conceived to express infinity and necessity of existence." Mereological simplicity cannot be inherited by the infinite modes *themselves* because, albeit they would possess it in virtue of their cause, they have a stronger ontological commitment to their

---

[65] *Letter 12* | G IV/53/12–14.

own essence.⁶⁶ Since infinite modes are, after all, modes, we must understand them as subject to the law of limitation that we have introduced in Chapter 1. As a reminder, something is limited if it might be constrained by another *id*, which must belong to the same realm of being. Infinite modes fall under this domain because their essence does not demand infinity; their cause does. Yet, substance causes an infinity of modes under each attribute,⁶⁷ and these modes belong to the same "realm of being." Thus, they are subject to limitation because they must be understood under the same attribute; bodies can limit each other, ideas are distinct from each other. In other words, since the essence of an infinite mode is a *mode's* essence, it must be subject to limitation, at least in principle; however, since its cause is an infinite thing, it is causally immune from finitude—therefore, its limitation manifests at a more virtual level, under the species of mereological compositeness.⁶⁸ In the following diagram (Figure 2.2), I show how multiplicity comes into being, under an expressive reading of Spinoza's metaphysics.⁶⁹ Under this reading, immediate infinite modes would also be mereological composites, which are composed by each "slice" of all their possible configurations. For example, in the case of motion and rest, we can understand it as the mereological composite of all its possible instantiations; that is, all the possible ways in which a total pattern

---

⁶⁶ This intuition came to me as I was listening to an extraordinarily profound conversation between Yitzhak Melamed and Eckhart Förster on the topic of infinity. I owe both a debt of gratitude.
⁶⁷ Cf. E1p16: "From the necessity of the divine nature there must follow infinitely many things in infinitely many modes."
⁶⁸ One remaining puzzle, if this picture is correct, is what to do of the mereological simplicity that Spinoza appears to attribute to "simplest bodies," which are nonetheless finite (see E2PhysDigA2"). I thank Sam Newlands for pressing me on this topic. Perhaps the distinction between virtual and nonvirtual limitation that I offer here might dispel some of the difficulties; however, I recognize the need to offer more than a sketch of Spinoza's physics under this new understanding of limitation, which will have to wait until further research.
⁶⁹ I am thankful to Sam Newlands for pressing me to formulate this interpretation in much more legible terms.

96 THE STRUCTURE OF SPINOZA'S WORLD

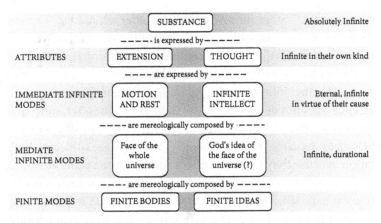

Figure 2.2 The flow of multiplicity in Spinoza's metaphysics

of motion and rest configurates a global state, known as the face of the whole universe (*facies totius Universi*).

The second text that represents a crucial passage in Spinoza's introduction of finitude is E1p28. After concluding his presentation of infinite modes, Spinoza explains how God is the one and only being whose essence involves existence (E1p24), and how necessity flows from God's essence to the essences of things, and from there to their effects (E1p25–p27). Necessity and finitude are the key themes of E1p28 and its demonstration, which I quote in full since it represents a keystone of Spinoza's aspect analysis.

> Whatever has been determined to exist and produce an effect has been so determined by God (by E1p26 and E1p24c). But what is finite and has a determinate existence could not have been produced by the absolute nature of an attribute of God; for whatever follows from the absolute nature of an attribute of God is eternal and infinite (by E1p21). <u>It had, therefore, to follow either from God or from an attribute of God insofar as it is considered to be affected by some mode.</u> For there is nothing except substance and its modes (by E1a1, E1d3, and E1d5) and modes (by

E1p25c) are nothing but affections of God's attributes. But <u>it also could not follow from God, or from an attribute of God, insofar as it is affected by a modification which is eternal and infinite</u> (by E1p22). It had, therefore, to follow from, or be determined to exist and produce an effect by God or an attribute of God <u>insofar as it is modified by a modification which is finite and has a determinate existence.</u> This was the first thing to be proven. And in turn, this cause, or this mode (by the same reasoning by which we have already demonstrated the first part of this proposition) had also to be determined by another, which is also finite and has a determinate existence; and again, this last (by the same reasoning) by another, and so always (by the same reasoning) to infinity, q.e.d. (emphasis is mine)

The proposition seeks to establish that while God is the ultimate cause of everything that exists,[70] finite beings *insofar as they are finite* must be caused by other finite beings.[71] In the demonstration, Spinoza obtains this distinction by means of the aspectual distinction between different expressions of the substance.

In E1p28d, Spinoza unleashes the full power of his hyperintensional understanding of causality. There is no doubt, from the setup of the *Ethics* thus far, that the substance must be interpreted as the only cause of everything that exists (both of their existence and of their essence, according to E1p24). Yet, the specific[72] understanding of the expression of the substance's

---

[70] Yovel has called this species of causation *vertical* cause (cf. "The Third Kind of Knowledge as Alternative Salvation," 160–162); Melamed has instead shown how the main characteristic of this kind of causation is that requires the effect to *inhere* in the cause, which represents an instance of *immanent* causation (*Spinoza's Metaphysics*, 25–27).

[71] This species of causation appears as *horizontal* cause in Yovel's taxonomy and as *transitive* (or transient) cause in Melamed's taxonomy. Another brilliant attempt at exhausting this topic has been produced by Di Poppa, "From the *Nihil ex Nihilo* Axiom to Causation as Expression."

[72] My use of "specific," here, follows Spinoza's idiosyncratic phrases, such as "under a species of eternity" or "under a species of duration," which will be further explored in the following chapter.

causality relies on a triplicity of aspects. Spinoza's causal expressionism opens three alternatives:

1. Things can be caused by the substance immediately. As we have seen in the case of the immediate infinite modes, this means that they retain the substance's infinity and necessity.
2. Things can be caused by the substance "insofar as it is affected by a modification which is eternal and infinite." This is the case of mediate infinite modes, which retain infinity and necessity, but are subject to limitation and thus lose mereological simplicity.
3. Things can be caused by the substance "insofar as it is modified by a modification which is finite and has a determinate existence." In this scenario, the finite and durational modes generated by the loss of mereological simplicity in the case above take the role of mediator causes, further modifying the substance and spawning further levels of modification.

This three-step gradient of causation represents the pathway from infinity to finitude paved by Spinoza. The "ontological jump" is justified through the introduction of parthood, made possible by the loss of mereological simplicity that the limitation of modes demands.

The essential demands of mode-hood (such as limitation, being conceived through another, and being caused by another) can only be satisfied through an hyperintensional account of infinite modes. Such an account allows them to be limited, insofar as they are subject to having parts—the very thing that is forbidden to attributes insofar as they are understood as expressing the essence of substance immediately. Thus, the expressionistic path of Spinoza's metaphysics is secured; the infinity of substance is not threatened because of the nontransferability of properties between aspects; and the bifurcation of causation that leads to finitude can exhibit its sufficient, justifying reason, satisfying the PSR.

2.6 Attributes at Work (Spinoza's Parallelism)

Once we have secured grounding for the conception of finitude in Spinoza, it is time to return to the attributes. The combination of aspectual distinctions and respect analysis provided in the previous sections should have convinced my readers of the viability of an understanding of Spinoza's attributes that sees them as facets of one and the same thing. This interpretation safeguards at the same time the unity of substance *and* the nontransferability of their individualizing properties. With this powerful tool in hand, Spinoza sets out to describe the world through a multifaceted lens that has fascinated scholars for centuries.

The informal name assigned to this metaphysical device is "parallelism." As many interpreters have rightly noted, Spinoza never used this term, which was instead introduced by Leibniz some years after. Nonetheless, the term fits Spinoza's doctrine so beautifully, that it would be a pity to ruin a good story with the truth. Let us continue to use this term, then, under the understanding that Spinoza does *not* aspire to build a so-called parallelism; his purpose is to account for the isomorphism and mutual independence of the aspects of substance.

The second part of the *Ethics* aims to account for the nature of the human mind and to explain its relationship with the human body. Faithful to his aprioristic and geometric methodology, Spinoza undertakes this task by first explaining the nature of *all* minds and bodies. The first definition of *Ethics* II (E2d1) affirms: "By body I understand a mode that in a certain and determinate way expresses God's essence insofar as [*quatenus*] he is considered as an extended thing." This definition reads as a practical application of the structure we have examined in the sections above. Let us break down Spinoza's steps. God's essence is the one unlimited power existing in the universe; by means of an aspectual distinction, we obtain a specification of this essence that allows us to conceive it as an attribute—namely, extension. Through a second expression layer, this attribute explicates itself in an infinite mode; in turn, the infinite mode of extension goes through an aspectual distinction to obtain its limited status—which is the reason why the resulting bodies, resulting from a mereological fractioning of this infinite mode, can be "certain and determinate."[73]

Spinoza offers further confirmation that the path from God to an individual body must run through this attribute-bound structure. After establishing that both extension and thought are attributes of God in a sense that make God "an extended thing" and "a thinking thing" (E2pp1–2), he goes on to shape what we can define as a causal and conceptual separation between modes of different attributes.[74] Remember that for most of *Ethics* I, while discussing the notion of mode, Spinoza was not particularly inclined to describe them as modes of particular attributes conceivably because *Ethics* I is dedicated to the notion of God *insofar as* God has all the attributes. By contrast, E2p6 establishes that "the modes of each attribute have God for their cause only insofar as he is considered under the attribute of which they are modes, and not insofar as he is considered under any other attribute." E2p6 has rightly been interpreted as a crucial text for the emergence of modes in individual attributes. In this proposition, Spinoza portrays an aspect-bound causal structure. For example: God insofar as he is extended does not cause minds and ideas; God insofar as he is thinking does not cause bodies. In other words, the thesis of this proposition is that the expression of different facets of God is opaque with respect

---

[73] It is possible to observe the expressionistic flow of Spinoza's metaphysics in the following, partially formalized, representation:

$$[\exists! x \to x\{e, t \ldots\} \to e\{e^1, e^2 \ldots\} \to e^2\{b1+b2+b3 \ldots\}].$$

If there is one and only one existing substance (whose existence is self-necessitated), then this substance must have all attributes (including extension). If the substance has extension, though, then it must express it through an infinity of infinite modes (e^1, e^2, etc.). However, the nature of these infinite modes—and in particular, the nature of mediate infinite modes—subjects them to limitation, that is, to be composed by an infinity of individual bodies (b1, b2, etc.), each of which expresses the nature of substance qua body in a certain and determinate way.

[74] Cf. Della Rocca, "Spinoza's Argument for the Identity Theory," 187–188.

to causality. Causality is not transitive, at least in the intensional way. God's causality is yet another hyperintensional notion.

Let us now consider the reasons that lead Spinoza to hold this thesis, before examining its consequences. In the demonstration to E2p6,[75] Spinoza relies on the causal axiom established at the beginning of *Ethics* I, which affirms that "The knowledge of an effect depends on, and involves, the knowledge of its cause." In other words, since the attributes are self-conceived (i.e., they cannot be conceived through another aspect of God's essence), then everything that is caused by God *insofar as* his essence is expressed by attribute x, cannot be conceived but through attribute x. Apparently, the causal and conceptional limits of attributes overlap. Michael Della Rocca has argued that this should be taken as a sign that, for Spinoza, conception and causation collapse on each other.[76] The theory guiding Spinoza's reasoning in this passage seems to be a strong interpretation of the PSR. Each thing must have a cause, and that cause must be intelligible. Since attributes can be conceived as the causes of their modes only insofar as they are understood (or conceived) through themselves, then cross-attributal conception is false—just as much as cross-attributal causation is impossible.

As we have seen in the previous sections, this does not just depend on conceptual containment. Attributes possess an explanatory role, akin to what Spinoza attributes to definitions (insofar as they are what the intellect conceives as constituting the essence of substance).[77] In this sense, it is important to mention that another axiom may play just as big a part in justifying E2p6. The axiom

---

[75] E2p6d reads: "each attribute is conceived through itself without any other (by E1p10). So, the modes of each attribute involve the concept of their own attribute, but not of another one; and so (by E1a4) they have God for their cause only insofar as he is considered under the attribute of which they are modes, and not insofar as he is considered under any other." The barrier erected between attributes is mostly conceptual in this passage, as Newlands notes (*Reconceiving Spinoza*, 241–244).

[76] Cf. Della Rocca, *Spinoza*, 65–68. An alternative option, which sees causation as collapsing on conception (but not vice versa), has been advanced by Newlands, *Reconceiving Spinoza*, 64–89.

[77] See above, Section 2.2.

I have in mind is E1a5, which reads "Things that have nothing in common with one another also cannot be understood through one another, or the concept of the one does not involve the concept of the other." When conjoined with E1p3 (the proposition establishing Spinoza's doctrine of homogeneous causality), this axiom clearly compounds causality with conception and subordinates both to homogeneity of aspect. Since attributes play the crucial expressive role of explicating the infinite causal powers of substance, they also regulate what kind of powers the substance expresses in each mode. The thinking power of substance, for example, will not be expressed by a body because bodies are not understood or caused through the essence of substance *insofar as* it is thinking. Thus, Spinoza's doctrine of expression allows him to put a seemingly conceptual notion—such as attributes—at work in a causal sense. Conception does equate causation under certain conditions, which I have described in the above sections of this chapter.

What is more, the aspectual conception of causation outlined by Spinoza at the beginning of *Ethics* II serves as a foundation for one of his most famous (and puzzling) doctrines: the parallelism of attributes. In E2p7, Spinoza affirms that "the order and connection of ideas is the same as the order and connection of things."[78] The demonstration of this proposition once again relies on Spinoza's causal axiom, subordinating the possibility of causation to the conceivability of the effect through the cause. Why is this called "parallelism"? Just like two parallel lines that behave in virtually isomorphic ways without ever touching, Spinoza's metaphysics

---

[78] A recent debate within Spinoza scholarship concerned the identification of two, separate doctrines of parallelism within Spinoza's metaphysics. The first one—affirmed by E2p7—would establish a parallelism between ideas and the objects they represent. The second one—affirmed by E2p7s—would concern the parallelism between modes of different attributes, regardless of what attribute they belong to (cf. Melamed, *Spinoza's Metaphysics*, 139-152). I agree with Melamed that this fascinating topic does deserve a profound analysis, and that there are relevant differences between E2p7 and its scholium. However, the structural parallelism that I discuss in this section can be applied to either one (and to both) of Melamed's two doctrines. I reserve a more comprehensive analysis of this topic for a more appropriate venue.

demands that the causal powers of substance, understood through irreducible attributes, generate equal effects without interacting. Their causal interaction is in fact forbidden by their conceptual separation.

However, it is in the scholium to E2p7 that things get interesting from the expressionistic point of view. Spinoza begins by reminding the reader that "the thinking substance and the extended substance are one and the same substance, which is now comprehended [*comprehenditur*] under this attribute, now under that."[79] Substantial monism and aspectual distinction are indicated as the key requirements for a proper understanding of the doctrine of parallelism. Spinoza comprehends the two aspects (thinking and extended) in one and the same substance, despite the incompatibility of their respective causal powers. The expression of the infinite power of substance must therefore involve all the attributes, even while denying them any possible interaction. But how does this affect individual modes? How are my mind and my body connected?

Spinoza's doctrine of parallelism demands a strict isomorphism in the *structural* components of reality. The "order and connection" of bodies must match the order and connection of ideas. This means that for each idea that results from the mereological decomposition of the mediate infinite mode of thought, there must exist a body that matches that idea in all its structural components (*ordo et connexio*), and that therefore results from the mereological decomposition of the mediate infinite mode of extension. In the next section, I explore what kind of questions this poses for our understanding of the numerical identity of individuals and their individuation.

---

[79] E2p7s | G II/90/6–8. I would like to note that in Latin, just like in English, *comprehendĕre* can mean both "to include" and "to understand." Therefore, an exclusively conceptual reading to this passage is only partially warranted by the text.

2.7 White Modes

The general outlook on substance described by the initial sentences of E2p7s is quickly integrated with the focus on modes that pervades *Ethics* II: "so also a mode of extension and the idea of that mode are one and the same thing but expressed in two modes [*duobus modis expressa*]."[80] The locution "so also" (*sic etiam*) explicitly equates the relationship between modes of extension and thought with the relationship enjoyed by extension and thought as attributes of the same substance.

The fractal structure, replicated at both levels, is a manifestation of the aspectual entailment we have described above. To render this in a clearer way, allow me to introduce an analogy. Imagine a windmill with each stripe colored differently; we have, now, what appears to be a composite object, with nonoverlapping sections that must be conceived separately. This is how Spinoza would conceive of the different modes under each attribute. Now, imagine that the windmill spins as fast as needed, until the colored stripes blur into one color. The windmill now appears white, and the individual stripes are not visible anymore.[81]

The structural entity that results from the sum of all the modes, as they are expressed by different attributes, is what we are accustomed to call "finite individuals" in our everyday discourse (e.g., human beings, animals, objects). I propose to assign to this entity the name "white mode," following a suggestion coming from one

---

[80] E2p7s | G II/90/8–9. Translation modified. While Curley's translation of the last line ("but expressed in two ways") is certainly correct, it underemphasizes Spinoza's suggestion toward a multiplication of the levels of modes involved in this expressionistic process, as I will demonstrate in the next section.

[81] Melamed (cf. *Spinoza's Metaphysics*, 83) proposed a similar understanding of modes. He calls the pre-expressive item "mode of God," which are the non-mereological totality of all the parallel "modes of the attributes" (the aspectual items). For Melamed, however, modes of God are posited in response to the "horizontal" issue of connecting corresponding modes in different attributes. My understanding of "white modes" is developed as an answer to *both* this horizontal problem and the "vertical" issue of explanatory expression.

of Spinoza's letters.[82] If x is a mode of the attribute of extension, it stands in an "aspect-of" relationship with y, where y is the white mode which corresponds to x. Given this case, every expression of y under the attribute of extension shall be exhausted by x; but the expression of y under any other attribute (e.g., the attribute of thought) would not entail x.

Thus, white modes comprehend (in the technical sense used by Spinoza above) all the individual modes of each attribute that express the power of substance in "a certain and determinate way." In this context, Spinoza puts to work the whole expressionistic machinery developed throughout *Ethics* I. The numerical identity between modes of different attributes, distinguished by means of an aspectual distinction, is a feat of expression, intended both as the explication of causal powers and as the explanation of definitory content.[83] Spinoza confirms this interpretation through an example: "a circle existing in nature and the idea of the existing circle, which is also in God, are one and the same thing, which is explained through different attributes."[84] Attributes function as a logical reduplication and an expressionistic specification of the causal powers of substance (since the essence of substance is nothing but its power).[85] Thus, since everything must be explained through its cause, the distinct modes of each individual attribute must be explained through substance *insofar as* it can cause them, that is, substance under a determinate attribute. As we have seen before, however, substance does not act immediately. Thus, each

---

[82] Cf. *Letter 9* | G IV/46/31–32.
[83] Cf. above, Section 2.2.
[84] E2p7s | G II/90/13–15. Spinoza's views on this topic seem to have undergone a slight evolution, since in the *TIE* he wrote: "A true idea (for we have a true idea) is something different from its object. For a circle is one thing and an idea of the circle another— the idea of the circle is not something which has a circumference and a center, as the circle does" (G II/14/14–17). However, the difference is not radical, considering that in the *TIE* the doctrine of parallelism was not yet fully formed.
[85] Cf. E1p34; see also Okrent, "Spinoza on the Essence, Mutability and Power of God," 71–84.

attribute possesses a chain of proximate causes that explains individual modes through other finite modes.[86]

Spinoza can then affirm that the substance causes finite modes both immanently or immediately, through its attributes which explain the individual mode; and mediately or transitively, through the order and connection of proximate causes.

> the idea of the circle can be perceived only through another mode of thinking, as its proximate cause, and that mode again through another, and so on, to infinity. Hence, so long as things are considered [*considerantur*] as modes of thinking, we must explain[87] the order of the whole of nature, or the connection of causes, through the attribute of Thought alone . . . I understand the same concerning the other attributes. Therefore, God is really the cause of things as [*ut*] they are in themselves, insofar as [*quatenus*] he consists of infinite attributes.[88]

As we have seen in this chapter, each of the two lines of causation (immanent and transitive) has an expressionistic justification. They preserve the order and connection of the whole of nature through an ordered succession of proximate causes, each of which expresses God's power insofar as it is understood to be modified in a finite mode through a certain attributal essence. White modes, under this paradigm, are the nexuses of God's causality under an infinity of attributes. Spinoza refers to these entities as "things in themselves" [*rerum ut in se sunt*]. *Pace* Kant, things in themselves

---

[86] As I understand it, this is the Spinozian concept of "structural causality" that Althusser discusses in his seminal work and is discussed by Hulatt, "Structural Causality in Spinoza's *Ethics*," 6–7.

[87] Notice once again, Spinoza's seemingly careless substitution of "exprimere" with "explanare."

[88] E2p7s | G II/90/22–29; translation modified. A similar reasoning is offered in E1p9: "The idea of a singular thing which actually exists has God for a cause not insofar as he is infinite, but insofar as he is considered to be affected by another idea of a singular thing which actually exists; and of this [idea] God is also the cause, insofar as he is affected by another third [NS: idea], and so on, to infinity."

are not beyond conception for Spinoza. Quite the opposite: they are *maximally* conceivable, since they involve all the attributes at once.

Yet, God is one and the same, albeit understood through aspectually distinct attributes. Therefore, a number of God's properties must remain unchanged as we range from one aspect to the next. As we have seen before, certain properties have "carry-over privileges" across aspectual distinctions. So far, we have isolated causation as one of these properties; the order and connection of causes (including proximate causes) must remain the same across attributes. We may refer to causal properties as "trans-attributal features" following a suggestion offered by Bennett, or "neutral properties" in the terminology proposed by Della Rocca.[89]

Neutral properties have the explicit task of allowing trans-attributal tracking of white modes, providing an individuation criterion that does not follow from any particular attribute.[90] In particular, I will take seriously a suggestion advanced by Schliesser, implying that the *essences* of modes must be attribute-neutral.[91] In the next two chapters, we will encounter two additional candidates for inclusion in the list of neutral properties, namely temporal features and compositional features. Before moving to that task, however, let us take stock of what Spinoza has shown us in this long metaphysical journey through the paths of expression.

---

[89] Bennett, *A Study of Spinoza's Ethics*, 141–142. Della Rocca, *Representation and the Mind-Body Problem*, 133–138.

[90] Let me immediately dispel one potential objection to this formulation. While Bennett claims that these "trans-attributal features" must be conceived without the involvement of *any* attribute, I second Melamed's criticism (cf. *Spinoza's Metaphysics*, 83) that in Spinoza's metaphysics nothing can be inconceivable, and everything must fall under some attribute. Thus, when I say that neutral properties do not follow from any particular attributes, I mean that white modes possess some properties *across all attributes*.

[91] Cf. Schliesser, "Spinoza's Conatus," 73–74. While Schliesser (at least explicitly) limits this claim to *conatus* as an attribute-neutral *and* essence-preserving concept, I believe that it makes sense to extend it to all the properties Spinoza uses—at different points in his arguments—as notions of the essence of modes. In the next two chapters, I examine compositional properties and durational properties under this assumption.

2.8 The Decalogue of Expression

The expressionistic structure that Spinoza provides in the *Ethics* functions as a scaffolding, tying together different sections of his ontology. While substance is initially established through self-causation (as we have seen in Chapter 1), its causal powers come to fruition mainly through expression. It is the expressionistic structure of substance that enables its definition to contain all the attributes; it is through the same expressionistic structure that attributes explain the substance, as aspectual components of its essence.

What have we learned about expression as a structure? Allow me to summarize our findings in a somewhat schematic way:[92]

(X1)[93] Expression is the structure that ties an individual x to its definition. Since definitions involve the essential features of the individual, expressive structures guarantee that y expresses x if and only if it existentially presents (at least one) of the essential properties contained in the definition of x.

(X2) Expression is not unique: y does not need to express all of x's essential properties in order to express x. In other words, x is hyperintensional with respect to its expressions, and expression is compatible with n^x intrinsically and mutually discernible aspects $(y, z, \ldots)$.[94]

(X3) Each aspect $(y, z, \ldots)$ expressing x is numerically identical with the other aspects of x. Yet, they are opaque to substitution, insofar as they express distinct essential properties of x. If y and y are distinguished by an aspectual distinction, they do not share all their properties.

---

[92] I motivate these results through a brief comparison with other metaphysicians of Spinoza's time in my "Spinoza and the Hybrid Distinction of Attributes."

[93] I use this notation for future reference to these theses and to avoid confusion with passages from the *Ethics*.

[94] On this point, see also Gartenberg, *Spinozistic Expression*, 3.

(X4) Some properties of x are transferred to its aspects. Most significantly, causal properties (and most structural properties) remain equal across aspectual distinctions.

(X5) Each expressive aspect of x is conceptually independent from all other aspects (but not from x, the individual that it expresses).

(X6) Each expressive aspect of x is causally independent from all other aspects (but not from x, the individual that it expresses).

(X7) Expressionism applies to all levels of Spinoza's metaphysics. The one existing substance is an x, whose essence is expressed through its attributes and by its modes. Each individual mode is an x (white mode), whose essence is expressed through its attributal aspects and by its second-order modes (and so on, through potentially infinite degrees of expression).

(X8) Following (X7), metaphysical structures are themselves subject to expression. I shall say more about this in the following chapter. For now, let us just pinpoint the thesis that since essences are expressed, and essences are results of structures, then structures are expressed through essences (see also X10).

(X9) Following (X3), distinct aspects of a mode ($y, z, \ldots$) can be said to be one and the same thing. Therefore, my mind and my body are one and the same thing (me as a white mode) explained through distinct aspects.

(X10) Following (X8), causality itself is subject to an aspectual distinction. While Spinoza's substance is the only cause of everything that exists, its causality is expressed through an infinite chain of finite modes *insofar as* the substance is understood through a particular attribute (horizontal causation). By contrast, the causality of substance is immediately expressed through all of its white modes *insofar as* the essence of substance is understood as causal power (vertical causation). These two kinds of causation overlap; since they are facets of one and the same causality, they are numerically identical but aspectually distinct.

As it has emerged from this sweeping reconstruction of some of Spinoza's key ontological tenets, Spinoza's structural metaphysics has no particular need for objects. Objects are useful—and meaningful—for Spinoza insofar as they constitute the crystallization of certain structural arcs. For example: my mind, under this expressionistic and structural paradigm, exists as the crystallization of God's causality insofar as it is expressed through an infinity of other minds (which horizontally cause my mind), which compose the infinite mediate mode of thought. At the same time, my mind also satisfies the requisites for crystallizing God's power insofar as it causes a white mode (which I self-define as "me") in the attribute of thought.

Individuals become nexuses of expression, meeting hubs for the intersection of horizontal and vertical causality. The harmony resulting in the parallel aspects of substance, and through the parallel aspects of white modes, must not surprise us. After all, they are numerically identical individuals, resulting from the output of the same expressionistic engine.

In the next chapters, we will observe just how important this outlook on structural expression can be for understanding other key notions of Spinoza's metaphysics, such as duration, individuality, and affects. A caveat for my reader: as we delve deeper in Spinoza's metaphysics of structure, I will investigate with growing attention the emergence of individuals from each of the metaphysical structure that we will encounter. I urge the reader not to consider this as a sign of my flaking commitment to the metaphysics of structure as primal. Individuals are, after all, the most significant intuitive obstacle to the development of a full-scale structural interpretation of Spinoza's metaphysics and ontology. If we can successfully trace back the origin and justification of individuality to the structures that support their essence, existence, and conceivability, we will have made great strides toward the goal of making a structural interpretation of Spinoza's philosophy more comprehensive and more palatable—which never hurts.

3
Unfolding Time
Eternity, Duration, and the Essences of Things

Before the mountains were brought forth,
or ever thou hadst formed the earth and the world,
even from everlasting to everlasting, thou art God.[1]

3.1 Time as a Construct

It may seem odd to include the discussion of an object-oriented property such as temporality in a book dedicated to the discussion of structural notions in the philosophy of Spinoza. Yet, as far as structures go, few are less important than modal notions. In this chapter, I will show in fact that eternity and duration are nothing more than modal properties for Spinoza. They emerge from his strictly structural understanding of causation and determination. Furthermore, I aim to show how they overlap with all the structural notions we have discussed so far (especially expression, causation, and limitation). Finally, investigating eternity and duration in Spinoza's thought will also provide insight on why philosophers interested in radical conceptions of temporality (such as Deleuze, Bergson, and McTaggart) have found in Spinoza fertile ground for their reflections.

Before beginning our analysis in earnest, however, it is appropriate to put forward a caveat. The notion of time (*tempus*) as such

[1] Psalms 90:2.

is just a figment of our imagination, according to Spinoza. What we call time is but a prism, a lens that makes it easier for humans to deal with concepts such as eternity and duration, an alternative viewpoint—which however has no metaphysical grounding except in the more sound notion of duration.[2] Both these notions, as we will shortly learn, are nothing more than modal structures in contemporary metaphysical parlance. Nonetheless, given that we are accustomed to describing eternity and duration in terms of "time" in our everyday experience, I will maintain the (albeit inexact) nomenclature of "temporal properties" when discussing these concepts.

Let us now commence our evaluation of Spinoza's philosophy of time. As in the previous chapters, I will begin with a survey of Spinoza's mentions of the relevant terms, starting from his juvenile works. There, Spinoza delivers some of his clearest arguments against the reality of time as we perceive it. Spinoza tackles the matter headfirst in the *Cogitata Metaphysica* (*CM*). As I have mentioned earlier, he includes time in his (short) list of beings of reason, which human beings devise and use to represent reality.[3] Time is assigned to the rendering of duration and specifically to the representation of relative duration: when x has a greater duration than y, we say that x lasts longer. In other words, time only arises from the comparison of the duration of distinct objects and must therefore display a relativistic and perspectival perception. Thus, Spinoza affirms that time "is not an affection of things, but only a mere mode of thinking, or, as we have already said, a being of reason."[4] Time does not modify the essence or the existence of things but merely our mental representation of them.[5]

---

[2] I am grateful to P. Ingallina for many enlightening exchanges on this topic.
[3] *CM* I, 1 | G I/234/14. The list also includes measure, number, and "perhaps others besides."
[4] *CM* I, 4 | G I/244/27-28.
[5] On this topic, see the excellent analysis provided by Baugh, "Time, Duration and Eternity in Spinoza," 214–215.

While not necessarily wrong (and sometimes useful), time does not provide us with information to be included in definitions, which (as we have seen before) contain only the true essence of things. In this sense, McTaggart was certainly right when he described Spinoza as denying the reality of time.[6] Yet, as we will see in the next section, he was certainly wrong in describing Spinoza as a denier of duration in toto. The reason why time is a mere being of reason is its parasitic connection with duration; duration has actual being (*esse* or reality),[7] while time belongs to the finite cognizer that describes it.[8]

In the *Ethics*, Spinoza takes a further step and completely collapses time on duration. He dedicates E1d8 to the definition of eternity, a crucial passage that we will analyze in detail below. In the explanation of this definition, however, Spinoza affirms that eternity is tied to the essential conception of things; and as such "cannot be explained by duration or time (*per durationem, aut tempus explicari non potest*), even if the duration is conceived to be without beginning or end" (emphasis is mine). It is interesting that Spinoza begins from the supposition that the essence of individuals must be explained (in the strong expressionistic sense elaborated in Chapter 2) by something that apparently is but a modification of those essences. We shall say more about it in the following sections, after completing our investigation on Spinoza's crusade against time.

The notion of *tempus* then entirely disappears from the text of the *Ethics*, until E2p44c1s. This text represents a crucial argument

---

[6] Cf. McTaggart, "The Unreality of Time." On this topic, see also Gorham, "Spinoza on the Ideality of Time"; and Melamed, "Hegel, Spinoza, and McTaggart on the Reality of Time."

[7] Cf. E2d6.

[8] See also *CM* II, 10 | G I/269/8–9, where Spinoza describes this thesis as "evident in itself." Moreover, in some remarks contained in the *CM*, Spinoza seems to explicitly consider duration itself as a mere mode of individuals (cf. II, 10 | G I/271/23–24, where he attacks those who "wish to set up a duration without created things, just as others invent an eternity outside God").

for Spinoza's modal understanding of duration and eternity, but once again, time is only assigned an imaginary nature. "No one doubts," says Spinoza, that "we also imagine time, viz. from the fact that we imagine some bodies to move more slowly, or more quickly, or with the same speed."[9] Imagining, for Spinoza, is far from knowing; it designates the mode of cognition that focuses on our human, finite and limited, point of view. As a result, all cognition deriving from imagination—including time—is relative and potentially inadequate. The text of E2p44c1s is not designed to deny the reality of movement. Spinoza, insofar as he is not an acosmist and he does assign a certain degree of reality to finite modes, must also accept movement. Instead, the scholium points at *speed* as the culprit, meaning by speed the relative understanding of movement that derives from the comparison of various bodies.[10] There is a scarcely surprising, but certainly noticeable, coincidence between this dynamic description of time and the relativistic understanding of the "measurement of duration" that we have observed in the *CM*. There, Spinoza had assigned time to the representation of relatively shorter or longer portions of duration; here, he delegates time to translate relatively faster and slower movements into a relative perspective. Once again, time does not have any reality apart from its grounding in duration, and it derives its robustness only from the strength of our imagination.

3.2 Modal Time

It is now time to fulfill my abundant promises and gestures toward a summarizing analysis of Spinoza's modal philosophy of eternity and duration.

---

[9] G II/124/26–27.
[10] See Spinoza's *Physical Digression*, E2PhysDigA2' | G II/97/21 and G II/97/21–27.

Some crucial notions of Spinoza's metaphysics underwent a significant evolution during his lifetime (such as creation, the inherence of attributes in the substance, and other important topics). By contrast, his views on the modal nature of eternity stayed monolithically consistent throughout his production. Already in the *Treatise on the Emendation of the Intellect* (*TIE*), Spinoza mentions that "eternal truths" are notions regarding those things "whose existence has a connection to their essence."[11] In the *Short Treatise*, he provides content for this general definition by affirming that "God's existence is [his] essence.[12] Therefore, [God's existence is from all eternity and will remain immutable to all eternity]."[13] The structural connection between essence and existence, which as we have seen[14] opens the *Ethics* as well, is explicitly attributed to God as an explanation for his belonging to the number of eternal beings.

To complete the triad of Spinoza's juvenile works, let us turn to the *CM*, which was appended to his rendering of Descartes's *Principles of Philosophy*. There, Spinoza connects the dots once again for the benefit of the reader:

> The chief attribute, which deserves consideration before all others, is God's Eternity, by which we explain his duration. Or rather, so as not to ascribe any duration to God, we say that he is eternal. For ... duration is an affection of existence, and not of the essence of things.[15] But since God's existence is of his essence, we

---

[11] Cf. *TIE* §100 | G II/36/28–29: "*earum existentia . . . habet connexionem cum earundem essentia.*"

[12] Melamed has a slightly different take on this thesis, as he expresses in his "Spinoza's Deification of Existence," 87–98.

[13] It is curious to note that Spinoza, here, is almost citing a recurring formula of the Bible, which appears—among several other places—in the Psalm quoted at the beginning of this chapter.

[14] Cf. E1d1 and Section 1.2 above.

[15] Cf. *CM* I, 4 | G I/244/29–32: "We should also note here—since it will be of use later, when we speak of eternity—that duration is conceived as being greater or lesser, and as composed of parts, and finally, that it is only an attribute of existence, and not of essence."

can attribute no duration to him. Whoever attributes duration to God distinguishes his existence from his essence. (*CM* II, 1 | G I/ 250/11–17)

The implications of Spinoza's reasoning in these three texts are clear. Duration pertains to things insofar as their essence differs from their existence. By contrast, eternity is defined as a coincidence between essence and existence; typically, Spinoza only attributes this congruency to God.

In the *Ethics*, this connection becomes—if possible—even more explicit. E1d8 reads: "By eternity I understand existence itself, insofar as it is conceived to follow necessarily from the definition alone of the eternal thing." As we have seen in Section 2.2, this procedural connection functions according to the rules of expressionism. The existence of an eternal being follows from the definition and expresses the essence contained in that definition.

Spinoza offers a remark validating this hypothesis, immediately after the definition. "Such existence, like the essence of a thing, is conceived as an eternal truth, and on that account cannot be explained by duration or time, even if the duration is conceived to be without beginning or end" (E1d8exp). Eternal truths are, however, an intricate issue in Spinoza's metaphysics. The only objects that Spinoza comprehends in this set are essences—with the notable exception of God's existence which, as he is fond of repeating, is identical with God's essence. The regular characterization of essences as eternal truths[16] has led many commentators to consider Spinoza as some sort of Platonist, who would attribute a separate and eternal kind of being to essences. By contrast, existences would have *esse* insofar as they have duration. I will examine the issues connected with this interpretation of the relationship between

---

[16] See, for example, E1p17c2s: "a man is the cause of the existence of another man, but not of his essence, for the latter is an eternal truth."

essence and existence in Spinoza in the remaining sections of this chapter and offer an alternative understanding.

However, before moving to the complicated task of establishing the ontological status of essence, I still must provide as complete a characterization of duration as available in Spinoza's works. In the *CM*, Spinoza equates duration and eternity, respectively, to non-self-necessitated existence and self-necessitating existence.[17] "From our earlier division of being into being whose essence involves existence and being whose essence involves only possible existence," he says, "there arises the distinction between eternity and duration."[18] Spinoza does not stop here but explicitly draws out the metaphysical consequences of this modal understanding of "temporal" properties: "duration is an attribute[19] under which we conceive the existence of created things insofar as they persevere in their actuality."[20] Thus, duration is described by the young Spinoza as the unfolding of the existence of finite beings; he is specific in attributing this unfolding through duration to their actual—not formal—being.

The seasoned Spinoza scholar will have recognized a special verb in the definition offered above. To *persevere* is a crucial word in Spinozian ontology, which returns into play when Spinoza offers his controversial definition of the essence of finite things in the *Ethics*: "The striving by which each thing strives to *persevere* in its being is *nothing but the actual essence* of the thing."[21] This striving is absolutely necessary insofar as the thing exists, as Spinoza establishes in E3p6 ("each thing, as far as it can by its own power,

---

[17] Cf. Chapter 1.
[18] *CM* I, 4 | G/I/244/13–15.
[19] In the *CM*, Spinoza still applies a nontechnical understanding of "attribute," which here means "property" in general, following the Cartesian use. A similarly vestigial term is "created," which in later works will be substituted by "determined" or just "finite," in reference to the modes of substance.
[20] *CM* I, 4 | G/I/244/19–20.
[21] E3p7, my emphasis. The Latin reads: "*Conatus, quo unaquæque res in suo esse perseverare conatur, nihil est præter ipsius rei actualem essentiam.*"

strives to persevere in its being"). The congruence between duration and actual essence is thus determined by their mutual expression in terms of perseverance. Things that are in duration—that is, anything but God—exist insofar as they persevere in expressing their actual essence.

Further evidence for this claim comes from the wording of the remainder of the quoted chapter of the *CM*. Spinoza claims that the existence of a given thing is distinguished from its duration *only* by reason (recall what we said in Chapter 2 about Spinoza's disdain for the metaphysical import of such distinctions). Why? Because "as you take duration away from the thing, you take away just as much of its existence."[22] This seems an almost trivial claim for a refined metaphysician such as Spinoza; after all, it is obvious in natural language that if a thing lasts less (if you take away its duration), it will exist for less (you take away "as much of its existence"). Yet, Spinoza is extremely careful with language, and this is no exception. Spinoza's definition of essence claims something extremely similar: "I say that to the essence of any thing belongs that which, being given, the thing is also necessarily posited; and which, *being taken away*, the thing is necessarily also taken away" (E2d2; my emphasis). While the verbs Spinoza uses in these two cases are slightly different (*detrahi* in the *CM*, *tollitur* in the *Ethics*), the meaning is surprisingly similar. Duration seems to constitute the very essence of the thing, insofar as the lack of duration implies a lack of existence, and insofar as the essence of things "posits" their existence.[23] In the language developed in Chapter 2, we could say that essence is *expressed* through existence just as much as it is expressed by duration.

We can thus conclude that Spinoza's understanding of the structural dimensions of eternity and duration is inextricably

---

[22] *CM* I, 4 | G/I/244/22–23.
[23] On this topic, see also the fruitful studies by Deveaux, "The Divine Essence and the Conception of God in Spinoza"; and Jarrett, "Spinoza's Distinction between Essence and Existence."

tied to what purists would consider more genuine metaphysical notions: essence and existence. In particular, there seems to be an edge in Spinoza's writings as he talks about eternal truths, on one side, and actual essence on the other. In the next few sections, we shall dive into this puzzle, to attempt a composition of all these jigsawed pieces. We will also keep an eye out for the structural notions we have indicated at the end of the last chapter as the cross-attributal markers of finite modes, "neutral properties." Clarifying the modal and ontological status of essences in Spinoza's metaphysics will also provide us with a more complete understanding of how modes are individuated.

3.3 The Aspects of Essences

As the previous discussion has shown, we need to illuminate Spinoza's distinction between the eternal and durational aspects of essences. In the following sections, I will argue that such distinction should be made through the use of the aspectual distinction I have developed in Chapter 2.

Two solutions along the lines I am proposing have recently been offered by Mogens Lærke and Valtteri Viljanen, and I shall use their works as useful introductions to this complicated topic. Viljanen employs a "realist" reading of the separation between formal and actual essences. Lærke, by contrast, rejects such a separation in favor of a "conceptualist" reading. In this section, I present their interpretations before proposing my own. My aim is to introduce a means of individuating modes through attribute-neutral properties, without falling into the error of "Platonizing" Spinoza's notion of essences.

Viljanen's analysis of the notion of essence in Spinoza's metaphysics attempts to bring it closer to a traditional "emanativist" reading.[24] According to Viljanen, Spinoza conceives reality as

---

[24] See Viljanen, "Spinoza's Essentialist Model of Causation," 412–437.

having two layers: the layer of essences and the layer of existence. However, Viljanen's account does not place essences in a separate abstract realm à la Plato. He separates the two layers by distinguishing two "registers," both already present in Spinoza's *Ethics*. The layer of essences belongs to the register (or to use Spinoza's terminology, to the *species*) of eternity, while the layer of existence belongs to the species of duration.[25]

The most significant feature of Viljanen's interpretation is the substitution of the internal and genuinely Spinozist distinction between duration and eternity for the Leibnizian language of *possibilia*. One advantage of this interpretation is that it refrains from attributing some sort of intellectualism to Spinoza. In other words, it avoids the drift from the intellect *thinking* of the formal essences into pure Platonism. In fact, it maintains that essences are attribute-neutral: "no matter under which attribute finite things fall, the formal essences and formal being of all finite modes—and thus the whole universe—to its finest detail, is fixed 'from eternity and to eternity', to borrow the words located in E1p17s."[26] Formal essences, according to Viljanen, are eternal and attribute-neutral.

However, the distinction between eternal and durational essences is less than immediately clear. How are we to interpret it, according to Viljanen? Following Koistinen, Viljanen proposes that formal essences are the eternal objects of truth that refer to singular modes.[27] In other words, they are "omnitemporally existing entities that function as the bearers of truths concerning finite temporal existents."[28] What is this view designed to achieve? First, it

[25] Viljanen, *Spinoza's Geometry of Power*, 21. Viljanen's position presents strong similarities to the ones proposed by Schmaltz, "Spinoza on Eternity and Duration," 205–220; and Scribano, *Guida alla lettura dell'*Etica *di Spinoza*, 55–88.
[26] Viljanen, *Spinoza's Geometry of Power*, 30. Admittedly, Viljanen is less clear about this point as he contemporarily contends that "true cognition of things proceeds through essences to which we can gain immediate cognitive access; sense perception of actually existing things is cognitively posterior" (16). However, he is straightforward in declaring this an epistemological claim.
[27] Cf. Koistinen, "On the Consistency of Spinoza's Modal Theory," 61–80.
[28] Viljanen, *Spinoza's Geometry of Power*, 31.

avoids the risk of creating shared essences based on commonalities of similar modes. Viljanen's Spinoza is still an individualist and not a specieist.[29] Essences are individual and not shared by all beings that belong to the same kind.[30] Second, it allows him to describe formal essences as the "prime layer of reality."[31]

To reconnect the two layers, Viljanen relies on epistemological tools. Drawing from Spinoza's geometrical examples, he interprets duration and eternity as different "ways of considering" the same thing, just as the same triangle can be considered as an isosceles triangle or as a triangle whose angles at the base are equal.[32] Viljanen thus reduces the distinction between eternity and duration to a perspectival distinction (a distinction of pure reason or reasoning reason). Nonetheless, he still claims that neither is an error nor an illusion: "as both seeings-as are evidently veridical, things really are both. If this sounds surprising, it is obviously only because we are most often trapped in our temporal viewpoint, which keeps us from seeing the eternal in us."[33] This distinction of pure reason maintains adequacy in describing the two temporal viewpoints.

Combining these two points, Viljanen concludes that formal essences are the blueprints for durational existence. What they lack—in comparison with their durational counterparts—is the relational properties that a thing gains during its existence, thanks to its being immersed in a universe rich in other things. These may be called "extrinsic properties," as Charles Huenemann proposes.[34]

---

[29] For a complete classification of the distinction between essences of species and essences of individuals in Spinoza, see Martin's recent essay "The Framework of Essences in Spinoza's *Ethics*."

[30] A fulgid attempt in this direction is the recent essay by James, "Spinoza on the Constitution of Animal Species." See also Strawser, "On the Specter of Speciesism in Spinoza."

[31] Viljanen, *Spinoza's Geometry of Power*, 11.

[32] The example is drawn from Lennon, "The Rationalist Conception of Substance," 12–30.

[33] Viljanen, *Spinoza's Geometry of Power*, 22–23.

[34] See Huenemann, "The Necessity of Finite Modes and Geometrical Containment in Spinoza's Metaphysics," 233.

Arguably, for Viljanen, the absence of those properties does not represent a significant ontological shortcoming. He claims that formal essences are the very basis of reality, and that actual beings follow from them. According to Viljanen, Spinoza's rationalism can be explained by attributing the order of the "whole of nature" to the fact that it follows the quasi-geometrical structure of the eternal and formal being of essences. He extends this claim so far as to conclude that "nothing deserves to be called real if it is not included in this infinite blueprint of reality."[35] Reality (even actual and durational reality) is regimented through formal essences.

Viljanen thus depicts the causal structure of Spinoza's reality as follows: causality flows "down" from the essence of God unto the eternal/formal essences of things.[36] Formal essences are quasi-identical—although lacking extrinsic properties—to actual essences. These essences in turn are modified in relation to the opposite powers of other existing things. The similarity between this model and the "emanationist" tradition is certainly striking and reasonably arouses the suspicion of having strayed too far toward Platonism.

This suspicion is voiced by Lærke, whose reading is, as I have noted, paradoxically close to Viljanen's. He, too, maintains that formal and actual essences are distinguished by a difference in viewpoint and posits a distinction of reason between the two. However, he criticizes Viljanen for expanding that distinction beyond its proper limits and therefore indirectly creating an "abstract realm" of ideas.

According to Lærke, the debate regarding formal and actual essences is merely an interpretative error created by the secondary literature. He maintains that Spinoza's metaphysics does not imply any separation between actual and formal essences. The difference

---

[35] Viljanen, *Spinoza's Geometry of Power*, 29.
[36] A similar model has been recently presented by Hübner, "On the Significance of Formal Causes in Spinoza's Metaphysics." Hübner, however, is a specieist with respect to the content of formal essences.

between the two, if any, lies simply in the emphasis put on one or the other aspect of a singular thing's essence. He opposes the dichotomy between the two species of essences, insofar as it creates "two different conceptual registers" and leads to "theorizing formal essences that are not actual essences, and furthermore, *a real distinction* between formal and actual essences, that makes them separate entities."[37]

How are we to understand, then, the relation between actual and formal essences? For Lærke, the distinction is one of pure reason, and it entirely depends on the mind of the perceiver. According to him, Spinoza uses the "actual" qualification with the intent of highlighting that he is talking about the essence of a thing as it is present to the mind and not as it is in itself. In other words, Lærke argues that "*actuality* reveals less about the concept of existence and more about the way the mind perceives that existence, as *present* or *not present* to it."[38] This solves the problem of the contrast between speciesism and individualism of essences; if Lærke is correct, essences of species are never actual for Spinoza.

However, there are still a few puzzles left. In Lærke's interpretation, the eternal essence is subordinate to the durational existence of the thing. He holds that formal essences (especially those of nonexisting things) have some degree of existence. This is because "even if non-existing things *are not* contained in the attributes *qua* existing, they are nonetheless contained in the attributes *qua* non-existing."[39] The formality of the essence of a mode refers to their structure or to "the relative configuration of its constituent parts." Formal essences, which Lærke maintains are "invariable and eternal," can be contained in the attributes as existent or nonexistent.

---

[37] Lærke, "La grande confusione: essenze formali ed essenze attuali in Spinoza," 89. Translation and emphasis are mine.
[38] Ibid., 88. Translation is mine, emphasis in the original.
[39] Lærke, "Aspects of Spinoza's Theory of Essence," 30. Emphasis in the original.

The upshot of Lærke's argument is that formal essences are defined by way of describing what brings them into existence—or, in the case of nonexisting modes, what prevents them from coming into existence. However, this means that the existence or nonexistence of the formal essence of a mode depends on the temporal and spatial position that the mode occupies. Here we seem to run into a problem, since Spinoza denies this claim on several occasions throughout the *Ethics*. At E2p44c2, things under a species of eternity are described as having "no relation to time"; at E5p23s, we are told that "eternity cannot be defined by time or be in any way related to time"; and at E5p29d, we learn that "eternity cannot be explained through duration." Thus, to apply the definition of "eternal" to essences, one must find a way to do so without referring to their durational existence as the ultimate reality. Yet, Lærke suggests that a formal essence exists in eternity as the "specific relative configuration of parts that defines the form and the individuality of the thing."[40] In other words, a mode exists as an individual instantiation of the "blueprints" introduced by Viljanen, in clear contradiction of this prohibition.

Although Lærke does not fully confront this objection, he does admit that there is one piece of textual evidence that does not fit his interpretation. This is E5p29s, where Spinoza makes an important distinction.

> We conceive things as actual in two ways: either insofar as we conceive them to exist in relation to a certain time and place, or insofar as we conceive them to be contained in God and to follow from the necessity of the divine nature. But the things we conceive in this second way as true, or real, we conceive under a species of eternity, and their ideas involve the eternal and infinite essence of God. (as we have shown in E2p45 and E2p45s)

---

[40] Ibid., 32.

This scholium introduces a tension between duration and eternity that Lærke hopes to reduce to a "terminological issue."[41] He argues that the use of "actual" in the passage is radically different from its use in other texts, where Spinoza discusses essences. In the case of essences, Spinoza is referring to things that are "present-to-the-mind"; in this passage, he is talking about actual existences.

This, however, reintroduces an equivocity into Spinoza's notion of existence. The arguments I have already offered demonstrate— in accordance with Lærke himself—that an equivocal notion of existence does not fit Spinoza's paradigm. Although this claim is not entirely uncontroversial, I think the evidence favors the view that Spinoza understands being as a univocal term. In other words, there is no more than one sense in which the term "being" is predicated, while there might be more than one sense in which the term "essence" is used.

Lærke's interpretation, far from reducing the tension between formal and actual essences, effectively increases it in the following way. If "actual," in the case of existences, means nothing more than "actually existent," then we would have a distinction between existences that are existent and existences that are *not actually existent*.[42] The latter notion is, I confess, unintelligible to me. The only way I can attempt to make sense of it is by supposing that existences that do not have duration must exist in some other sense. Unfortunately, this would mean reintroducing an "abstract realm," this time a realm of existences instead of essences. I agree with Lærke that the risk of a Platonizing tendency in Spinoza's scholarship is real: so real, that Lærke struggles to avoid it. As I have argued, he drifts unwillingly in a Platonist direction by admitting some sort of duality of existence, of being, and of essence.

As an alternative solution, I propose that we can reconcile eternal and durational essences through the notion of aspectual

---

[41] Lærke, "La grande confusione," 89.
[42] Ibid.

distinction we have elaborated in Chapter 2. If we apply that lens to this case, we can understand Spinoza's distinction between *essentia actualis* and *essentia formalis* without having to concede that things exist in two senses.

Like Lærke, I maintain that we need a unitary notion of essence. Essence is one and only one. However, it does have different aspects, and to resolve the debate about formal and actual essences, we need to treat the distinction between the eternal and the durational as a difference between aspects. To put the point another way, we are dealing with a difference *in rebus*, which is not a distinction *de rebus*.[43] According to the interpretation I defended in Chapter 2, we have an aspectual distinction when the adequate intellect makes a distinction that captures something that is independently true.[44] In this case, the intellect distinguishes two aspects of the essence of a finite mode, one durational and the other eternal.

A singular mode is, or exists, in both these registers— durationally, as part of the infinite chain of modes, and eternally as an expression of the infinite power of the substance. In many ways, these two registers are parallel to the twofold conception of causation I described above.[45] Durational modes are connected to transitive/horizontal causation, while eternal modes are connected to vertical/immanent causation.[46]

Furthermore, the essence of a singular mode can also be conceived through both lenses. Since there is a one-to-one correspondence between essence and existence (due to the individualism of essences), we are allowed to switch between these aspects. This does not imply identity between the two, as it is a tenet of Spinoza's metaphysics that a singular mode's essence is not the

---

[43] I am thankful to A. Douglas for his generous help and advice in developing this argument.

[44] On the topic of independent truth in Spinoza, see also Santinelli, "*Assidua meditatio, propositum constantissimum*," 95.

[45] Cf. Section 2.7.

[46] Cf. Gilead, *A Rose Armed with Thorns*, 47–58.

same as its existence.[47] However, both share the same aspectual distinction: in one sense, they are eternal, while in another sense, they are durational. Therefore, essence and existence are "parallel," in the sense that they each possess two temporal registers. In the next section, I expand on this parallelism and compare it with the parallelism of attributes.

The advantage of this interpretation is that it allows us to make better sense of what Spinoza means in the passage quoted above, E5p29s. "We conceive things as actual in two ways: either insofar as we conceive them to exist in relation to a certain time and place, or insofar as we conceive them to be contained in God and to follow from the necessity of the divine nature." Things are indeed actual (in the sense alleged by Lærke, of "actually existing") in two registers. Under the first aspect, we conceive of them under a species of eternity, and we see their immediate connection with God's essence and power. Under the second aspect, we conceive of them under a species of duration; their essence is determined by the time and space they exist in and the neighboring modes that limit their power.

However, just like the trans-attributal identification of white modes needs to be justified in terms of neutral properties, the trans-"temporal" individuation of essences across eternity and duration needs to be justified. In the following sections, I offer arguments toward the clarification of my position and the forestalling of some important objections.

---

[47] For more on this issue, see Chapter 1. The reference is to the difference between God and the modes. God's essence is the same as its existence (E1p20: "his existence and his essence are one and the same"), whereas a mode's essence is not the same as its existence. Cf. Okrent, "Spinoza on the Essence, Mutability and Power of God"; see also Jarrett, "Spinoza's Distinction between Essence and Existence," 245–252.

3.4 The Onto-Temporal Grid

In the previous sections, after presenting two recent attempts at solving the puzzle of the ontological status of essences in Spinoza's metaphysics, I have offered my alternative: insofar as this difference is understandable to us, its interpretation must rely on an aspectual between the durational and eternal aspects of the same mode.

Does this argument help my thesis, namely, that the individuation of modes is always structural, and it runs along relational pathways? I maintain that it does, insofar as it creates a methodological grid for the individuation of modes. On the first axis, one finds the attribute-dependent expressions of a single white mode that I called "modes of the attributes." Such expressions are differentiated in terms of attributal properties ("extrinsic" properties in Huenemann's definition) but unified by the fact that they share what I have called trans-attributal properties. This axis is "ontological": it expresses the ways in which modes exist and can answer the ontological question: what kinds of things exist in the world?

The "temporal" distinction of aspects represents the second axis of individuation. In this section, I shall show that temporal properties might be after all considered attribute-neutral. Temporal properties operate across attributes, provided that we can show how the eternal mind parallels the eternal body and the durational mind parallels the durational body. In other words, I aim to demonstrate how, for each attributal aspect of a white mode, there is a temporal aspect from the point of view of duration that parallels another temporal aspect of the same attributal aspect from the point of view of eternity.

There are, I suggest, four aspects of *the same* white mode. To illustrate this claim, I shall focus on the two attributes that Spinoza most explicitly discusses: thought and extension. However, it is clearly implied that the same structure applies to other attributes, for each of the infinite attributes of Spinoza's substance. In what

	Eternity	Duration
Thought	δ	β
Extension	γ	α

Figure 3.1 The onto-temporal grid

follows, I employ the term "ontological aspect" to represent a mode's position on the ontological axis. By contrast, I employ "temporal aspect" to indicate a mode's position on the temporal axis (be it durational or eternal). The combination of these two criteria generates a grid (see Figure 3.1) that identifies the aspects of a singular entity, which I have described as a white mode.

Aspect α: a finite body existing in duration, conditioned and determined by the bodies it encounters, is the expression of the actual essence of a white mode under the attribute of extension.

Aspect β: a finite mind/idea existing in duration, conditioned and determined by the ideas it encounters, is the expression of the actual essence of the same white mode under the attribute of thought.

Aspect γ: a finite body understood under the temporal aspect of eternity, that is, determined by the expression of the substance as its proximate cause, through the infinite modes of extension, immediately connected with the essence of substance as immanent cause.

Aspect δ: a finite mind/idea, which is understood under the temporal aspect of eternity, and connected immediately to the substance's essence; δ is "contained in God's attributes," which in turn constitute the substance's infinite essence.[48]

---

[48] E2p8s.

Aspects α and β belong to the same white mode, in virtue of the parallelism of aspects discussed in Section 2.7 and according to the numerical identity of aspects claimed by thesis (X3 in Section 2.8). Their identity is guaranteed by their sharing trans-attributal properties, such as causality.[49] Furthermore, the above list clarifies how these four aspects (ontological and temporal) all express the essence of the same white mode.

This account of modes is likely to provoke three objections. The first objection denies the existence of γ (a finite body understood under the temporal aspect of eternity). The second objection denies that γ and δ (a finite mind understood under the temporal aspect of eternity) constitute the temporal aspects of one and the same thing. The third objection denies the cross-temporal identity of (γ and δ) and (α and β). In other words, it rejects the claim that a mind and its corresponding body, understood under the temporal aspect of eternity, are identical with the same mind and body viewed under the temporal aspect of duration. In doing so, it rejects the coherence of my claim that formal and actual essences exist in distinct temporal registers.

Let me address these objections in turn. I begin by defending my claim that γ is the eternal aspect of a finite body. One strategy to criticize this claim would be to deny the existence of intrinsically eternal bodies and straightforwardly rule out γ.[50] This issue is indeed controversial. Many commentators have debated whether Spinoza's claim that "something" of the mind which "remains . . . eternal" after the destruction of the body can be understood as a nod toward the immortality of the soul.[51] However, I suggest that,

---

[49] I take this to be sufficiently established by previous arguments offered throughout Chapter 2.
[50] There may be some similar perplexity regarding δ, insofar as it is understood as a finite, personalized, mind. I shall offer some remarks on this topic in Chapter 5.
[51] See E5p23: "The human mind cannot be absolutely destroyed with the body, but something of it remains which is eternal." Some excellent recent discussions of this issue can be found in Garrett, "Spinoza on the Essence of the Human Body"; Klein, "Something of It Remains"; and Lærke, "Spinoza on the Eternity of the Mind."

interpreted in another way, this passage is consistent with the view that Spinoza is committed to the eternity of the body, in the specific manner that I shall describe below.

In E5p29, Spinoza offers some useful remarks about the eternity of the body (γ). "Whatever the mind understands under a species of eternity," he says, "it understands not from the fact that it conceives the body's present actual existence, but from the fact that it conceives the body's essence under a species of eternity." Since Spinoza repeatedly affirms that when the mind understands something under a species of eternity, it understands it adequately, the mind's perceptions of "the body's essence under a species of eternity" must be adequate.

My aim is not to determine whether this "something" is eternal. To argue in that direction would drag us back into the debate about whether the distinction of the formal and actual essences is real or rational. Instead, the hypothesis that the distinction between the eternal body and the eternal mind is aspectual allows us to accept Spinoza's hint that the essence of the finite body has an eternal aspect.[52] As he says, the mind "conceives the body's essence under a species of eternity" (E5p29). Further support for this view can be derived from the scholium to this proposition, where Spinoza explicitly states that to conceive of things under a species of eternity is to conceive of them as "true, *or* real."[53] I think this gives us sufficient reason to set aside the first objection and conclude that Spinoza countenances eternal essences of bodies. In doing so, he paves the way for my claim that a finite body viewed under the species of eternity (γ) can be understood as identical with a finite mind viewed in the same way (δ).

---

[52] Diodato suggests something similar when he affirms that essences of bodies have a distinct and eternal existence in their formal aspect, which is rooted in their relationship with God's infinite intellect. According to this interpretation, "the happening of things in duration does not add anything to their formal essence" (Diodato, *Sub specie aeternitatis*, 43–44).

[53] E5p29s; emphasis in the original.

As I have signaled above, however, my contention that γ and δ coincide is also vulnerable to a second objection. I have argued that the coincidence of the eternal aspects of minds and bodies results from Spinoza's parallelism. But an opponent might argue that, even if we accept that both the body and the mind have eternal aspects, they are not—to borrow Spinoza's words from E2p7s— "one and the same thing."

An objection along these lines has been put forward by Marshall, who argues that mind and body are 'components' of the same object. This view would be committed to understanding the mind and the body of a singular mode as parts of the same object. According to Marshall, this doctrine would prove that Spinoza's view is continuous with a hylomorphic or Cartesian solution.[54] Furthermore, this option would entail a lighter commitment toward the identity (or parallelism) of the body, considered as a mode of extension, and the mind, considered as a mode of thought. In other words, mind and body, under this interpretation, would not be aspects of the same thing. Instead, they would constitute two *parts* of the same object, and as a result, would hold independent (attribute-neutral) properties. Thus, the eternal aspect of the mind and the eternal aspect of the body (respectively, δ and γ in my classification) would not be one and the same thing.

First, in order to entertain this hypothesis, one needs to deny that the relationship holding between modes of different attributes is isomorphic with the relationship holding between different attributes of the substance. This would make the substance divisible into parts and thus contradict Spinoza's monism. Even if mind and body were parts of the same object (a mode), thought and extension could not be parts of the same substance because substance is indivisible.[55]

---

[54] Marshall, "The Mind and the Body as 'One and the Same Thing' in Spinoza," 913.

[55] E1p12: "No attribute of a substance can be truly conceived from which it follows that the substance can be divided." Moreover, in Section 2.6, I have presented my argument for holding that the two relationships are isomorphic.

Furthermore, this interpretation is hard to square with the text of the *Ethics*, where Spinoza repeatedly indicates that parallelism is a real feature of *Natura naturata*. Even if we set aside the arguments for this doctrine in the secondary literature,[56] we can find support for it in the demonstration of E5p29 (the proposition quoted above), where Spinoza clearly states that "the nature of reason is to conceive things under a species of eternity (by E2p44c2), and [that] it also pertains to the nature of the mind to conceive *the body's essence* under a species of eternity (by E5p23)." Beyond these two, Spinoza concludes, "nothing else pertains to the *mind's essence*."[57] The passages I have emphasized provide further evidence for my argument. Spinoza is effectively proposing a parallelism between the essence of the body under a species of eternity, namely γ, and the essence of the mind under a species of eternity, namely δ. The mind's essence, under a species of eternity, consists in nothing more than the eternal essence of the body.

In the demonstration of E2p44c2, Spinoza is even more explicit. "It is of the nature of reason to regard things as necessary and not as contingent (by E2p44). And it perceives this necessity of things truly (by E2p41), that is (by E1a6), as it is in itself. But (by E1p16) this necessity of things is the very necessity of God's eternal nature." There are therefore ample grounds for concluding that there is a parallelism between the eternal aspect of the mind and the eternal aspect of the body.

Finally, to establish the onto-temporal grid, we also need to rebut the third objection: the claim that eternal aspects (γ and δ) and durational aspects (α and β) cannot be distinct aspects of the same essence. My reply to this objection rests on the claim that durational

---

[56] For example, consider Melamed's two types of parallelism. Whether we consider mind and body to be subject to ideas-things parallelism or to attributal parallelism, the requirements that would establish their metaphysical 'contemporaneity'—that is, a parallelism of species of eternity/duration—remain crucial. For more on the two types of parallelism, see Melamed, *Spinoza's Metaphysics*, 139–152.

[57] E5p29d; emphasis is mine.

and eternal aspects coexist in the same essence. This, I propose, is how Spinoza escapes the twin threats of Platonism on one side and pure materialism on the other. My central aim in this chapter is to establish that formal and actual essences are aspects of one and the same thing. They are distinguished as aspects. Yet, they remain numerically identical. For this conclusion to hold, we must be able to identify γ and δ as the trans-attributal forms of the eternal essence of α and β, which are in turn the attributal forms of a white mode's durational essence.

Strong support for this contention comes from Spinoza's *Letter on the Infinite*. Here, Spinoza distinguishes durational (including infinite duration) from eternal existence.[58] According to the text, which is reminiscent of a theory presented in the early *CM*, the distinction is dependent on the difference between beings whose essence entails existence and beings whose essence does not; in other words, between substance and modes.[59]

This relationship provides a strong backbone for my argument. The continual reference to the ontological distinction between substance and its modes cannot be reduced to a merely projected one—a temptation that would arise if one were to follow Lærke's interpretation. According to his view, the distinction between eternal and durational (or formal and actual) essences is a distinction of reason. Spinoza clearly asserts that there is a real distinction between what is in itself and what is in another. However, the definitions of substance and mode (E1d3 and E1d5) remind us that the distinction between these entities is also a difference of conception. In these two definitions, Spinoza states that the substance is "conceived through itself," while modes are "conceived through another." Therefore, I maintain that my thesis diverges from Lærke's in that the distinction between eternity and duration must be—as

---

[58] Interestingly, Spinoza seems to equate eternal existence and eternal being in the text: "the infinite enjoyment of existing [*existendi*] or, in bad Latin, of being [*essendi*]."

[59] Interesting remarks on why and how *Letter 12* echoes the *CM* are presented by Schmaltz, "Spinoza on Eternity and Duration."

I interpret it—an aspectual distinction, which maintains at once numerical identity and nontransitivity of all properties.

One of the aspects of modes—their durational, or actual, essence—is entirely confined within duration; as Spinoza declares, "it is only of modes that we can explain the existence by duration."[60] However, Spinoza does not maintain that this aspect excludes its opposite. In fact, we can understand modes as direct expressions of the immanent and vertical causality of the substance, and thus as included in the eternity of substance, since it is the finite intellect that forces finite modes to be exclusively durational. In fact, Spinoza states that

> if the modes of substance themselves are confused with beings of reason [*entia rationis*] of this kind, or aids of the imagination, they too can never be rightly understood. For when we do this, we separate them from substance, and from the way they flow from eternity, without which, however, they cannot be rightly understood.[61]

In this passage, Spinoza asserts that modes—insofar as they are not separated from substance—flow from eternity, which allows for their conception (as required by E1d5).

Thus, the distinction between durational modes and modes that exist eternally *as immediate manifestations of the substance* has some of the characteristics of a real distinction (modes really are in duration) and some of the features of a distinction of reason (we separate modes from the eternity of substance from which they flow).[62]

---

[60] *Letter 12*, G IV/55.
[61] *Letter 12*, G IV/57–58.
[62] Admittedly, in this passage Spinoza appears to entertain the hypothesis that the durational essences of modes are illusory (*entia rationis*). This interpretation is connected to an "acosmist" reading of Spinoza's metaphysics of modes. As we have seen in Chapter 2, however, Spinoza's expressionism strongly denies this possibility.

It is important to note that the relationship between duration and eternity is not a part-whole relation—a finite duration is not a part of eternity. I have applied the same clarification to modes, which are not in a part-whole relation with the substance.[63] Instead, duration and eternity are different *ways* of existing or aspects of existence. Eternity pertains to substance and to the formal essences of things (not just ideas or modes of thought) as particular determinations of the infinite productive power of *natura naturans*.[64] Duration pertains to modes and to their actual essences as particular manifestations (or parts) of the infinite chain of expression that is *natura naturata*.[65]

This section has clarified the role played by the layers of temporality (eternity and duration) in Spinoza's metaphysics of modes. The individuation of modes is the result of many factors, some of them attributal and others trans-attributal. In this section, I have suggested that these factors can be schematically represented in an onto-temporal grid with two axes: the first recomposes the modes conceived under different attributes; the second recomposes them under different temporal species, in their durational existence and in their immediate dependence on the substance. Modes have duration but are also present under a species of eternity. I now move on to demonstrate how the individuation of modes is built on structural notions.

In the next section, we will dive into eternity and its complicated metaphysical structure. But first, let us discuss the connection between the durational aspect of modes and trans-attributal properties.

---

[63] See Chapter 1.
[64] A similar idea has been recently expressed by Baugh, "Time, Duration and Eternity in Spinoza," 213.
[65] The durational account can be applied to both infinite modes (Spinoza does not rule out infinite duration but simply differentiates it from eternity) and finite modes; see *Letter 12*, G/IV/54 and 60–61.

3.5 An Essence in Time

In the previous section, I concluded that Spinoza's notion of essence is twofold, in that it is expressed in duration as much as in eternity. I have suggested that this dualism is an example of aspectual distinction.

The durational aspect of essence, I maintain, is the expressed power of the substance, or *natura naturans*, as it unfolds through time in accordance with eternal laws, and equally in accordance with the encounters of each individual mode.[66] Such encounters are, by their nature, not eternal but durational. Spinoza describes duration at several points in the *Ethics*, but his most straightforward account is to be found in the *Physical Digression*. In what follows, I provide a reconstruction of the *Digression* compatible with the principles of relational individuation that I have established for the actual essences of finite modes. In the context of the *Digression*, I shall isolate Spinoza's treatment of two main "neutral properties" as individuation criteria for finite modes and explain their application to the attribute of extension as a particular case of attribute-neutral individuation.

The *Digression* is exclusively concerned with the impacts, reactions, and inertia of extended objects or bodies. However, the doctrine of parallelism asserted just a few propositions earlier in *Ethics* II allows us to understand that what is true under one attribute must (in some way) be true under the others. In other words, the *Digression* provides us with information about the structural feature of modes in all the attributes in virtue of their isomorphism.[67]

As I have argued, the properties identifying white modes escape the constraints of attributal constriction and are simultaneously

---

[66] The language of "encounters" has been developed to describe a finite mode's durational existence by Deleuze in *Spinoza: Practical Philosophy*; see, for example, ibid., 19.

[67] For the sake of this argument, I do not believe it is important to distinguish between the ideas-things parallelism of E2p7 and the ideas-bodies parallelism of E2p7s.

valid in all attributes. But we can extract information about white modes from some of the passages where Spinoza refers to the general characteristics of modes conceived under a given attribute, as he does in the *Digression*. In describing the physical structure of modes of extension, Spinoza characterizes them as constituted by their relations on both quantitative and qualitative levels. What, if anything, can this tell us about white modes?

I maintain that Spinoza intends the conclusions of the *Digression* to be applicable—mutatis mutandis—to each aspect of a white mode. After introducing the concept of movement, E2l1 of the *Digression* declares that the individuation—or distinction—of bodies lies in the differences in their motion (together with its speed).[68] Thus, the individuation of modes of extension therefore relies on a property that seems to be as far as possible from attribute-neutral. However, this appearance is dispelled on a more careful reading. The demonstration of E2l3 reverses this picture. "Bodies are singular things," Spinoza says, "which are distinguished from one another by reason of motion and rest; and so, each must

---

[68] E2l1: "Bodies are distinguished from one another by reason of motion and rest, speed and slowness, and not by reason of substance." Spinoza considers the individuation of modes in the attribute of extension to be dependent on two criteria, namely (1) their motion or rest and (2) their speed. However, a case could be made to ultimately reduce from (2) to (1). In other words, speed is merely the numerical (and apparent to a less refined observer) expression of variations in motion. In E2l2, Spinoza maintains that the fundamental properties of bodies are, firstly, to involve the concept of one and the same attribute—the attribute of extension. Secondly, that they "can move now more slowly, now more quickly, and absolutely, that now they move, now they are at rest." Spinoza describes speed as the relative (as opposed to absolute) understanding of motion and rest. *In primis*, the very concept of speed is a relational one as its determination involves reference to a nonempty environment (E2l3c: "when I suppose that body A, say, is at rest, and do not attend to any other body in motion, I can say nothing about body A except that it is at rest"). A first and quick implication of this argument is that speed is trivially relational; a monad in an empty universe would have no speed. A deeper interpretation would object that the argument does not do justice to Spinoza's conviction that demonstrative philosophy should be established beyond the determinations made by observers. As a general strategy, he rests his cases on purely rational, a priori demonstrations (see Schliesser, "Spinoza and the Philosophy of Science," 155–189). It could not be the case, for example, that the relationality of speed depends on an idea of imagination. Therefore, the determination of whether speed is a relational concept falls back on the understanding of motion.

be determined necessarily to motion or rest by another singular thing, namely, by another body." In this passage, he affirms that the individuation of bodies relies on mode-to-mode (horizontal) causation or, in his own words, "communication."[69]

E2l3 is a vital component of Spinoza's argument in the *Digression*. This lemma directly correlates motion-and-rest with causation. Bodies, being finite modes, cannot determine themselves to motion and must therefore be determined by something else. To prove this doctrine, Spinoza refers us to E1p28. "Bodies," he argues, "are singular things which are distinguished from one another by reason of motion and rest; and so (by E1p28), each must be determined necessarily to motion or rest by another singular thing, namely, by another body" (E2l3d). In E1p28, Spinoza had demonstrated that "every singular thing... can neither exist nor be determined to produce an effect unless it is determined... by another cause, which is also finite and has a determinate existence." In this passage, Spinoza establishes the horizontal line of causation that connects finite modes in each attribute.

We can thus argue that E2l3 of the *Digression* represents a "translation" of E1p28 in the language of bodies. In other terms, E2l3 is the application to extended reality (an attribute-dependent account of bodies) of a metaphysical law (an attribute-neutral account of white modes). Spinoza argues for the physical application of causation—a neutral property. This focus on the horizontal side of causation emphasizes its relational aspect. Ostensibly, this is also true of the physical description of E2l3. Spinoza presents the body-to-body transmission of motion as a structural determination.[70] As such, each instance of this determination must involve more than one body to cause any shift in the motion/rest ratio. We can thus

---

[69] E2l7: "each part retains its motion, and communicates it, as before, to the others."
[70] On this crucial point, see the acute and extensive study produced by Toto, *L'individualità dei Corpi: Percorsi nell'Etica di Spinoza*.

conclude that the individuation of modes of extension (bodies) proposed by Spinoza in the *Digression* is intrinsically relational.[71]

However, one fundamental objection to my account remains unaddressed. Even if the *ratio* of motion and rest that identifies a mode in the attribute of extension is fundamentally connected to the body's essence,[72] why should we maintain that this essence is relational? Spinoza offers an answer to this question in E2a1″.

All the ways[73] in which a body is affected by another body follow both from the nature of the body affected and at the same time from the nature of the affecting body, so that one and the same body may be moved differently according to differences in the nature of the bodies moving it. And conversely, different bodies may be moved differently by one and the same body.

This axiom establishes a key principle: for Spinoza, (durational) essences can—and do—interact. Arguably, the nature of bodies can be interpreted to be coextensive with their actual essence, which is the durational aspect of their essence. In E2a1″, Spinoza indicates that the outcome of an affection involves both the actual essence of the "causing" body and the actual essence of the "caused" body. In other words, bodies are determined constantly from within and from without, giving rise to an interactive and relationally individuated physical world.

---

[71] A similar conclusion is reached by Deleuze. Ironically, he presents his view in the definition of "eternity" included in his index of the main concepts of Spinoza's *Ethics*. "Duration is expressed only insofar as the existing modes realize relations according to which they come to be and cease to be, enter into composition with and decompose one another" (*Spinoza: Practical Philosophy*, 66). Thus, Deleuze's account connects the durational relations of finite modes with compositional properties, a position that I shall defend shortly.

[72] For a more detailed discussion, I encourage the reader toward Winkler's excellent study, "The Conatus of the Body in Spinoza's Physics."

[73] Curley translates *omnes modi* with "all modes." I emended the translation as my version avoids confusion between modes of the substance (i.e., in the extended attribute, bodies) and modes of modes (i.e., properties of modes).

The application of this principle can be pursued even further. If one interprets the ratio of motion and rest as the actual essence of bodies, this essence becomes susceptible to being modified through its interaction with the expression of other actual essences. If this interpretation of E2a1″ is correct, then the actual essences of modes under the attribute of extension determine the outcome of their interaction. However, they are also determined by their encounters with the essences of neighboring modes. Thus, we can conclude that in the *Digression*, Spinoza establishes causality as a relational property responsible for the individuation of modes of extension and their actual essence.

Let us now move to the analysis of another structural and attribute-neutral property: composition. Does composition have a connection with the actual essences of modes of extension? I argue that it does.[74] A large portion of the *Digression*, in fact, is dedicated to the compositional properties of extended modes. From the definition present after E2a2″, we learn that "bodies are united with one another" and that "they all together compose one body or individual" when they are determined by other bodies to "communicate their motions to each other in a certain fixed manner."[75] While it could be obvious to consider composition a relational property, or a structure, the involvement of relationality in establishing the "nature" of modes is less trivial.[76] I will expand on this topic in the next chapter, where I explore the nature of Spinoza's mereology.

For now, let us focus on the relationality of the nature of modes, which is precisely what Spinoza goes on to defend in E2l4: "If, of a body, or of an individual, which is composed of a number of bodies, some are removed, and at the same time as many others of the same

---

[74] In the next chapter, I expand on the structural importance of composition for the individuation of modes in Spinoza's metaphysics.
[75] G II/99/26–100/4.
[76] A more extensive analysis of the nature of compositionality as constituting essences shall be the object of the next chapter, where I examine Spinoza's *Letter 32* as a case study of the individuation of finite modes under both temporal aspects.

nature take their place, the individual will retain its nature, as before, without any change of its form."

The first item of interest of this lemma is the locution "a body, or an individual," which confirms that Spinoza wants to apply the principles expressed in the *Digression* beyond the limited realm of extension, as attribute-neutral features. Second, the nature of the composite individual—which we have seen to be determined by the bodies' constant interaction and determination—has a sort of "resilient" property, which rests on its internal interconnection.[77] Spinoza defends this doctrine in E2l7, which explicitly states: "The individual so composed retains its nature, whether it, as a whole, moves or is at rest, or whether it moves in this or that direction, so long as each part retains its motion, and *communicates it*, as before, *to the others*."[78] The durational survival—or perseveration in existence—of the composite body rests on its ability to have internal connections, relations, and interactions. Thus, we can conclude that composition—as a structural property—constitutes a crucial criterion for the individuation of the actual and durational essence of finite modes. Not so from the point of view of eternity, where the immanent and formal connection between a thing's essence and God's essence justifies its existence in a more immediate manner.

This analysis of the *Digression* confirms that the trans-attributal properties of modes (e.g., causality and composition) are better described as structural properties.[79] These properties are the ones guaranteeing the individuation of a mode across attributes, and they determine the actual or durational essence of a finite mode—in this case, a mode of extension.

---

[77] For the use of "resilience" in the context of Spinoza's compositional physics, see my "Uno Spinoza sistemico" [A Systemic Spinoza]; see also Merçon, "La filosofia de Spinoza y el pensamiento sistémico contemporáneo," 83–101.

[78] Emphasis is mine.

[79] I have investigated the nature of causation in the previous chapters; I shall go on to focus on composition in the next chapter.

Could the same argument be made for the durational mind? My answer is in the affirmative. Given the previously proved parallelism of durational mind and durational body, the properties individuating the durational mind must be structural or relational. However, a more complete answer would need to consider Spinoza's identification of the singular mind with a unity of the affections of the singular body, and the relationality that this doctrine entails.[80] That is the task that awaits us in the next two chapters.

3.6 The Fleeting Laws of Time

Before moving on, let us take stock. In the last few sections, I have connected the relational, attribute-neutral properties of modes with their durational essence (or actual essence). This substantiates my claim that (at least) the durational essences of modes must be defined in terms of their structural properties. Therefore, the individuation of modes in Spinoza's metaphysics of duration is described as fundamentally dependent on the observation of their relational properties. Furthermore, my analysis has made it more plausible that the eternal aspect of essence can be analyzed in terms of relationality or structural features.

The plausibility of a thesis, of course, does not entail its truth. It remains for me to prove that Spinoza considers individuality as the result of structural features under the species of eternity as well as under the species of duration. Furthermore, it is an intuitive consequence of this interpretation that rational beings should be able (in principle) to switch between these aspectual understandings of the structural unity of finite beings. Is that goal compatible with Spinoza's epistemology? In the next chapter, I will dive headfirst into this question, arguing that Spinoza believes the world an

---

[80] A crucial proposition in this sense is E2p23: "The mind does not know itself, except insofar as it perceives the ideas of the affections of the body."

epistemologically rich place, full of aspectual understandings that are not mutually exclusive.

However, the interpretative theses developed in the present chapter entail one more consequence, which might leave a bitter aftertaste in the mouth of some seasoned navigators of Spinoza's metaphysical oceans. According to my interpretation, eternity and duration are nonmutually exclusive modal properties of finite beings. Even though modes are finite and ultimately durational insofar as they are modes, I have argued, they are also eternal and infinite. These apparently inconsistent statements are compatible insofar as modes are the determinate expression of one of God's modifications, and insofar as their formal essence represent a mereological part of God's intellect (the infinite mode of thought). The structural understanding of expression developed in Chapter 2 comes now to my aid, allowing me to argue that Spinoza intends infinite modes as the immediate expressions of the attributes; their eternity is a *proprium* deriving directly from the essence of God explained through the attributes.[81]

Spinoza's modal laws of time do not apply univocally to finite beings, insofar as they are subject to aspectual causation. They are essentially caused in two distinct regimens (the regimen of duration that causes their actual essence; and the regimen of eternity that causes their formal essence). Thus, their essential being is aspectually distinct as well, modally positioning them in two worlds (or species) at once.

This also implies that a white mode exists across several aspectual distinctions at once. Its essential being is situated on a double "temporal" level, since it possesses a species of eternity *and* a species of duration. Its attributal specification, however, possesses a multiplicity of facets as well—one for every attribute that is expressed in a finite manner by that specific mode. Human beings express the attribute of thought and the attribute of extension in a finite and

---

[81] See Figure 2.2 above.

determined way. Therefore, human modes showcase two facets—a mind and a body—each of which will be available for essential comprehension under a species of duration and under a species of eternity. How can Spinoza's epistemology account for this wide array of possible conceptualizations of one and the same mode, let alone one and the same substance? This challenge will guide us in the next chapter, as we undertake an analysis of Spinoza's epistemology of finitude in terms of its composition.

4
To Build a World
Individuals, Composition, and the Universe as a Whole

> How happy is the little stone
> That rambles in the road alone,
> And doesn't care about careers,
> And exigencies never fears;
> Whose coat of elemental brown
> A passing universe put on;
> And independent as the sun,
> Associates or glows alone,
> Fulfilling absolute decree
> In casual simplicity.[1]

4.1 Questioning Individuality

In the last three chapters, we have plunged the depths of Spinoza's philosophy to provide a coherent picture of some key metaphysical structures. The ubiquity of these structures (causation, inherence, conception, parallelism, expression, essential conditioning) in the secondary literature as well as in Spinoza's network of definitions, axioms, and propositions proves that they are indispensable for our understanding of his thought. From the substance to the attributes, from the infinite modes to the many facets of the universe, structural

[1] Dickinson, *Complete Poems*, XXXIII.

features run deep in Spinoza's metaphysics and condition virtually any aspect of his philosophy. Yet, there is at least one more structural notion that we have so far only marginally mentioned: composition. This structure constitutes a solid foundation for Spinoza's conception of individuals, but it also represents a blueprint for the relationships between individuals and their environment.

Individuality is perhaps one of the most intuitive, and at the same time most carefully analyzed structures in the history of philosophy (in particular, in its declination in continuity over time). However, examining what constitutes the criteria for the identification of an individual seems almost futile: I can *see* that what is in front of me is a table, can't I? I can see that it resists my efforts of moving it, and that it constitutes a solid block of wood. Why should I bother to investigate the conditions for calling it an individual, and why do these conditions matter to anyone but philosophers?

In recent years, the seemingly untouchable notion of individuality is coming under stress from multiple sides. Object-oriented ontology, which claims that the world is constituted by "objects," coinciding (more or less) with the *things* that populate our everyday experience, appears to be less and less obvious at each attack. One important front in this debate was opened by the partisans of neo-materialism. Theorists of this persuasion, such as Jane Bennett, accuse object-oriented ontologies of creating a fictional distinction between "objects and their relations," ultimately preferring hypostatizing "mysterious objects" over the recognition of "complex systems of relations."[2] Moreover, Bennett attempts to reduce the distinction between objects and larger systems (which we would intuitively designate as a group of objects) because of our phenomenological observations regarding causality. In fact, our everyday "experience routinely identifies some effects as coming from individual objects and some from larger systems (or, better put, from individuations within material configurations and from

---

[2] Bennett, "Systems and Things," 226–227.

the complex assemblages in which they participate)."³ Yet, discriminating between these two kinds of causality is only justifiable if we take a prejudicial stance regarding the status of individuals as causes, as we have discussed in Chapter 1. Statements such as "this hatred is caused by society" and "this fear is caused by my past behavior" need not be distinct on an ontological basis. The effects of societal patterns and of my individual behavior are just effects: they do not offer us any evidence toward a potential preference for individual causality.

Just like causation, composition is another structure that has been traditionally used to suggest a "natural" inclination toward object-oriented individuality. In fact, the most basic example of ontological composition is the assimilation of nutrients by organisms. Intuitively, we recognize how the process of "eating" is comparable to the incorporation of new parts into an already existing individual. This natural inclination toward the organic understanding of part-whole composition, however, risks to lead us astray insofar as it may constitute an inflexible paradigm. Inorganic objects and structures showcase compositional properties, too: the self-organization patterns shown by crystals are just the most accessible level of such properties.[4] Reality is filled with entities organized (and what's more important, *self*-organized) into compositional structures that lead to bigger, more complex, more capable items. The ontological flexibility showcased by these structures should lead us to question the individualistic paradigm dictated by object-oriented ontology.

A different route to this same task has been explored by the proponents of "ontic structural realism" (OSR). While neo-materialism stems from conclusions drawn from phenomenology

---

[3] Ibid., 227.
[4] Cf. DeLanda, *A Thousand Years of Nonlinear History*: "inorganic matter-energy has a wide arrange of alternatives for the generation of structure... even the humblest forms of matter and energy have the potential for self-organization," 16. See also Bennett, "The Force of Things," 351–352.

and continental philosophy, theorists belonging to the OSR camp derive their ontological framework from findings in contemporary physics, particularly in the field of quantum mechanics. Since most quantum theories do not offer an account of intrinsic individual properties capable of providing a sufficient reason for numerical identity and individuation, OSR proposes to let go of our object-oriented prejudice to embrace a more relational outlook on physical reality. Thus, "fundamental physical objects are parts (*relata*) of a physical structure in the sense of a network of concrete physical relations." The consequence of this approach is that objects "do not have any existence—and in particular not any identity—independently of the structure they are part of."[5] As a consequence, some OSR metaphysicians argue that the distinction between objects and relations is merely conceptual, without grounding in reality. Others claim that objects are mere epiphenomena, knots in the network of asymmetric relations that constitute the scaffolding of the physical world.[6]

Some of these claims should ring familiar to my reader, since in this volume I have been arguing for an interpretation of Spinoza's metaphysics that is compatible with the theses advanced by both neo-materialism and ontic structural realism. Over the course of this chapter, I aim to show how Spinoza's account of composition and whole-part causality provides us with an understanding of individuality that can step beyond the naturalist temptation of object-oriented ontology. In doing so, I shall also offer a relational understanding of Spinoza's epistemology, arguing for we will call an "aspectualist" reading of truth and individuality.

---

[5] Esfeld and Lam, "Ontic Structural Realism," 143.
[6] OSR partisans can be distinguished according to the degree of eliminativism they support. Some of them argue that objects should be eliminated from our metaphysical furniture, while others are less drastic. However, the overall treatment of relations on par with objects is the threshold commonly accepted for inclusion in the OSR framework.

4.2 Knowing Individuality

As we have mentioned several times in this volume, Spinoza maintains that there are three kinds of cognition. In a crucial section of the *Ethics*, he announces that human beings most commonly access the world through one *inadequate* form of cognition,[7] imagination. This kind of cognition derives, firstly:

> from singular things which have been represented to us through the senses in a way which is mutilated, confused, and without order for the intellect; for that reason, I have been accustomed to call such perceptions cognition from random experience.[8]

And secondly:

> from signs, for example, from the fact that, having heard or read certain words, we recollect things, and form certain ideas of them, like those through which we imagine the things; these two ways of regarding things I shall henceforth call cognition of the first kind, opinion or imagination.[9]

The combination of the two above passages provides us with a description of imagination that overlaps with both sensory experience and "internal sensation" as empiricist philosophers of the Early Modern period call it. The main feature of these kinds of cognition is that the formation of ideas is based on images, which are

---

[7] In the English-speaking literature, it has become customary (since at least Curley's translation) to translate Spinoza's *cognitio* with "knowledge." Albeit intuitive, this translation has the unfortunate side-effect of suggesting that imagination (the first kind of cognition) is knowledge. However, contemporary accounts of knowledge designate it as "justified true belief." This is trivially false for Spinoza since imagination does not have a necessary or analytic connection to truth. For this reason, it is preferable to maintain the translation more neutral and indicate imagination as a kind of cognition.
[8] E2p40s2 | G II/122/4–7.
[9] Ibid., | G II/122/8–12.

either directly or indirectly acquired through the senses. According to Spinoza, however, this route presents significant obstacles in the process of any real knowledge, since it does not conform to the rules that bind the production of ideas in the intellect. Moreover, an idea produced by the cognition of the first kind involves the idea of the act of perception, as Lewis argued: "in imagining we perceive an affection of our body, and we form an idea of our body and of external bodies in their varying affection-causing interactions."[10] In other words, imagination relies on our body as a primary access route to experience, privileging the relation between our body and the perceived bodies, without taking into consideration the gap that necessarily exists between a body and its idea or mind.[11]

Next, Spinoza moves to the discussion of *adequate* forms of cognition. The most common form of adequate knowledge derives "from the fact that we have common notions and adequate ideas of the properties of things. This I shall call reason [*ratio*] and the second kind of knowledge."[12] In other texts, Spinoza frequently hints at the fact that this is the sort of knowledge we acquire from abstract reasoning, geometrical deductions, pure philosophy, and mathematics. The method of *ratio*, in fact, involves proceeding from a clear and distinct idea to the next.[13] Furthermore, reason enables us to gain adequate knowledge of the essences of things through what they have *in common*. The very notion of commonality, however, prima facie appears to imply an intrinsic substantial pluralism; or is an analysis of modes all that reason can achieve?

---

[10] Lewis, "Spinoza on Having a False Idea," 25.
[11] See E2p41: "Knowledge of the first kind is the only cause of falsity, whereas knowledge of the second and of the third kind is necessarily true." Cf. Lewis, "Spinoza on Having a False Idea," 25: "an idea involved in imagination is not inherently false but is false—when it is so—because of the surroundings of the idea."
[12] Ibid., | G II/122/12–14.
[13] An open debate within Spinoza's interpreters struggles to assess whether this first degree of adequate knowledge (*ratio*) is limited by the scope of the objects it can refer to and investigate, or if its subjection to the third kind of cognition (described below) is dictated by uniquely methodological issues, such as its mediacy against intuition's immediacy. For an excellent perspective on this debate, see Soyarslan, "The Distinction between Reason and Intuitive Knowledge in Spinoza's *Ethics*."

This would be a rather disappointing limitation for human knowledge.

Luckily, Spinoza guarantees that there still is a third step available to human beings. The third kind of cognition (which we will explore in depth in the next chapter) has attracted a great deal of scholarship, despite the fact that it is described in a rather mysterious way and not expanded in detail by Spinoza (or perhaps, for this very reason). This is how he defines it:

> In addition to these two kinds of knowledge, there is another, third kind, which we shall call intuitive knowledge. And this kind of knowing proceeds from an adequate idea of the formal essence of certain attributes of God to the adequate knowledge of the [NS: formal] essence of things.[14]

So, to sum up: the first kind of cognition is imaginative, and it involves inadequate ideas and sensory experience. The second kind of cognition involves adequate ideas, and it proceeds through the inference from a clear and distinct idea to the next clear and distinct idea. The third kind of knowledge is rather mysterious. From these short notes, all we know that it is intuitive, and that it involves the relationship between "formal essences" and God's essence. Spinoza also maintains that this latter kind of knowledge is only seldom reached by human beings, who mostly move between the first and second, between imagination and reason. The rarity of the intuitive kind of knowledge is affirmed in the closing lines of the *Ethics*, where Spinoza declares that "what is found so rarely must be hard [to reach]."[15] In his other major work (the *Theological-Political Treatise* [TTP]), he behaves similarly, attributing the plenitude of the third kind of knowledge exclusively to Jesus Christ.[16]

---

[14] Ibid., | G II/122/15–19.
[15] E5p42s | G II/308/25.
[16] *TTP* chapter 1 | G III/21/5.

Be that as it may, one important result of this investigation of Spinoza's epistemology is that each level of cognition—including the two kinds of knowledge described—exclusively interacts with individuals. Spinoza famously rejected the existence of species (and the exclusive existence of individual essences); consistently, he maintained that knowledge must be knowledge of particulars. This thesis is hypostatized in the famous Spinozian *dictum*, according to which "the more we understand singular things, the more we understand God" (E5p24). The proportionality between one's knowledge of individuals and one's knowledge of God (even within the third kind of cognition, which is the object of the fifth part of the *Ethics*) is dictated by the intrinsic relationality of all knowledge, which in turn derives from Spinoza's fundamental belief in the relationality of reality, as I shall demonstrate in the following sections of this chapter.

4.3 The Definition of Individuality

How is the above epistemological analysis helpful in our analysis of Spinoza's concept of individuality and mereology? I argue that seeing individuals through the multifaceted lens provided by Spinoza's epistemology is the most efficacious way to make sense of one of his most crucial texts about individuality, the *Letter 32* to Oldenburg. Despite its being one of the most studied texts of Spinoza's relatively contained opus, its richness allows us to discover new angles at each reading. The origin story of the letter is quite straightforward. In 1665, Henry Oldenburg, secretary of the Royal Society, asked Spinoza a question about compositional properties, on behalf of himself and of Robert Boyle, the famous Irish chemist who was at that time living in London and that was part of Spinoza's circle of correspondents. "If your investigation has shed any light," Oldenburg says, "on that difficult question concerning our knowledge of how each part of Nature agrees with its whole and in what way it agrees with other things, we ask you, most affectionately, to communicate it to us."[17]

A month later, Spinoza replied, putting a particular gloss on Oldenburg's query. "I presume you are asking for the reasons by which *we are persuaded*, that each part of nature agrees with its whole, and coheres with the others."[18] As Spinoza admits, his interpretation of the question is motivated by ignorance. "I don't know [absolutely] how they *really* cohere and how each part agrees with its whole. To know that would require knowing *the whole* of Nature and *all* of its parts."[19] Thus, in this text he separates two distinct perspectives: one of which he claims to be ignorant of, and one of which he proceeds to explain.

In this chapter, I aim to distinguish these two perspectives. I claim that the "real" perspective—the one Spinoza claims to be ignorant of—is the perspective of the third kind of knowledge, the more "mysterious" of Spinoza's approaches to truth. Identifying this perspective with intuitive knowledge helps us to make sense of two important points. First, if the knowledge Spinoza claims to lack is intuitive knowledge, we also know that knowledge of this kind is, as he reminds us in E5p42s, "difficult" and "rare." Second, the letter makes it clear that the knowledge Spinoza lacks is holistic; this is a typical feature of the third kind of knowledge, as well.

By contrast, "the reasons by which we are persuaded that each part of nature agrees with its whole and coheres with the others" belong to the second kind of knowledge, the rational or scientific sort of knowledge. Acquiring knowledge of this kind is a matter of arriving at clear and distinct ideas by way of definitions and demonstrations. It is important, however, to note that both kinds

---

[17] *Letter 31* | G IV/167/11–14.
[18] *Letter 32* | G IV/170a.
[19] Ibid; emphasis is mine. The Latin text reads: "*Nam cognoscere, quomodo revera cohæreant, et unaquæque pars cum suo toto conveniat, id me ignorare dixi... quia ad hoc cognoscendum requireretur totam Naturam, omnesque ejus partes cognoscere.*"

of knowledge are adequate, and both focus on the interaction between parts and wholes.

If we assume that the *Letter* is concerned with the second kind of knowledge, it makes sense that Spinoza should open his discussion with a definition: "By the coherence of parts, then, I understand [*intelligo*] nothing but that the laws or nature of the one part so adapt themselves to the laws or nature of the other part that they are opposed to each other as little as possible."[20] The use of the verb *intelligo*, which is applied throughout the *Ethics* where Spinoza provides definitions of key terms at the beginning of each book, signals that we are in the presence of an adequate definition of the *definiendum* "coherence of parts." In the definition, Spinoza stipulates that parts agree with each other when they do not oppose each other, which is equivalent to adapting to each other. In other words, we can only understand how wholes are mereologically formed of parts through a knowledge of the relations that connect the parts.

Nevertheless, the phrasing of the definition is odd. Spinoza only tells us that parts do *not* oppose each other, without providing the reader with the reason for this absence of opposition.[21] Fortunately, the problem can be clarified by referring to the *Ethics*. In E3p5, Spinoza affirms that "things are of a contrary nature, that is, cannot be in the same subject, insofar as one can destroy the other." Things cannot be parts of the same whole if they *completely* disagree. That would destroy the composite object (E3p4).[22] We may still ask: what about the opposite case, where the parts completely

---

[20] *Letter 32* | G IV/170a/12.
[21] An alternative reading of this passage can be found in Sangiacomo's brilliant analysis, *L'essenza del corpo: Spinoza e la scienza delle composizioni*, 124–139.
[22] E3p5d: "For if they could agree with one another, or be in the same subject at once, then there could be something in the same subject which could destroy it, which (by E3p4) is absurd." E3p4 reads: "No thing can be destroyed except through an external cause."

agree? In this case, the monist Spinoza would probably conclude that they would become one and the same thing.[23]

While this analysis goes some way toward clarifying the notions of "agreement" and "disagreement," difficulties remain. In the *Physical Digression*, as well as in *Letter 6* to Robert Boyle, Spinoza seems to understand "agreement'" in purely mechanistic terms, as a chain of interaction between parts that exchange motion and rest.[24] In *Letter 32*, however, we are offered a picture of parts that, by adapting to one another, form complex wholes. For a whole to be formed, the parts in question must agree to some extent, without agreeing entirely. Thus, "parthood" must be a fluid balance of agreement and disagreement, perfectly described by the Latin *convenire* (to encounter, or come across each other). The partial agreement and disagreement of parts is, for Spinoza, a necessary condition of their being able to combine into wholes. Moreover, as I shall shortly demonstrate, this condition also allows finite beings to be both parts and wholes, depending on the intensity of the agreement between them and the point of view of the observer.

With this fluidity in mind, let us return to Spinoza's discussion of the nature of parts and wholes in *Letter 32*.

> I consider things as parts of some whole insofar as the nature of the one so adapts itself to the nature of the other that so far as possible, they are all in harmony with one another. But insofar as they are out of harmony with one another, to that extent each forms an idea distinct from the others in our mind, and therefore it is considered as a whole and not as a part.[25]

---

[23] I agree with Della Rocca, who maintains that Spinoza implicitly endorses the Principle of Identity of Indiscernibles; see Della Rocca, *Spinoza*, 47.

[24] For a more detailed study of these two texts, see Buyse, "A New Reading of Spinoza's Letter 32 to Oldenburg"; and Dukić, "Individuation of Finite Modes in Spinoza's *Ethics*."

[25] *Letter 32* | G IV/170a/16–171a/2.

In this passage, Spinoza shifts away from the adequate language of definitions. *Intelligo* ("I understand") becomes *considero* ("I consider"). He also introduces the locution "insofar as" (*quatenus*). When Spinoza uses these terms, as I have demonstrated in Chapter 2, he is entering a hyperintensional kind of discourse, which makes heavy use of the notion of "aspect." Remember that with the term "aspect," I indicate elements of one and the same thing that can be recognized, or discovered, by an adequate intellect. Aspects are numerically identical with the individual they belong to, but they are nontrivially distinct from each other, and thus they are opaque to substitution.

Therefore, such elements are not a mere figment of imagination, and they are not *created* by the intellect (as for the duplication of subjects present in the proposition "Paul is *Paul*"). In this sense, when we claim that Spinoza considers parts and wholes as real entities that are aspectually distinct, we are recognizing that this distinction highlights elements that really exists *in rebus*, although the categories of parts and wholes do not constitute the (univocal) real essence of a given thing.

According to the passage quoted above, then, "to be a part" and "to be a whole" are aspectual properties of an individual.[26] Depending on which aspect we are considering, the same singular thing can be either a part or whole. Depending on whether it "adapts" harmoniously to its neighboring modes, we consider a certain mode as a part of a bigger whole or as an independent whole. As we will soon see, Spinoza maintains that it is possible

---

[26] Toto ("Convenienza e discrepanza," 163–190) offers a diametrically opposite reading of this passage. As I understand his claims, he argues that once Spinoza introduces the concept of "universal nature of the blood," he is not entitled to perspectival reasonings anymore because of his commitment to universality as unchanging. In light of my development of the theory of aspectual distinction in Spinoza, however, I think that the agreement of parts—despite its fundamental ontological value—can acquire a shifting logical meaning, aligned with Spinoza's general use of *quatenus* and logical reduplication of the subject, which in the *Ethics* applies to substance itself (the most universal lawmaker).

to shift between such aspectual readings, depending on the point of view we assume, while rejecting a subjectivist genealogy of such perspectives.

Further support for this interpretation comes from a parallel text, E2d7, where he defines singular things [*res singulares*], a concept that must be at least a cognate to the concept of individual, if not its congruent counterpart. "By singular things, I understand [*intelligo*] things that are finite and have a determinate existence. And if a number of individuals so concur in one action that together they are all the cause of one effect, I consider [*considero*] them all, to that extent, as one singular thing."[27] The language used here perfectly echoes that of *Letter 32*. In this case, Spinoza begins by providing a definition of "singular things," using the verb *intelligo*. He then provides us with the mereological rules that allow a "singular thing" to combine with others to form a higher-level composite.[28] The respective causal actions of the singular components adapt to each other, concurring to form one and the same effect.[29] Analogously, in *Letter 32*, Spinoza offers a similar (noncausal, yet still structural) understanding of the agreement of parts of the same individual, claiming that the adaptation that allows the composition of a higher-level individual takes the form of "harmony."[30]

---

[27] Emphasis added.
[28] One could also consider E2p24d as a third example of this strategy. There, Spinoza argues that "the parts composing the human body pertain to the essence of the body itself only insofar as they communicate their motions to one another in a certain fixed manner, and not insofar as they can be considered as individuals." Here, too, we can observe a shift between the two aspectual readings, claiming that only an understanding focusing on individuals as parts can conceive of them as harmonizing within the same body. However, due to the lack of a straightforward definitory claim in this passage, I have preferred excluding it from my main argument. For a more detailed analysis, see Newlands, *Reconceiving Spinoza*, 152.
[29] See Melamed, *Spinoza's Metaphysics*, 75, for an interesting interpretation of this criterion.
[30] However, it is important to note that Spinoza is not talking about the universal mechanism, *harmonia universalis*, described by Leibniz—Spinoza's understanding of agreement does not admit of any teleology. The parts of a Spinozian whole do not agree because some sort of final cause drives them to join efforts or *convenire*. Instead, their agreement or disagreement depends exclusively on efficient causality. Spinoza only admits of two types of causality: the immanent and vertical causality of the substance,

Thus, the mereological definition offered in Spinoza's epistolary exchange with Oldenburg and the causal explanation offered in the *Ethics* coincide perfectly, and both rely on structural properties of modes.[31]

As these two passages indicate, the structures of causation (more evident in E2d7) and composition (more evident in *Letter 32*) are integral to the structure of parts and wholes. Thus, even though Spinoza mainly discusses the part-whole relations of extended modes, we can infer that the same individuation criteria must apply across attributes (i.e., it must apply to minds as well). We can therefore tentatively formulate the following criterion for the individuation (IC) of a finite individual:

IC: A singular thing x is an individual if and only if the parts that compose x agree with each other to some extent and have compatible trans-attributal properties (i.e., they cause or are caused together, they compose higher-level individuals together, their modes of the attributes share the same "temporal" properties).[32]

The above IC is a flexible criterion for establishing the individuality of a singular being, and as we have seen, it mainly rests on the

and the horizontal and transitive causality of neighboring modes. Both immanent and transitive causality fall under the scope of efficient causality, thus safeguarding Spinoza's rejection of final causality. On this subject, see also my analysis of the distinction between Leibniz's and Spinoza's mereologies in "Whole-Part Relations in Early Modern Philosophy."

[31] As John Carriero helpfully pointed out to me, there could be more to say regarding the intrinsic biological/organic nature of the examples chosen by Spinoza.

[32] The need for a so-called trans-attributal individuation of finite individuals is generated, within Spinoza's metaphysics, by the claim that "the mind and the body are one and the same individual, which is conceived now under the attribute of thought, now under the attribute of extension" (E2p21s). As I have discussed above, this difference in conception is arguably recognized through an aspectual distinction, which accounts for the opacity to substitution and numerical identity of the two aspects of the individual without separating it into parts. Cf. Newlands, *Reconceiving Spinoza*, 51–55. "Temporal" properties, of course, indicate the species of duration and eternity identified through my "onto-temporal" grid in the previous chapter.

notion of a "harmony" among parts. This harmonical structure is what allows parts to compose a higher-level individual, thus respecting the compositional requirements for the individuation of individuals. Furthermore, the harmonization of their causal properties guarantees that they share the same position in the chain of causal connection, thus respecting the causal requirements for the identification of individuals under the paradigm of horizontal expressionism.

What can this understanding of harmony tell us about the structural notions of part and whole? By conceiving individuals through this flexible notion of harmony, we conceive them to be constantly shifting between a hyperintensional status of part and one of "whole-ness."[33] In this sense, we can infer that the concept of harmony employed by Spinoza in *Letter 32* serves as a guide for the mind to favor one aspectual reading of reality over another, as proven by the remark "insofar as they are out of harmony ... each forms an idea distinct from the others in our mind." As we have already seen above, aspects are generated in the mind by a *real* feature of an object. The hyperintensionality of Spinoza's philosophy emerges, as we have seen, through the conjunct presence of a reality rich in aspects and an adequate mind that conceives them through a hybrid distinction, not limited by the dichotomy of real distinction and distinction of reason.

Because of this aspectual framework, we find adequate understandings to be interacting with mereological reality through the index provided by the agreement of parts, which generates wholes. Thus, when the harmony between an individual and its adjacent modes is weak, the mind will view the individual as a

---

[33] I admit that this conception of the individuality of finite modes is likely to raise concern as it appears dangerously close to a view that rejects the reality of the finite, the so-called acosmism of Hegelian ascendance. However, the fact that individuals are individuated by reason (which is an adequate kind of knowledge) should be enough to dispel such doubts in this context. For more arguments regarding Spinoza's wholesale rejection of acosmism, see Melamed, *Spinoza's Metaphysics*, 79–82.

whole. When the harmony is stronger, the mind will view the individual as a part. It is important to keep in mind, however, that while it may be conceived as a part or a whole by an adequate mind, the individual retains the same degree of reality. This aspect-rich mereological reality constitutes our provisional conclusion, which in the next section I will illustrate through an example provided by Spinoza himself in *Letter 32*. The focus of this example will be a shift from the third-person point of view adopted so far to a first-person perspective, which acknowledges the participation of finite individuals in the mereological processes that they observe.

4.4 Shifting Structures

So far in this chapter, I have shown how Spinoza's interpretation of the concepts of part and whole depends on an aspectual reading of the composition that allows several finite beings to combine in a higher-level individual. In virtue of IC, each individual is, at the same time, a whole insofar as it is composed by other individuals, and a part insofar as it harmonizes with neighboring modes to compose a higher-level individual. To interpret a finite being as a part, I maintain, is a matter of recognizing its advanced degree of agreement with neighboring modes. By contrast, to interpret the same finite being as a whole is a matter of recognizing its comparatively limited agreement with neighboring modes. Consequently, individuals (as Spinoza conceives of them) can only be isolated through a loose process of individuation.[34] In other words, individuality is not a fundamental structure in Spinoza's metaphysics. Instead, it is a second-order structure that relies on causality and composition to emerge. I shall now go on to show how the concept of relational knowledge impacts this notion of individuality in *Letter 32*.

---

[34] Cf. Melamed, "Acosmism or Weak Individuals?," 89.

In fact, in the text of the letter, Spinoza does not just provide general criteria for the notions of part and whole. He also includes a clarificatory example, designed to elucidate how these notions operate in the formation of our concepts. The example stipulates that human blood is not a simple fluid but is composed of different parts, such as "lymph" and "chyle." It is a nonhomogeneous whole. This being so, its parts must (to some extent) adapt to each other. If the motions of the different particles were able to adapt to each other to the point of "complete agreement," blood would become homogeneous. Note that this notion of "complete agreement" is incompatible with the existence of lymph and chyle as wholes, as it would reduce them to the exclusive role of parts.

At this point, however, Spinoza immediately offers a qualification: "But insofar as we conceive the particles of lymph, by reason of their shape and motion, to differ from the particles of chyle, to that extent we consider them as a whole and not as a part."[35] The elements that we had assumed to be parts can also be interpreted as wholes. Two points are relevant here.

First, in order to articulate the sense in which the particles are wholes, rather than parts, Spinoza employs the terminology I have already highlighted above. He says that we consider [*consideramus*] the particles as wholes, insofar as [*quatenus*] they differ from each other. As we have noted before, this language indicates that he is making an aspectual distinction, drawing our attention to an aspect of reality.

Second, Spinoza adds a new and puzzling element to his description of the whole of which chyle and lymph are parts: he remarks that the parts constitute a whole when they *completely*[36] agree with each other. This claims starkly contrasts with the definition he has already offered us, namely that things cannot completely agree (on pain of being assimilated to each other). Elements, we were told,

---

[35] *Letter 32* | G IV/171a/7–9.
[36] "*Plane*" in the Latin text.

are parts of the same whole to the extent that they agree with one another *as far as possible*.[37] While IC had established a partial criterion for the agreement of parts (especially heterogeneous parts) in a whole, the example of the blood sets a far more demanding standard.[38] For parts to constitute a whole, they must be in *complete* agreement.[39] How can we make sense of this apparent contradiction? Which kind of "agreement" should we be looking for in investigating the nature of composite individuals? And what bearing does this have on the issue of the individuality of finite beings?

In order to answer these questions, let us follow Spinoza a little further. In fact, he goes on to offer a different perspective on the same scenario by picturing a "little worm" that lives in the blood. The worm, according to the example,

is capable of distinguishing by sight the particles of the blood, of lymph, etc., and capable of observing by reason how each particle, when it encounters another, either bounces back, or communicates a part of its motion, etc. Indeed, it would live in this blood as we do in this part of the universe and would consider each particle of the blood as a whole, not as a part.[40]

---

[37] "*Quoad fieri potest*" in the Latin text.
[38] This is what Newlands describes as the "*eating* model of composition, in which individuals or wholes are consumed once they become parts" (*Reconceiving Spinoza*, 162).
[39] The first criterion seems more in tune with Spinoza's proclamation of ignorance regarding the absolute nature of agreement and coherence, stated in the letter's *incipit*. The second hints at the formation of an individual in the sense described in the *Physical Digression* of *Ethics* II, where the "union of bodies" is obtained through a "communication of motion." There is an open debate in the literature about whether this should be considered as an "inertial" reading of *conatus* in Spinoza's physical theory. For more information about this debate, see Newlands, *Reconceiving Spinoza*, 166; Rice, "Spinoza, Bennett, and Teleology," 248–249; Viljanen, *Spinoza's Geometry of Power*, 106; and Winkler, "The Conatus of the Body in Spinoza's Physics," 102–104.
[40] *Letter 32* | G IV/171a/11–16.

We learn that the worm—an explicit metaphor for human beings—shares two distinctly human cognitive capacities: imagination (exemplified by the sense of "sight") and reason.[41] Moreover, the worm and human beings are perfectly aligned in their understanding of parts and wholes. Humans live in "this part of the universe," paying more attention to the differences between the several beings that compose it than to their harmony and agreement. As a result, humans consider these parts as wholes, just as the worm considers the parts of the blood—chyle, lymph and so on—as wholes. However, as Spinoza goes on to specify, the worm is ignorant ("could not know") of

> how all the parts of the blood are regulated by the *universal nature* of the blood, and *compelled* to adapt themselves to one another, as the universal nature of the blood requires, so that they agree with one another *in a definite way*.[42]

The "universal nature" mentioned in this passage represents the nature of the whole, formed by the blood's parts as they adapt to one another through a process of mutual interaction. The passage therefore resonates with the declaration of ignorance at the opening of *Letter 32*. The worm is ignorant of how the parts "are regulated by the universal nature of the blood," just as Spinoza had claimed to be ignorant of "how [parts] really cohere and how each part agrees with its whole." The worm, like Spinoza, does not possess knowledge of the third kind; it only has "sight" and "reason." Thus, it is not capable of uniting the infinite plurality that exists in "the whole of Nature and all of its parts."

---

[41] See Gaspari, "The Curious Case of the *Vermiculus*," 78.
[42] *Letter 32* | G IV/171a/17–20; emphasis is mine. Interestingly, "in a definite way" reads *certa ratione* in the Latin text, reminding us of the notion of *ratio* of motion and rest necessary for the preservation of an individual in the *Physical Digression* of the *Ethics*. Therefore, the "universal nature" referred to in this passage must not be interpreted as some sort of Platonic "form."

The third kind of knowledge can unify the horizontal interconnections joining the plurality of beings. At the same time, this unified plurality can be connected with the vertical relations deriving from the expression of God's essence. Failing this, we can still have adequate knowledge of the horizontal level (as demonstrated by the adequate language of definitions employed by Spinoza in *Letter 32*). But this knowledge must proceed carefully by examining the interactions between each finite individual and its neighboring parts. The second kind of knowledge, in fact, proceeds from one clear and distinct idea to the next and cannot immediately grasp the "universal nature" of the whole.

Reason seeks to understand the world through an analytic process, investigating the common features of objects (in the *plural*) and unifying them through an act of the understanding. As Viljanen has recently argued, the formation of a clear and distinct idea through the second kind of knowledge rests on the possibility of the twin processes of analysis and synthesis. In the first, the object of an idea is reduced to its components or parts; in the latter, where the object of an idea is reconstructed through its components.[43] Conversely, the third kind of knowledge has as its sole purpose that to unify reality through the reconduction of parts to their essential reality, and from there to the essence of God—the attributes. Intuitive knowledge does not need to abide by the same rules of reason and can therefore ignore the common notions and properties of the parts, immediately seeing their agreement within the whole.[44]

Ultimately, for Spinoza, every finite individual in the universe is but a part of the totality of Nature. And yet, if in order to grasp such truth the philosopher was required to proceed carefully through the procedures of reason, it would never achieve the total

---

[43] Viljanen, "The Young Spinoza on Scepticism, Truth, and Method," 137. Cf. *TIE* §69 | G II/26/15–25. See also Sangiacomo, "Fixing Descartes: Ethical Intellectualism in Spinoza's Early Writings," 348.

[44] This description of intuitive knowledge is based on Spinoza, *KV* II.1 | G I/54/10–14.

understanding[45] required to obtain immediate knowledge (and enjoy beatitude, as the fifth part of the *Ethics* reminds us). Intuitive knowledge, then, is necessary to accept the ultimate reality about the mereology of the universe. "thus it follows that every body, insofar as it exists modified in a definite way, must be considered as a part of the whole universe, must agree with its whole and must cohere with the remaining bodies."[46] The third kind of knowledge simply cannot be ignored in the understanding of Spinoza's endgame in *Letter 32*. Without intuition, the infinitely complex agreement of the universe would be desperately beyond human reach.[47]

This interpretation helps us to make better sense of the opposition between the two ways in which Spinoza characterizes the notion of "agreement." As I have pointed out, there seems to be an utter incompatibility in Spinoza's position: on the one hand, he argues that the agreement between wholes can never be more than partial; on the other, he seems to claim that the agreement between two parts must be complete if they are to constitute a whole. I suggest that, by reading these two terms through the lens of a structural epistemology that focuses on knowledge of the mutual interactions between objects, we can explain this apparent contradiction. If

---

[45] With this term, I intend to capture an understanding-of-totality, not universal understanding.

[46] *Letter 32* | G IV/173a/2–5.

[47] John Carriero has friendly objected to this thesis, pointing to the fact that if agreement is the mark of wholeness, then God—who only has knowledge of inadequate ideas through his knowledge of finite minds—would not have an adequate idea of agreement, since wholeness is a being of reason—according to the *KV* and other passages in Spinoza's works. If, then, our intuitive knowledge is modeled after God's own knowledge, it should similarly not feature wholeness and parthood. My answer to this objection rests on the fact that agreement and disagreement are real features of the individuals known through the third kind of knowledge, which ground parthood and wholeness in the same way in which the common notions of several individuals might ground the definition of a universal concept, which for Spinoza is a being of reason. In other words, what I defend here is not a rehabilitation of the notions of part and whole at the level of intuitive knowledge. Instead, I am arguing that mereological structural notions such as agreement and disagreement must feature in the third kind of knowledge, insofar as they regulate the behavior, the duration, and the essential modifications of individuals such as finite and infinite modes (see Figure 2.2, in Chapter 2, for a reference to how mereological composition must be involved in our conceptualization of infinite modes).

we view the problem through this lens, we can interpret both the concepts of 'as far as possible' and 'completely' as aspectual readings of the same finite being.

Each of the aspects described above "picks up" on an aspect of reality. Parts of a whole agree "as far as possible" because, as modes, they are specific singular expressions of the substance. As Spinoza states in E2d1, "by body I understand a mode that in a certain and determinate way expresses God's essence insofar as he is considered as an extended thing." Even when they are included in a higher-level individual, finite beings are expressions of God's essence, which is immediately connected with their formal essence. We learn about this connection when we know things *sub specie aeternitatis*, in the third kind of knowledge. Therefore, they cannot be entirely annihilated in the process of forming a higher-level mode, and they can only agree "as far as possible." Each part is a whole. As such, it cannot completely agree with other wholes on pain of disappearing in a process of adaptation, which would make it impossible for its essence to be known *sub specie aeternitatis*. If a mode's essence is immediately connected with the immanent causation of substance—as the eternal character of formal essences demands—it cannot completely disappear in the process of adapting to neighboring modes.

By contrast, from the point of view of higher-level individuals (i.e., wholes), Spinoza must commit to an agreement of parts that is "complete." Due to the restraints formulated in E3p4 and E3p5, the notion of agreement employed in the forming of wholes must dispel any doubts about an eventual disagreement between the parts of a composite, on pain of endangering the survival of its structure.[48] How should we then conceive of individuals? As Spinoza demonstrates with the example of the worm in the blood,

---

[48] In this sense, the ethical component of Spinoza's mereological theory is also clear, as described by Newlands in *Reconceiving Spinoza*, 208: "insofar as Peter and I jointly compose a single individual through cooperative activity, the threat of conflict between us disappears, according to Spinoza."

these two aspectual readings of the agreement of the parts of the human blood are both adequate, and yet do not contradict each other. Our confusion is generated by our exclusive focus on one or the other level of modes, and by our ignorance about the relations between the components.

As a result, our everyday understanding of individuals—which we naturally see as wholes—cannot be underwritten by Spinoza in its entirety. The conception of individuals that results from a structural understanding of Spinoza's epistemology calls for an understanding of modes as relationally dependent individuals, that can be both part and whole at the same time, in an overlapping of mereological states, depending on which structure assumes prevalence.

Since it has great bearing on the notion of individuality, this understanding of mereological structure would already be enough to claim that Spinoza's core metaphysics rests—once again—on a structural or relational bedrock. Yet, Spinoza pushes his analysis even further. He claims that ultimately everything can (and should) be understood as a mereological component of a macromode, which encompasses the whole infinite universe. The explosive metaphysical consequences of this claim are going to be our topic in the next section, where we will need to employ our aspectual and structural tools again, in order to tease out Spinoza's endgame.

4.5 The Face of the Whole Universe

As the reader might suspect, Spinoza's unapologetic metaphysical determination does not allow him to stop his mereological analysis at the finite bodies of our everyday life (may they be worms, particles of blood, complex organisms, or whirring machines). The reason behind this determination is probably the Principle of Sufficient Reason (PSR). If one is committed to the full explainability of reality, and if a considerable portion of the explanatory burden of individuality is carried by composition, then a sufficient reason for the halting of explanation through composition is required. Such a sufficient reason, however, does not seem available. How would a larger body differ from a smaller body, with respect to its metaphysical laws?

The consequences are foreseeable. In the following lines of *Letter 32*, Spinoza pushes his argument ever forward, concluding that "every body, insofar as it exists and it is modified in a definite way, must be considered as a part of the whole universe."[49] Thus, the whole universe is aspectually conceivable as a mereological composite, regulated by the same laws that apply for smaller composites (such as the blood or the human body).[50] This is a weird claim for Spinoza, since he maintains that an infinite addition of finite elements can never generate an infinite sum.[51] Given his general distrust for the concept of summatory infinity, we may be tempted to write off this claim as a fluke, generated perhaps by the fact that the text we are examining is a letter. After all, who doesn't get a little heated when trying to argue a point with a friend? Spinoza's generalization in this context might be justified, or excused, by the fact that he is trying to showcase to Oldenburg the stretching capacity of his mereological theory.

However, this generalization appears in other texts, where Spinoza demonstrates the deep homogeneity of mereological structure that unites the world of modes. In the *Ethics*, the so-called *Physical Digression* appearing after E1p13 is wholly dedicated to the discussion of bodies, as we have seen in Section 3.5. Here, Spinoza focuses in particular on how extended modes get together to form larger bodies. A curious text appears around halfway through the

---

[49] *Letter 32* | G IV/173a/3–4. Translation modified.
[50] The adverb "aspectually" in this sentence is meant to preserve the potential for perspectival readings of mereological composites. This is coherent with what we have evidenced in the previous sections of this chapter, which is highlighted by Spinoza, in this passage, through the locution "insofar as it exists and it is modified in a definite way."
[51] Cf. *Letter 12*, and my discussion of these themes in Section 2.5.

Digression. It bears the name of "definition," although it has no clear *definiendum*; and in contrast to what we have observed so far in this chapter, it does not contain the verb *intelligo*, but only *dicemus* ("we say" or "we call it"). The definition reads:

> When a number of bodies, whether of the same or of different size, are so constrained by other bodies that they lie upon one another, or if they so move, whether with the same degree or different degrees of speed, that they communicate their motions to each other in a certain fixed manner, we shall say [*dicemus*] that those bodies are united with one another and that they all together compose [*componere*] one body or Individual [*individuum*], which is distinguished from the others by this union of bodies. (E2PhysDigD | G II/99/26-100/5; my emphasis)

Prima facie, the object of this definition could appear to be the concept of "one body, or individual." In other words, an *id* or item. However, on closer look, Spinoza is undertaking a different enterprise. The *definiendum* of this text is the *union* of the bodies that form an individual, which also provides the ground for its distinction from other bodies [*a reliquis per hanc corporum unionem distinguitur*]. Just like in *Letter 32* Spinoza focused his attention on the notion of "agreement" or "coherence" of parts, here he pinpoints a structure—union—as the key concept necessary for the identification of an individual.

The metaphysical criterion for the individuation of a singular body, for Spinoza, does not come from the individual properties of the thing. Instead, such criterion is provided by the structural unity that internally connects its parts. Thanks to this criterion, we can now provide a new interpretation of E2PhysDigl4,[52] which

---

[52] "If, of a body, or of an Individual, which is composed of a number of bodies, some are removed, and at the same time as many others of the same nature take their place, the [NS: body, or the] Individual will retain its nature, as before, without any change of its form."

we had observed before as an example of horizontal expression. Spinoza here affirms that modifying the composing elements of a body, or individual, does not necessarily imply a change in the "nature" or "form" of the individual (provided that the substitute bodies are homogeneous with the ones they replace). In other words, Spinoza claims that the structural unity of individuals does not depend on its parts (in what could be seen as a form of mereological mechanicism). On the contrary, "what constitutes the form of the Individual consists [NS: only] in the union of the bodies."[53] Structural unity generates the conditions for assimilation of the parts that compose an individual, in a paradigm that follows the laws of mereological organicism.[54]

Spinoza further claims that it is not necessary for the mereological unity of an individual that its parts are homogeneous among themselves. They might possess different "natures" (and they do, as we have seen in Chapter 3). They could all be distinct individuals, each possessing its own structural unity. In advancing such claims, Spinoza can be seen as endorsing a parsimonious mereological view. He maintains that things can be part of one and the same thing despite their belonging to different natures, without any modification in their relation of parthood with respect to the whole they compose. In other words, he defends a univocal notion of parthood. While parts are in themselves heterogeneous, they compose individuals in a nonambiguous manner, without any distinction between different sorts or *kinds* of parts.[55] There is no "dominant monad" or "essential core" in Spinoza's egalitarian understanding of composition.

---

[53] E2PhysDigl4d.
[54] For more on this, see my "Whole-Part Relations in Early Modern Philosophy."
[55] In doing so, I assume Spinoza rejects ambiguous compositional structures such as (neo-)Aristotelian parthood of form and matter, or Lewis's four-dimensionalism. Spinoza's univocal mereology of heterogeneous parts is closer—in contemporary terms—to the view delineated by Koslicki in her wonderful volume, *The Structure of Objects* (see 167–199, in particular).

Thus, Spinoza's parts are homogeneous *insofar as* they are parts—they belong to a shared attribute, for example. By contrast, individuals composed by parts that are heterogeneous *insofar as* they have distinct natures or essences are not metaphysically problematic, for Spinoza. In fact, he attributes to this kind of individuals a superior power to be affected, which—as we will see in the next chapter—implies a superior power to act.[56] Knowing Spinoza and his tendency to bring every metaphysical reasoning to its extreme consequences, then, it will not be difficult for my reader to guess his next move. Since the composition of heterogeneous bodies does not constitute an obstacle to their structural unification in one and the same individual, and since Spinoza is committed to the universal applicability of all metaphysical laws, he can easily conclude that every finite body is unified in a universal body or individual. "If we proceed in this way to infinity," he says, "we shall easily conceive that the whole of nature is one Individual, whose parts, i.e., all bodies, vary in infinite ways, without any change of the whole Individual."[57] For Spinoza, the compositional structure of the world allows every individual to retain at once its individuality and its mereological position in a unifying totality, thanks to the possibility of alternative aspectual readings of one and the same state of affairs (as demonstrated in *Letter 32*).

Thus, the structural unity of Spinoza's individuals is not anchored to the homogeneity of their parts. This mereological independence, joined with the aspectual perspective implied by any process of individuation, ensures the modularity and replicability of individuality in Spinoza's metaphysics. Each individual assumes both the role of whole and that of part at any given moment, provided that it respects the requisites of structural unity. My liver, for example, is an individual resulting from the union or agreement of

---

[56] E2PhyDig17s | G II/102/1–4: "if we should now conceive of another [Individual], composed of a number of Individuals of a different nature, we shall find that it can be affected in a great many other ways, and still preserve its nature."

[57] E2PhyDig17s | G II/102/11–13; my emphasis.

the cells that compose it. In turn, my body is a composite individual resulting from the union or agreement of all the organs that compose it. As an organism, I participate in an ecosystem that relies on me to be a (hopefully responsible) predator and—with a bit of luck, a day far away—a prey for saprophytes. Thus, I am part of a union or agreement that qualifies the ecosystem as an individual (according to Spinoza's IC). And so on. The system is replicable until infinitely big (and infinitely small) individuals are identified.[58]

If we still had doubts about Spinoza's commitment to this universal declination of his mereological theory, we could look at the only other text where he refers to E2PhyDig17s. In a letter addressed to G.H. Schuller, composed two years before his death, Spinoza answers to his friend's request, which concerned mediate infinite modes and the possibility of conceiving an infinite modification of God. Spinoza happily complies, affirming that "an example of the [things produced by the mediation of some infinite modification] is the face of the whole Universe [*facies totius Universi*], which, however much it may vary in infinite ways, nevertheless always remains the same. On this, see L7s before E2p14" (our very scholium). Spinoza here calls "*facies totius Universi*" the infinitely composite individual that mereologically summates all the bodies in the world. As we have proved in this chapter, this infinite mode perfectly coincides with "the whole universe" described in *Letter 32*,

---

[58] There is one possible exception: in the *Physical Digression*, Spinoza mentions the existence of something that he calls "simplest bodies" (*corpora simplicissima*). These might not be subject to the same rules of universal compositionality. However, Spinoza does not discuss or mention them elsewhere, and he does not affirm specifically that they are *not* composites. Several commentators believe that the *corpora simplicissima* might even be mere beings of reason, introduced to establish a conventional starting point (e.g., see Buyse, "Corpus," 190–191; Lermond, *The Form of Man: Human Essence in Spinoza's "Ethics"*, 78–80). Others see it as vestigial evidence of the derivation of Spinoza's physics from Hobbes's, for example, Santinelli, "*Conatus e corpora simplicissima*. Hobbes e Spinoza sulla natura e origine del moto," 383–406. In either case, their threat to Spinoza's implication that all nature should abide by the same rules does not seem significant enough to demand a revision of Spinoza's general theory of individuality.

which is explicitly described as an aspectual understanding of an arrangement of individuals united through a harmonic structure.

Spinoza's trail of implicit and explicit quotations provides us with a poetic and fascinating ontological image. Individuals come in agreement (or union), thanks to a majestic dance of parts and wholes that are but mere facets of the complexity of the whole universe, a vertical expression of God's essence as *Natura naturans*. In a nutshell, this is the structure of Spinoza's world.

4.6 The Puzzles of Infinite Individuals

As grandiose as it may sound, the picture of Spinoza's mereology that I painted in the section above is vulnerable to at least two objections, one considerably more robust than the other. The first would prejudice the compatibility between Spinoza's understanding of individuals and the impossibility of a universal mereological whole. This objection is kinder, in the sense that it at least takes seriously the IC I have formulated in this chapter. The second objection, more dangerous for the view that I have been spelling out in this volume, would bring me to task regarding the notion of limitation that I described in Chapter 1. If limitation is the structure that establishes what it is to be a mode, how can we take seriously Spinoza's suggestion of such an unbound individual, which would embrace everything that exists under a certain attribute? The combination of these two objections would certainly be a lethal punch for my interpretation. If we want to defend Spinoza's universal mereology, we had better get to work to solve them.

Let us consider the apparently kinder objection first. Does the "face of the whole universe," as we have described it so far, withstand the scrutiny provided by the IC that Spinoza had set for individuals earlier in *Letter 32*? As a reminder, IC claimed that x is an individual if and only if its parts showcase a certain agreement and share a coherent array of trans-attributal properties (including causal, compositional, and "temporal" properties). Is the whole universe the kind of object captured by this criterion? It should be, according to Spinoza's naturalism—the belief that everything is bound by the same natural laws. The compositional criterion is easy enough—after all, Spinoza builds his whole theory of mereology upon this universalizing feature. The "temporal" criterion is not an unsurmountable obstacle, either. Modes are by definition not eternal, and they have an eternal essence only insofar as they are conceived to immanently express God's power. Therefore, if *a* and *b* are two bodies that both belong to the universal individual body, they will both share of eternity in the same way—conditionally.[59] However, it is not immediately clear that the whole universe of bodies (to pick an example out of the infinite pool of attributal modes) can constitute a coherent causal individual. For what would be the effect of such a behemothic causal individual?

First, let us clear the table from an obvious concern. How do we *know* that there must be some effect at all to the whole world, if conceived as an individual? Spinoza offers us some certainty regarding this topic in a beautiful line, which closes *Ethics* I and reads: "Nothing exists from whose nature some effect does not follow" (E1p36). I am fond of calling this proposition Spinoza's Principle of Sufficient Effect (PSE), as it establishes a rationalist tenet that is as universal in its application as its more famous sibling, the PSR. For something to exist, it must have an effect. Given our natural interpretation of the word "effect," this can be translated as "if x exists, x causes."[60] Of course, this does not take away from the view we fleshed out in Chapter 2, maintaining that in virtue

---

[59] Cf. Section 3.4 above.
[60] This natural reading of "effect" implies its binary correspondence with the notion of "cause." Even though it is not necessary for an effect to have *one* cause (i.e., many causes can concur to generate one and the same effect), it still seems natural and philosophically sound to say that it is necessary for an effect to have *a* cause, within the domain of rationalism to which Spinoza clearly belongs.

of Spinoza's expressionism, God is the only immanent cause in the universe. The demonstration attached to E1p36 proves that Spinoza is thinking along these lines. "Whatever exists expresses the nature, or essence of God in a certain and determinate way, i.e., whatever exists expresses in a certain and determinate way the power of God, which is the cause of all things" (E1p36d). We thus have a textual confirmation that *if* our universal individual exists, it must be a causal agent in some way. Yet, I still must answer that all-important question: does the universe cause anything?

To make the reasoning easier, let us limit our example to the "mere" universe of extended modes. By definition, the gargantuan individual we call "face of the whole universe" must include every body in existence. This apparently innocent affirmation generates a puzzle that will be recognizable to my reader if she has familiarity with set theory. To respect the PSE, our individual—let us call it u—must cause something. Yet, a body a cannot exist outside u because u is by definition the body that mereologically includes all bodies. Our body a would thus be a part of u, and u would enjoy some form of reflexive causality. Where is the contradiction here? Recall our very first argument in Chapter 1. Spinoza maintains that the first and foremost distinction between substance and everything else is that substance enjoys a special structure, self-causation. Thus, we must reformulate our PSE: if x exists, x must cause y, and y must be different from x. It is true that u and a are not identical, since a constitutes a proper part of u and is therefore (infinitely) smaller. But still, for u to cause a, it would mean for u to cause itself, or a part of itself, in some sense. No new body can thus be caused by the universal individual including all bodies. How about other modes that do not belong to the realm of bodies? Unfortunately, due to Spinoza's causal separation of attributes, that is an obvious nonstarter.

So what solution are we left with? Our universal body u cannot cause itself, cannot cause another body, and cannot cause a mode of another attribute. Luckily for us, Spinoza is not a set theorist (or at least, I am not aware of any undeniable source that affirms that), and his mereological wholes are not sets. Thus, the individual consisting of all bodies is not identical to a hypothetical set of all bodies *at all times*. Let us take for example the *facies totius universi* as it appears at a given moment in duration, for example t^0. Each of the parts that constitute u as a mereological whole causes something, in accordance with Spinoza's PSE. Thus, the mereological whole at an instant successive in time, for example t^1, is not identical to u at t^0. It is still the same individual, even though all of its parts have undergone some change, if it maintains the same *ratio* of motion and rest, as we have learned from the *Physical Digression*. If u at t^0 is not identical to u at t^1, then u at t^0 can legitimately cause the latter without "idolatry" —that is to say, without threatening God's position as the one and only being that is *causa sui*.

Moreover, the fact that any change in u's *ratio* of motion and rest is internally generated helps Spinoza to justify his tenet that the world of modes has an eternal duration (which, I remind the reader, is distinct from eternity). This tenet is the logical result of Spinoza's engagement with the Scholastics.[61] Even in the young days when he was apparently or ironically posing as a creationist, Spinoza denied that creation could have happened at a given time. Time, just like duration, is the exclusive domain of modes; infinite duration is accordingly the exclusive domain of infinite modes. This important distinction (probably elaborated at some point in 1663, as proved by Schmaltz's excellent study) is maintained in the *Ethics*.[62] However, the infinite duration of infinite modes has another result. As we have seen, Spinoza denies that a mode's destruction can come about through an internal cause.[63] Thus, the fact that the whole universe can be conceived as a whole (and that no mode of the same attribute exists outside of it) also means that

---

[61] See my "Spinoza and Scholastic Philosophy" (§1), as well as Scribano's intensive study "Spinoza e la Scolastica sull'eternità del mondo."
[62] Schmaltz, "Spinoza on Eternity and Duration." Cf. E1pp21–23.
[63] Cf. E3p4.

no mode can destroy the universe. The rejection of this possible "closure" of the universe as a mereological whole pairs nicely with Spinoza's rejection of teleology. As Klein puts it, "persevering in a ratio of motion and rest is not incompatible with transformation and reconfiguration."[64] Spinoza's total individual (u) is capable of causal action insofar as it can reconfigure itself through discrete instants of duration.[65]

In conclusion, we have the answer to our first objection. The "face of the whole universe" can be defined as a legitimate individual, according to IC: its parts are harmonized in terms of their causal, compositional, and "temporal" properties.

Let us now move to the second objection. Is it credible on my part to represent the universe as an *infinite* individual after I have built the structure of limitation into the very heart of Spinoza's conception of modes? More generally: can my interpretation of Spinoza account for infinite modes? The answer, in short, is yes. However, this challenge will require me to stretch the understanding of limitation I proposed in Chapter 1 to its limits and perhaps (a little) beyond.

As you will recall, I introduced limitation, in Section 1.2, following Spinoza's definition (at E1d2) of a finite thing as the object resulting from a metaphysical structure that depends on two criteria. At that point, the two criteria for understanding x as a finite object demanded that x and its fellow limited being y both belong to the same kind *and* that y can possibly act on x to limit x. As we already noted in Chapter 1, this definition implies some kind of structurally oriented existence. In other words, x cannot exist as limited without at least formally implying the existence of an equally and oppositely limited y. However, in the course of this book I have repeatedly employed "finite thing" as shorthand for "finite mode,"

---

[64] Klein, "By Eternity I Understand," 316.
[65] Again, this implies denying that Spinoza is a four-dimensionalist and affirming that he is committed to a mereological homogeneity of parts qua parts.

and I have partially based my understanding of individuals on the definition of "singular thing" provided by Spinoza. "By singular things," he affirms at E2d7, "I understand things that are finite and have a determinate existence." Thus, it seems that the notion of finitude is built into the notion of limitation, which in turn is the basis on which we construct the very idea of individuals as structurally imbued of relationality. Are we entitled to export this notion to the world of infinite modes, and in particular to the mereological case of the *facies totius universi*?[66]

There are two possible solutions to this puzzle. The first would require us to step forward in the organicist world. As we have seen above, one of the possible models of composition that generates higher-level individuals from lower-level ones is the organic model. Spinoza's individuals would behave as living beings, absorbing lower-level individuals through a progressive harmonization of their *ratio* of motion and rest with their own. In this case, we could imagine the infinite individual composed by all the finite modes of one attribute as a leviathan, constantly absorbing smaller individuals in its infinitely large body (for example). However, following the example of the worm, we could maintain that even when so absorbed, finite modes retain a sufficient level of individuality. Thus, the face of the whole universe would be internally limited, insofar as it encounters a hypothetical resistance from the finite bodies that it has subsumed. This is a fascinating solution, which has been adopted by several prominent Spinoza scholars.[67] However, I maintain a form of friendly skepticism about it because of what I consider two substantive threats to its full adoption. First, it is too heavily indebted to the world of bodies and organism—it

---

[66] Melamed deals with a parallel problem when he analyzes the notion of God's infinite intellect (*Spinoza's Metaphysics*, 179–191). He also argues that the infinite mode of thought represents a special case in Spinoza's metaphysics. However, since I take Spinoza to hold a nonpreferential version of expressionistic parallelism, I will take his conclusions regarding infinite modes to apply generally across attributes.

[67] See, for example, Jonas, "Spinoza and the Theory of Organism"; Di Poppa, "Spinoza and Process Ontology"; and Merçon, "Relationality and Individuality in Spinoza."

is far from clear what would it mean for a mind to "absorb" smaller minds, even leaving aside the worries about modes of unknown attributes. Second, it requires anchoring our notion of limitation in the durational world, since every process of assimilation would always be a process, developing in duration. From my point of view, this would endanger the scheme of eternal aspects that I have developed in Chapter 3.

Let me propose an alternative solution, entirely grounded in the formal requirements set by Spinoza's definition of limitation. In E1d2, Spinoza spells out limitation as the structure characterizing individuals that "can be limited by another of the same nature. For example, a body is called finite because we always conceive another that is greater."[68] In this formulation, Spinoza tells us nothing about the *actual* limitation of finite individuals. Instead, he insists on the *formal* aspect of this structure, devising a sort of transcendental argument *ante litteram* in which the finitude of things is based on their potential limitation. Thus, it is not required of our infinite individual to be actually limited. It is sufficient that its body, even though infinite, is subject to potential limitation by another body. Similarly, it is not required that "God's intellect" (the infinite mode of thought) be actually limited by our puny minds for it to be captured by the criteria set for its classification as an individual. Remember that Spinoza's *Letter on the Infinite* distinguishes between beings that are infinite in virtue of their essence and beings that are infinite in virtue of their cause. As we know, infinite modes belong to the second group. Thus, their essence can allow for them to be formally limited even in spite of the fact that they are never actually limited. By contrast, God's essence, which implies infinity and eternity, would not allow God to ever be formally limited. Consequently, God cannot be considered an individual according

---

[68] In the Latin, E1d2 reads: "*Ea res dicitur in suo genere finita, quæ alia ejusdem naturæ terminari potest. Ex. gr. corpus dicitur finitum, quia aliud semper majus concipimus. Sic cogitatio alia cogitatione terminatur. At corpus non terminatur cogitatione, nec cogitatio corpore*" (my emphasis).

to the criteria set by this chapter. As I had anticipated, this solution might be seen as stretching the technical boundaries of Spinoza's concept of limitation. Yet, I maintain that this kind of "ride or die" solution is in line with the bold spirit of Spinoza's metaphysics, and that it does not violate the specific formulations that he offers in any of his texts.

Let us look back for a moment. In this chapter, I discussed Spinoza's complex views on individuality, configuring the criteria that allow him to distinguish discrete individuals despite his substantial monism. To establish these criteria, we have seen how Spinoza recurs once more to structural notions, and in particular to what I have described as ontological composition. Under my interpretative lens, individuals do not form ties insofar as they are individuals; rather, they are individuals insofar as they form ties.

To defend this view, I faced several mereological puzzles, such as the possibility of overlapping distinct compositional states— to which I have proposed a solution, thanks to our old friend, Spinoza's aspectual distinction; and such as the possibility of infinite individuals, capable of capturing the entire multiplicity of finite modes. To unravel this latter puzzle, I have invoked the notion of (mere) formal limitation, which has allowed us to run with Spinoza's hares and hunt with his hounds, too. With this final adjustment to the notion of formulation, I conclude my treatment of Spinoza's metaphysics of structure from the third-person point of view. In the next and conclusive chapter, I will leave behind the safe shores of ontology to face the open seas of psychology and anthropology, in search of Spinoza's Promised Land: beatitude.

5
The Human Point of View
Action, Passion, Striving, Affects

And though you were of the hot-tempered kind,
or of the lustful, or of the fanatical, or the vengeful;
in the end, all your passions became virtues,
and all your devils, angels.
Once you had wild dogs in your cellar:
but they changed at last into birds and charming singers.
Out of your poisons you brewed
soothing ointments for yourself.[1]

We have finally reached the apex of our metaphysical wanderings. In Chapter 1, we started our analysis of Spinoza's metaphysical system from the simplest notions of structure available in his landscape (limitation, conception, inherence, and causation). We then climbed the steep hills of expression and conceptual entailment, only to find ourselves in need of more climbing to achieve a more accurate grasp of Spinoza's notions of eternity, duration, composition, and individuality. Each of these structures has added more detail to our understanding of Spinoza's philosophy, allowing us the wonderful sight of a complex and dynamic world. In order to gain such heights, we have adopted the point of view suggested by Spinoza: a bird's-eye view, subsuming the whole world under the

---

[1] Nietzsche, *Thus Spoke Zarathustra* I.5, 25.

same set of rules (the attitude I have described as naturalism) and the same structures.[2]

In this chapter, while maintaining this general naturalistic attitude, I will partially abandon the global point of view adopted so far. We will plunge into the world of particularized and individual things, casting aside even the holistic safety rope that we had carried with us during our survey of composition and harmonization. The reason for this partial change of strategy is the naïve methodology that I had outlined at the beginning of Chapter 1. In the *Ethics*, Spinoza dedicates the entirety of the first (and most of the second) part to general issues of metaphysics and epistemology. By the time we reach *Ethics* III, however, he begins a situated analysis of the human condition. Despite this restricted emphasis, however, Spinoza never renounces the privileged attention reserved to general structures. In fact, a wide portion of the analysis developed throughout *Ethics* III, IV, and V focuses on the structural connections between distinct modes in each attribute and their reciprocal interaction. In this sense, while Spinoza's philosophy is strictly amoral (since it does not provide prescriptions), it concerns human behavior in the purest sense. In contemporary terminology, we could describe such attitude as a philosophical *ethology*, the science concerned with providing behavioral descriptions and explanations.[3] In this chapter, I shall examine the main structures involved in such ethology. Namely, we will encounter action, passion, striving, and *amor Dei intellectualis*, or intellectual love of God. To be sure, I cannot hope to exhaust in these pages the sophisticated analysis of humanity, and human character, that Spinoza deploys throughout his masterpiece. As before, I aim solely to provide a streamlined reconstruction of the structural tendencies of Spinoza's philosophy; in particular, my goal in this chapter is to

---

[2] Cf. E3Pref | G II/138/13–14: "for nature is always the same, and its virtue and power of acting are everywhere one and the same."
[3] I am indebted to Idit Dobbs-Weinstein for this insightful *dictum*.

highlight the metaphysical doctrines that underpin Spinoza's ethics and philosophy of action. As it has been customary in the previous chapters, I shall focus primarily on what I have established in Chapter 1 as the most fundamental structure of Spinoza's metaphysics: causation, limitation, conception, and inherence. These structures, as I will show in what follows, are exercised by Spinoza in the construction of a relational network that can function as a blueprint for the observation, study, and understanding of the behavior of individual things. In this sense, Spinoza's metaphysics of individuals is exemplified in the crucial notions of action, passion, and striving—all of which constitute the building blocks of Spinoza's ethology. As for the notion of *amor Dei intellectualis*—a prerequisite to Spinoza's idea of beatitude—we shall see how it represents a structural notion itself, even though in a more derivative sense. The main reason for its inclusion in this gallery of fundamental structures is historical; Spinoza clearly assigns to it an outstanding importance, almost capable of enacting an essential transformation in "passionate" individuals. As beatitude patently represents the nonteleological goal of the *Ethics*, it is only appropriate that we adopt it as our own finishing line, in a parallelism of intentions that is respectful of Spinoza's master plan.

5.1 Reducing Action

The foundation of Spinoza's ethology is constituted by the tryptic of definitions that opens *Ethics* III. In these three definitions, Spinoza outlines his theory of action and cashes out the complex texture of structures built in *Ethics* I. E3d1 establishes the concept of "adequate causation," and it reads: "I call that cause adequate whose effect can be clearly and distinctly perceived through it. But I call it partial, or inadequate, if its effect cannot be understood through it alone." Prima facie, this definition affirms an equation of adequate causation and conception. Spinoza stipulates that x is an adequate cause of *y* if and only if *y* is caused by *x* and *y* is "understood through" (conceived through) *x*. This definition of adequate causation, on the face of it, can apply equally to all forms of efficient causation—both immanent and transitive.[4]

This initial impression is confirmed by Spinoza's actualization of this general principle in E3d2, which defines "action [*agere*]."

> I say that we act when something happens, <u>in us or outside us</u>, of which we are the adequate cause, i.e. (by E3d1), when something in us or outside us <u>follows from our nature</u>, which can be clearly and distinctly understood through it alone. On the other hand, I say that we are acted on when something happens in us, or something follows from our nature, of which we are only a partial cause. (G II/39/6-13; my emphasis)

Action is thus equated with "adequate causation." Spinoza specifies that such causation can happen either "in us or outside us," thus dispensing with the suspicion that inherence might play a major role in his understanding of adequate causation. Furthermore, the effect of an adequate causal process is described not only as that which joins efficient causation with conception through the cause but also as that which "follows from" the nature of its cause, in a reprise of the essentialist model of expression that I have analyzed in Chapter 2.[5] As I concluded in Chapter 1, if this dual model of conception and causation was to be joined by inherence, we would obtain immanent causation. Yet, immanent causation does not ipso facto mean "naturare." For *x* to be the *naturans* of *y*, Spinoza requires that *x* causes (and conceptually grounds, and provides the substrate of inherence) both the essence and the existence of *y*. As we saw in Chapter 1, that is certainly the case of the relationship

---

[4] Cf. *KV* I.3 | G I/39/15–22.
[5] A similar interpretation of this passage is advanced by Viljanen, *Spinoza's Geometry of Power*, 49.

between substance and modes. However, E3d2 is limited to a much more general case, one that lacks the requirements of both causation of essences and inherence of effects in their causes.

Further expanding on this general case, Spinoza proceeds to determine that by "affect I understand affections of the body by which the body's power of acting is increased or diminished, aided or restrained, and at the same time, the ideas of these affections. Therefore, if we can be the adequate cause of any of these affections, I understand by the affect an action; otherwise, a passion." Two points are of interest here. First, Spinoza confirms once again the cross-attributal nature of his general metaphysics, by providing a general model that can be applied to both modes of extension and modes of thought (respectively, bodies and ideas). Each of these orders of modes is modified according to their distinct attributal nature. Yet, the model of modification or affection *in se* (or in itself) is identical, since both are modifications of substance, as demanded by Spinoza's parallelism in E2p7s. Second, we learn that "affect" is the general name that indicates anything that engages with a finite mode—a body or a mind—in such a way that it engenders a mutation in that mode. Such mutation can be either "positive" or "negative" (both highly relative terms, for Spinoza) from the point of view of the mode. The positive value of affects is captured under the term "action," which corresponds to an affect that sees our individual point of view as congruent with the adequate cause of the effect (of that affect). By contrast, the negative value of affects is designated as a "passion," following the etymological meaning of "*passio*"—to suffer, or be subject to, something else.

In this chapter, one of my main goals will be to establish an interpretative understanding of the twin notions of "action" and "passion" as perspectival outlooks on one and the same causal interaction. In doing so, I must admit I am partially capitulating to the reductionist attitude that I have often criticized in the course of this book. Not without reason, one could accuse me of inconsistency, or even interpretative hypocrisy. In Chapter 1, I have offered several arguments to support structural pluralism and to reject the reduction of dependence relations to either causality or conception (reducing them all to inherence is not an option that I am aware of—but it goes without saying, I would oppose that, too). In Chapters 2 and 3, I have offered more reasons to doubt structural reductionism by adding notions such as expression, entailment, and modal hyperintensionality to Spinoza's metaphysical toolbox. In Chapter 4, I have enriched this understanding by "structuralizing" our very notion of individuality, pointing to a possible detachment of causality and conception due to the involvement of a partial, perspectival point of view. So far, this book has outlined a consistent picture of antireductionist metaphysics. And now, in the final chapter, I am proposing to consider the possibility that Spinoza might be willing to reduce action and passion to causation, after all. Why would I do that? What changed?

Well, the simple answer is everything. The fundamental outlook that Spinoza had embraced in the first two parts of the *Ethics*, where he was concerned with the establishment of the structural scaffolding of reality, is superseded in *Ethics* III by the specific outlook typical of human beings. Spinoza is leaving behind the perspective of eternity to delve into duration, with the hope of returning to eternity once more after his investigation of finitude. Moreover, while *Ethics* I (and in a lesser way, *Ethics* II) never explicitly called for a reduction of one structure to another, the opening lines of *Ethics* III appear to imply such reduction in a forceful manner. Finally, Spinoza switches from the range of eternity and necessary connections to the language of modifications, affections, and contingency. This switch is testified by Spinoza's language. In *Ethics* III, he makes ample recourse to the first plural person "we," indicating a finite and human perspective. As Susan James affirms, the ideas discussed in these pages "do not tell us how things are independently of their relations."[6] The phrase "if we can be the adequate

---

[6] James, *Passion and Action*, 143.

cause [*adæquata possimus esse causa*]" (my emphasis) inserted in E3d3 further highlights such a switch, which also implies the mere *possibility* of adequate causation (instead of the necessary causation typical of substance).

Thus, we witness here a content change, a textual change, and a modal change. These three changes are, in my opinion, enough to warrant the consideration of an eventual reduction of action and passion to causation, in a way that was not warranted when only so-called first-order structures were concerned. Before, Spinoza's attention was focused on how modifications of the substance are originated, and how those modifications align with his substantial monism. By contrast, he now takes interest in how those modifications (which remain modifications *of the* substance, according to all the meanings of dependence illustrated above) affect other modifications, *from their point of view*; and how finite modes can be involved in this causal and conceptual structures. With my conscience clearer, I can follow Spinoza down this partially reductionist path, without compromising my pluralistic framework.

5.2 God as *Agens* and *Patiens*

The lines that open *Ethics* III have provided us a straightforward (even too much, perhaps) picture of Spinoza's philosophy of action. The structural lines that tie together Spinoza's world have crystallized in a net of causes and concepts that effectively cover anything happening in nature. A question that might come naturally, at this point, is "which nature"? Since Spinoza has just announced that he is focusing on human beings,[7] which belong to the aspect of *Natura naturata*, are we to take the definitions of *Ethics* III as

---

[7] Cf. E3Pref | G II/138/24–27: "I shall treat the nature and powers of the Affects, and the power of the Mind over them, by the same Method by which, in the preceding parts, I treated God and the Mind, and I shall consider human actions and appetites just as if it were a question of lines, planes, and bodies."

indicative of a restricted domain, or do they apply to God as well? After all, Spinoza must have had well in mind the consolidated Aristotelian and Scholastic tradition that identified the first attribute of God as "*actus purus*," pure act.[8] The impossibility of God's undergoing any kind of change (and thus becoming *subjectum*) was commonplace in philosophy and theology in Spinoza's time. It was certainly one of the bedrock theses of Moses Maimonides, which we could well consider his foremost philosophical reference.[9]

Spinoza takes up this question in the convoluted demonstration that follows E3p1, which applies the general principle of action as adequate causation and conception to the human mind. Specifically, Spinoza affirms that our mind "insofar as [*quatenus*] it has adequate ideas, it necessarily does certain things, and insofar as [*quatenus*] it has inadequate ideas, it necessarily undergoes other things" (E3p1). It is tempting to read these lines as an indication of a direct causation of ideas over things, as a direct contradiction of Spinoza's parallelism as affirmed in E2p7. However, it must be noted that Spinoza does not deploy a causal connection here (which would be the Latin *quia*) nor a grounding one (which he generally signals through the adverb *vi*, "by force of" or "in virtue of"). Instead, he recurs to the aspectual connective we have witnessed before, *quatenus*. The precise meaning of this connective is appropriately laid out in the demonstration.

> From any given idea some effect must necessarily follow (E1p36), of which effect God is the adequate cause (see E3d1), not insofar as he is infinite, but insofar as he is considered to be affected by that given idea (see E2p9). But if God, insofar as he is affected by an idea that is adequate in someone's Mind, is the

---

[8] However, it must be kept in mind that even classical Scholastics might have been less than firm on considering God's *actus* as pure unity; on this topic, see the brilliant study by Matthews Grant and Spencer, "Activity, Identity, and God: A Tension in Aquinas and His Interpreters."

[9] See Maimonides, *The Guide for the Perplexed*, I.52, 62a.

cause of an effect, that same Mind is the effect's adequate cause (by E2p11c).[10]

This demonstration is a crucial text for Spinoza. In just a few sentences, he manages to defy both occasionalists and theologians of transcendence by radicalizing his understanding of immanent causation. These are conceivably the very lines that inflamed Pierre Bayle, who penned a scorching entry about Spinoza in his *Dictionary*, declaring Spinoza's "monstruous" doctrine guilty of making God a party in "all the follies, all the dreams, all the filthiness, all the iniquities of the human race."[11] According to Bayle, such monstrosity derived from Spinoza's conception of God as both "agent and patient, efficient cause, and subject."[12] While it is an open debate in the literature how sincere Bayle's indignation really was, his *Dictionary* entry certainly catalyzed a widespread feeling of scandal about Spinoza's identification of God as an agent *and* a patient.[13]

In light of all the fuss made about it, it behooves us to ask: how legitimate was this scandal? Does Spinoza actually identify the agent God and the patient God? The answer, as my reader probably guessed, is in the negative. The aspectual analysis elaborated in Chapter 2 allows us to see how Spinoza can distinguish between God qua agent and God qua patient along the same lines that distinguished *Natura naturans* and *Natura naturata*. God (*sive Natura*) constitutes the grounding of action and passion insofar as he is either considered in himself—adequately—or considered in his modifications. In contrast to what he has maintained so far in the *Ethics*, Spinoza might seem here to be suggesting a partitioning of reality, since "part" of reality—the individuals of *Natura*

---

[10] E3p1d | G II/140/17-22.
[11] Bayle, *Historical and Critical Dictionary*, 311.
[12] Ibid., 301 (N).
[13] On the topic of Bayle's disputable sincerity and his instrumental use of Spinoza, see Benigni, *Itinerari dell'Antispinozismo*, chapter 4.

naturata—is potentially subject to passion or passivity. With the help of the conceptual analysis developed in Chapter 4 through the examination of *Letter 32*, however, we can affirm that this partitioning is only valid through an individualist point of view, which Spinoza assumes in *Ethics* III to account for variety of the human experience.

If read through this perspectival lens, E1p3d does not challenge any of the metaphysical claims of Spinoza's *Ethics*. Take the mind of Anakin Skywalker to be our sample mind. The idea of Obi-Wan Kenobi, as generated by Anakin's mind, would be adequate if and only if *Natura naturata*—exclusively insofar as it is modified by Anakin's mind—were the adequate cause of Obi-Wan Kenobi's idea.[14] That is probably not true, considering that Kenobi is his own individual, and that he is a separate modification, with equal standing in the universal order of *Natura naturata*. Thus, the idea of Kenobi in Anakin's mind is at least partially caused by Kenobi himself. Anakin's mind cannot be an adequate cause of the idea of Kenobi, and the resulting idea will be therefore inadequate. Anakin is thus condemned to inadequacy and passivity. That is probably why he shouts at Kenobi, with truly little evidence, "from my point of view, the Jedi are evil!," falling into the same moral perspectivism that Spinoza condemns as the origin of most human suffering.[15]

What is the alternative offered by this aspectual, structural reading of E1p3d? God qua *naturans* is the immanent adequate cause of any and all things "which can fall under an infinite intellect" (E1p16c1). Thus, God qua *naturans* also possesses an adequate idea of any and all ideas of those things. In E1p3d, Spinoza offers the important clarification that it is not sufficient for a

---

[14] If my reader has missed out on the fascinating masterpiece that is *Revenge of the Sith*, they are welcome to substitute Obi-Wan and Anakin with the more canonical Socrates and Plato, for less fun and more clarity.
[15] Cf. E1app | G II/82/19–22: "the ignorant... believe all things have been made for their sake; and call the nature of a thing good or evil, sound or rotten and corrupt, as they are affected by it."

mode of God to belong to *Natura naturata* to enjoy access to this adequacy. The aspectual barrier instituted in *Ethics* I between *naturans* and *naturata* effectively functions as a veil of inadequacy, preventing human modes from accessing the adequate ideas of things that they do not cause.

By contrast, the paradigm of mental activity involves adequate conception. In this sense, God qua *naturans* cannot but be active. As Di Poppa affirms, for Spinoza "God's power is that in virtue of which infinitely many things exist: that is, anything that can be *produced*, or anything that can be *conceived* by an infinite intellect." However, she takes this equivalence to mean that "there is nothing that is *conceived* that is not actually *produced*," thus establishing a de facto priority of causation over conception.[16] In the context of the structural pluralism that I have described in this book, and especially in Chapter 1, this instantiation of causal priority would mean that conception can be reduced to causality. As a response to this attempt, we must again stress that Spinoza does not establish the correlation between causal and conceptual priority as a grounding relation (in either direction). The *quatenus* connective of E3p1d merely establishes an aspectual equivalence between conception and causation—in line with the ideas-things parallelism of expression delineated in E2p7. The simple fact that *mental* activity involves conception can be explained through the fact that conception *is* the work of the mental, in its representational structure. Thus, Spinoza is correct in attributing activity to God's mind insofar as it *conceives* the things his power *causes*; but the infinite and all-embracing extension of this activity depends on God's infinite power of conceiving and not on his infinite power of causing—even though the two are coextensive.

This aspectual barrier between conception and causation is confirmed by Spinoza in E3p3. There, he affirms that "the actions of the Mind arise from adequate ideas alone; the passions depend on

---

[16] Di Poppa, "Spinoza on Causation and Power," 311.

inadequate ideas alone" (my emphasis). Adequate conception and adequate ideation are thus linked, in the realm of the mind, because the mind's very activity as a modification is nothing over and above ideation. By attributal contrast, we can deduct that adequate bodily causation entails an adequate (i.e., exclusively caused) modification of the arrangement of bodies that are involved in a thing's identity. Thanks to this aspectual distinction, the attributal barrier is safe, as well as the structural divide between conception and causation. What is, then, Spinoza's response to Bayle's accusation? The distinction between *Natura naturans* and *Natura naturata* allows Spinoza to differentiate, within one and the same action, the two aspects of *agens* and *patiens*. God (the God Bayle means, at least) is safely on the side of action; God's mind cannot but have adequate ideas, and God's unlimited power of causation guarantees his adequate role in all causal processes.

The issue is quite different for finite modes—minds and bodies alike. Finite minds possess a limited power of conception, and finite bodies have a limited physical causal power. As a result, they will be partial or inadequate explanations (on the conceptual or the physical side) of the respective effects in which they are involved. Action and passion are second-order structures; they rely on adequate conception and causation. Thus, they inherit whatever adequacy they have from their "parent" structures, meaning that "controlling" the passions and actions of the mind and the body without intervening on the causal and conceptual structures of which they are but phenotypes is impossible. In God's case, contra Bayle, such causal and conceptual structures are adequate by definition; the *naturans* God can never be subject to external action, that is, *patiens*.[17]

As we have just seen, Spinoza's philosophy of action demands that the *agens* and the *patiens* enjoy a robust aspectual distinction, to avoid conflating them into reflexive agency that would contradict

---

[17] Cf. Sangiacomo and Nachtomy, "Spinoza's Rethinking of Activity," 107.

God's absolute role as *naturans*.[18] Having once again assured God's safety from inadequacy and limitation, it is finally time for Spinoza to turn to less absolute things, into the very heart of the world.

5.3 Striving for Action

As I have mentioned in the first section of this chapter, Spinoza designs a large portion of his *Ethics* as an ethology, a study of behavior. Yet, this descriptivist stance quickly turns into a truly Newtonian dynamics, a study of the causes of action. In this latter sense, a notion tightly correlated to the twin structures of action and passion is the so-called striving that occupies a central position in the development of *Ethics* III.

E3p6 and E3p7, the two propositions that officially introduce this structure in Spinoza's argumentation, constitute together one of the most fundamental building blocks in his metaphysics of individuals; we have already encountered them in this latter guise in our investigation of the concept of actual essences.[19] The propositions read respectively:

> E3p6: Each thing, as far as it is in itself, strives to persevere in its being [*Unaquæque res, quantum in se est, in suo esse perseverare conatur*].[20]

---

[18] Along with Di Poppa's causal reductionism, this internal differentiation allows my pluralistic Spinoza to rebut his alter ego, Della Rocca's Eleatic monism of action. According to Della Rocca, Spinoza's rationalistic monism would require him to "transcend the unintelligible distinctions between individual actions or between actions and mere events." In virtue of this transcendence, "the one action remains, and individual actions (and events) do not"; Della Rocca, "Steps toward Eleaticism in Spinoza's Philosophy of Action," 31.
[19] See above, Section 3.2.
[20] Translation modified. Curley justifies his translation, "Each thing, as far as it can by its own power, strives to persevere in its being," by referring to a Latin idiom, which is a reasonable if speculative hypothesis (see n15). In the absence of deciding evidence, I maintained the English translation closer to the literal Latin, to avoid undue interpolation.

E3p7: The striving [*conatus*] by which each thing strives to persevere in its being is nothing but the actual essence of the thing.[21]

In this diptych of propositions, Spinoza presents the fundamental structure that characterizes the durational existence of finite beings. Things, insofar as they possess an actual essence which is the result of its durational being, are inserted in a rich tapestry of similar durationally bound items to which they are joined in the process of composing higher-level individuals (as we saw in the previous chapter).

The actual essence of things coincides with their striving, as we learn in E3p7. With this memorable formula, Spinoza captures the instinct for survival that is shared by all things, even the inanimate ones. As James puts it, God himself is no stranger to this process, insofar as he is a thing (*res*) too, whose infinite *esse* is unbound as it is extraneous to limitation. "Substance itself, the causal subsystems that it contains, and particular things, all strive to persevere in their being. The whole of nature exhibits this striving or *conatus*, which constitutes the essence of the whole and each of its parts, so that everything possesses some power to maintain itself and resist destruction."[22] The crucial word in this formulation is "some," associated to the notion of power. Spinoza's understanding of the *conatus* structure is relative at its core, despite its ubiquitous presence in the infinite multiplicity of *res*—or rather, because of it.

As we have seen in the previous sections of this chapter, Spinoza's definitions of adequacy and action in E3d1 and E3d2 most eminently rely on structural notions such as causation and conception. The phrase "as far as it is in itself," inserted in E3p6, serves instead

---

[21] While "striving" is a highly deserving translation insofar as it maintains the specular connection with E3p6's "*conatur*," the Latin term *conatus* has enjoyed such a success and proliferation in Spinozian and post-Spinozian secondary literature that it deserves highlighting. In what follows, I will employ "striving" and "*conatus*" as synonyms.

[22] James, *Passion and Action*, 146.

the double purpose of evoking both inherence and limitation in Spinoza's understanding of striving. The proposition argues that the *conatus* of each thing (and by extension, its capacity for acting) is directly proportional to its self-inherence and absence of limitation. If a thing is less limited, it maximally inheres in itself and it strives for a longer duration; if a thing is more limited, by contrast, its inherence is placed outside of itself (*in alio*), and its striving will come to a sooner end.

This association of striving with inherence and limitation makes perfect sense when understood through the general framework of Spinoza's metaphysics. As we know from E1d2, Spinoza understands limitation as a reciprocal structure; things are limited insofar as they can be limited by something else. The declination of this notion in the dynamic structure of *conatus* entails that "no thing can be destroyed except through an external cause" (E3p4), as we saw in our analysis of composition. Just like limitation implies a negative interaction *ab alio*, then, the interruption of striving (i.e., destruction) also entails the interference of an external cause, since things cannot bring *in se* the seeds of their own annihilation. It is interesting to note in this context that E3p4d does not appeal to the notion of limitation directly but instead argues that "the definition of any thing affirms, and does not deny, the thing's essence, or it posits the thing's essence, and does not take it away." Once again, Spinoza recurs to definitions as the "explanations" of essences.[23] Conversely, the process that leads from the essence of a thing to its instantiation is the familiar structure of expression, which equates a thing's power to its essence, as we have seen in Chapter 2. At the same time, since we are after all discussing the uncertain world of individuals, Spinoza does reaffirm the perspectivity of this understanding of striving, as he adds "while we attend only to the thing itself, and not to external causes, we shall not be able to find anything in it which can destroy it." This apparently innocent clause in

[23] Cf. above, Section 2.2.

Spinoza's demonstration for E3p4 dissimulates the harsh reality of finite things. Insofar as the world of composition is open to alternative understandings of one and the same configuration of bodies or ideas, the focus on its own essence and power is the only safeguard protecting a thing's striving toward a potentially infinite duration.[24] Once we enlarge our point of view to include other finite beings, the competitive striving of things "contrary in nature" reinserts the risk of conflict and destruction into the world of individuals. Thus, the open-ended preservation of being and the unlimited expression of essence appear as unattainable goals for finite individuals.

The reasons for this sad state of affairs is the concomitant adversity of each of the first-order structures we analyzed in Chapter 1. Things strive successfully and persevere in their being insofar as they are not limited, and they inhere in themselves. As we know, Spinoza understands finite beings as modes, inhering in the one substance—God. Thus, their insufficient logical status prevents them from reaching an infinite striving. Further along this line of thought, limitation provides the grounds for the interruption of the striving itself; a given thing *a* would never interrupt its own striving (Spinoza actually argues that this is metaphysically and ethologically impossible).[25] It is only because of the external (and reciprocal) intervention of another finite thing *b*, that this limitation takes place. The limited ontological status of finite things such as *a* and *b* further exposes them to passivity, insofar as neither of them is cause of itself or conceived through itself, as Spinoza affirms in E3d2. Their lack of self-caused and self-conceived acting results in their impossibility to indefinitely preserve their striving.

---

[24] Cf. E3p8: "The striving by which each thing strives to persevere in its being involves no finite time [*tempus*], but an indefinite time."
[25] The ethological impossibility of self-destruction in Spinoza has given rise to a fascinating debate on his understanding of rational suicide. Two recent examples of this debate are Nadler's "Spinoza on Lying and Suicide" and Grey's "Reply to Nadler: Spinoza and the Metaphysics of Suicide," where the argumentation verts on the (im)possibility of obtaining an adequate idea of one's own death.

Several commentators have observed that this multi-structural approach to *conatus* allows Spinoza to elaborate it as a notion that admits of degrees.[26] Spinoza's *conatus* appears in the *Ethics* as a quantitative notion not just in terms of the measurability of its actual duration but also in terms of how intense its self-sufficiency can be, given its first-order structural underpinning.[27] The graduality of *conatus* constitutes a pivotal point for Spinoza's development of his metaphysics of individual essences as coextensive with the power of finite things. Through this notion, Spinoza elaborates a theory of action that admits of different degrees of self-sufficiency. He can thus describe a spectrum of activity whose maximization represents the didactic goal of the *Ethics*. Under this metaphysical paradigm, striving to preserve one's being is not a mere instinct for survival but an attempt to augment one's power of acting, in order to reduce one's exposition to the whim of external causes, conceptions, subjections.

Such structural interpretation of the *conatus* of finite things constitutes the starting point of Spinoza's metaphysics of action as an embodied relation between *res* which compete, ally themselves, and clash to achieve whatever approximation to sempiternal duration they can access. Action becomes the metaphysical standard that certifies one's striving to minimize limitation and increase independence in causal, logical, and conceptual terms. Action is the translation of one's *conatus* in the metaphysical language of first-order structures. This understanding of action approximates finite things to God insofar as the gradual augmentation of the adequacy of their acting equals a similarly gradual approach to (finite) immanent causation. This idolatrous interpretation can rely, apart from the texts of the *Ethics* that we have already examined, on the

---

[26] See, for example, Naaman-Zauderer, "Human Action and Virtue in Descartes and Spinoza," 30; Viljanen, *Spinoza's Geometry of Power*, 50; Sangiacomo and Nachtomy, "Spinoza's Rethinking of Activity," 111–112.
[27] Cf. Schliesser's reading of *Letter 12* in "Spinoza and the Philosophy of Science," 173–174.

often-neglected *Compendium of Hebrew Grammar* that Spinoza left unfinished (and unpublished). In this metaphysically rich text, Spinoza analyzes the structure of reflexive verbs as exemplars helpful to understand the notion of immanent causation.[28] In this sense, when an agent acts immanently, she "does something to itself," generating a reappropriation of the process of causation and inherence. This can be understood as "a function of the identity of the patient it is acting on ... it is because an immanent cause 'is acted on by itself' that its effect is 'in itself.'"[29] Thus, we could argue that acting adequately makes the agent godlike, since it eliminates the ontological gap between agent and patient while leaving untouched the aspectual divide between the two (as I have observed in the previous section).

Spinoza can rightly claim, then, that "the power by which singular things preserve their being is the power itself of God, or Nature" (E4p4d). Action progressively assimilates finite things to God, insofar as they expand the adequacy of their causal scope and incorporate their effects as miniature immanent causes. In the specific case of human beings, as Naaman-Zauderer argues, "the human power of acting or striving (*conatus*) constitutes a part of God's infinite power or essence only to the extent to which the human mind is 'active' in Spinoza's technical sense (E3d2), and thus perceives things adequately."[30] We can thus claim to have uncovered the first-order structures that constitute the base of Spinoza's understanding of adequacy and action, by examining the metaphysical and structural prerequisites of the preservation of one's striving.

---

[28] Cf. *CHG* 12 | G I/342–343, translated by Zylstra, in "Spinoza on Action and Immanent Causation," 33: "Infinitive nouns, or actions, express an action either as it is related to the agent or as it is related to the patient. [...] But because it frequently happens that the agent and the patient [of an action] are one and the same person, [...] it was necessary to devise another form of infinitive which would express an action as it is related to the agent, or immanent cause."
[29] Zylstra, "Spinoza on Action and Immanent Causation," 33.
[30] Naaman-Zauderer, "Human Action and Virtue in Descartes and Spinoza," 30.

The question that still lies ahead, however, is pressing and looms ever larger. Once we have understood how important it is to reclaim our adequacy in order to gain this "active" status, what are we to do? How does this translate in our limited control over the everyday interactions that populate our life? The answers to these interrogatives occupy the rest of Spinoza's *Ethics*. In the following sections, I will undertake an analysis of those answers from a structural point of view, seeking to highlight their relationship to the overarching picture of Spinoza's metaphysics.

5.4 The Con-Struction of Affects

As we have learned in the previous section, throughout his development of the essential nature of striving Spinoza theorizes a flexible structure, which admits of degrees and is fundamentally protean in character. Its lack of internal specification allows Spinoza to furtherly determine *conatus* within a relative and relational paradigm, which in turn responds to the nonsolipsistic reality of finite things.

This relational paradigm comes to the forefront of Spinoza's metaphysics of individuals in E3p11, which establishes the parallelism of affections according to object-oriented specification. As the proposition reads, "the idea of any thing that increases or diminishes, aids or restrains, our body's power of acting, increases or diminishes, aids or restrains, our mind's power of thinking," it appears immediate that Spinoza relies for this structural association on the ideas-things parallelism of E2p7, as he readily announces in the proof.[31] Thus, the *conatus* of the body and the *conatus* of the mind are affected in parallel ways by the parallel impediments or

---

[31] Cf. E3p11d: "This proposition is evident from E2p7, or also from E2p14." The latter proposition, which appears immediately after the *Physical Digression*, reads: "the human mind is capable of perceiving a great many things, and is the more capable, the more its body can be disposed in a great many ways."

boosters that they may encounter in their respective domains of striving. These affections cannot, of course, leave either the mind or the body unbothered. Each of these two aspects of the human mode reacts by welcoming and anticipating its boosters (the favorable encounters) and eschewing its impediments (the unfavorable encounters). As Spinoza puts it:

> when this striving is related only to the mind, it is called will; but when it is related to the mind and body together, it is called appetite. This appetite, therefore, is nothing but the very essence of man, from whose nature there necessarily follow those things that promote his preservation. And so, man is determined to do those things. (E3p9s | G II/147/28-32)

Through this process, the protean nature of *conatus* is specified and oriented in a centrifugal motion of objectual relationality with a potential "partner" for affective engagement. To be sure, this engagement is far from passive from the point of view of the *conatus*. The objectual relation between the striving individual and the external things that it progressively objectifies is a hermeneutic relation. The ideas of external things that our mind objectifies, and the bodies that our body interacts with, are not received passively and impartially. Instead, they are "nuanced interpretations of the capacities of things around us to sustain or damage our power to persevere in our being." As such they are considered and evaluated in interaction with the *conatus* that is the perspectival barycenter of this oriented relationship.[32]

This extroverted nature of the structure of *conatus* is immediately put to work by Spinoza. In the following propositions, and in the fascinating catalog of the *Definitions of Affects* that follows *Ethics* III,[33] he devices a complex configuration of pathways, which function

---
[32] James, *Passion and Action*, 146.
[33] Cf. G II/190–205.

as regularly observed connections between an individual striving and its objectual counterparts. These structures are organized according to a "con-structing" paradigm, in the etymological sense of the term. The Latin root *"struĕre"* indicates an accumulating or stratifying development; the prefix *"con-"* emphasizes instead the togetherness and internal cohesion of this process. Under this interpretative lens, we can observe how Spinoza defines joy (*laetitia*) as the passion "by which the mind passes to a greater perfection," that is, the passive affect associated with an augmentation of the *conatus* of the mind. By contrast, sadness (*tristitia*) is identified as the passion "by which [the mind] passes to a lesser perfection," that is, the passive affect associated with a diminishment of the *conatus* of the mind.[34]

It is noteworthy that from the beginning, Spinoza describes these affective understandings of the augmentation and diminishment of the *conatus* as passions. Albeit positive in its effect on the striving, the mere augmentation of being does not equal a more adequate role in the process of causation and conception of the ensuing effect, as we have observed in the previous sections of this chapter. Spinoza makes this abundantly clear in his subsequent definition of love (*amor*) as the passion that accompanies the augmentation of the striving of the mind and the body *joined by the idea of an external cause*. Similarly, hatred (*odium*) is the passion accompanying the diminishment of our striving, joined by the idea of an external cause.[35] The crucial definition, here, is that of love. While it may be trivial to assume (according to E3p4 and E3p5) that the diminishment of power and *conatus* cannot be endogenetic, and must come from an external cause, the emphasis on love as a passion—not an action—uncouples the empowerment of the striving from the adequacy of causation and conception. This adequacy, by contrast, is directly proportional when it comes to

---

[34] E3p11s | G II/149/1–4.
[35] Cf. E3p13s | G II/151/5–8.

the relationship between the two aspects of the human mode—the body and the mind; as Carriero puts it, "the more causal reality found in the body, the more intelligibility found in the idea of the body."[36] Adequacy—or as we shall begin to call it, action—is thus a structure that is virtually independent of the increasing and diminishing of the amount of power that a mode enjoys. Surely, an increased power of action equates a more durable striving. However, the most important feature in the adequation of a mode's causality is its activity, which is beyond the immediate satisfaction that can be provided by love and joy.

In fact, *laetitita* and *amor*—even though they reflect an augmentation of power, and thus a pleasure—give rise to a cascade of other passions, often less pure. In Spinoza's constructive process, *amor* takes the role of a building block, functional to the completion of a taxonomy of all the ways in which human modes are entangled in the inadequate world of passions.

For example, Spinoza pinpoints hope (*spes*) and fear (*metus*) as two of the most pernicious passions. Their most damaging character is that they encourage humans to withdraw from the often-difficult present to live in the future, projecting their desires and worries toward something as yet inexistant. They both expose their subject to insecurity, despite hope's technical belonging to the realm of positive affects, which is associated with the increase of one's power. In fact, by dwelling in hope, humans are merely delegating their power to satisfactions coming from "an inconstant joy" arising "from the image of a future or past thing whose outcome we doubt."[37] The impossibility of grounding stable power and self-reliance on this uncertain terrain appears to play a large role in Spinoza's distrust of hope and its cognates.

Similarly, Spinoza has less than kind words about dwelling in magnifying images of oneself or one's loved ones that are not

---

[36] Carriero, "Spinoza on the Primary Affects," 88.
[37] Cf. E3p18s2.

grounded in reality. Even though such images and affects can often function as a flywheel, stimulating the growth of one's power of acting, the unsure footing on which they rely makes Spinoza highly skeptical of them. Spinoza's ethological methodology recognizes that we do in fact "strive to affirm, concerning ourselves and what we love, whatever we imagine to affect with joy ourselves or what we love."[38] However, the commentary provided in the scholium clarifies that this affect is not as innocent as it seems. "When this imagination concerns the man himself who thinks more highly of himself than is just, it is called pride [*superbia*], and is a species of madness." Spinoza denounces the detachment from reality that pride encourages, insofar as the person subject to pride "cannot imagine those things which exclude the existence [of his success] and determine his power of acting."[39] Spinoza here offers an insightful take on "madness" (*delirium*), which he portrays as the refusal to admit the ontological status of the human mode as subject to passivity; logically inherent *in alio*, causally determined *ab alio*, conceptually included *in alio*, humans (as all finite modes) are consistently limited and determined.

Ever the realist, Spinoza refuses to acknowledge as positive the human inclination for self-deception, however apparently empowering it may seem. Despite his recognition of the pleasantness of the delusions deriving from hope and pride—two different ways of deviating from one's actual structural alienation from power—he does not encourage them. The pernicious side-effect of these affects is that they enhance the human state of subjection, in its etymological sense of *sub-jectum*, thrown under or downtrodden, under the comfortable disguise of an increase of underserved power. Love, hope, and pride are but effects of man's subjection to external causes and reinforce the state of uncertainty to which finite modes are apparently condemned.

---

[38] E3p25.
[39] E3p26s | G II/159/25–30.

We have apparently reached a standstill, an almost paradoxical notion.[40] Human modes are denied power insofar as they are structurally limited in their action because they are finite modes. They are also denied by Spinoza the aspiration to increase their power through dwelling on positive (i.e., affirmative) affects, since such affects are uncertain and feed into their state of external dependence. What are we to do, then, to *actually* increase our power, if we are to cast off the yoke of passions, which Spinoza describes as outright slavery [*servitus*]?[41] How can we escape this spiral of self-deception, if the very things that deceive us are the same affects that provide our everyday relief? Spinoza offers us two distinct pathways to securing freedom from the bondage of passions, in line with his acknowledgment of a plurality of adequate kinds of knowledge. As we have seen in Chapter 4, Spinoza's epistemic pluralism allows him to recognize that there are at least two ways to conceive of things adequately: according to reason and according to intuitive knowledge.[42] Thus, the first of Spinoza's pathways to human freedom relies on reason, and it takes particular notice of the human state as an individual thing, inserted in a structural network of empowering and disempowering relationships. The second, by contrast, relies on the immediate connection that humans have—as finite modes—with their immanent cause, God. In the following two sections, I will briefly analyze each of these proposals, to uncover the metaphysical structures that validates them as compelling alternatives in Spinoza's eyes. One methodological caveat is in order; to attain our goal, we shall now definitely abandon our naïve approach, to allow ourselves greater reach and gather the clues that Spinoza disseminated throughout the final pages of the *Ethics*.

---

[40] See my "Spinoza's Metaphysics of Freedom and Its Essential Paradox" on how the notion of essence elaborated by Spinoza might impede the achievement of a univocal sense of freedom.
[41] Cf. the title of *Ethics* IV, which Curley translates as "On Human Bondage, or the Powers of the Affects."
[42] See above, Section 4.4.

5.5 Acting Freely

At the very end of *Ethics* V, Spinoza introduces an important figure in the context of his ethology of human beings—the notion of the wise person (*sapiens*). This figure is arguably intended as an *exemplum*, a paradigmatic inspiration to show us that his ethical project is not unattainable and can be enacted during an actual life. This exemplar goal functions in harmony with another crucial (if gender-blind) figure that Spinoza had already introduced in *Ethics* IV, the free man (*homo liber*).[43] At the end of the previous section, we had encountered an ethological standstill, triggered by the apparent impossibility of transforming our passive existence into a more adequate activity, due to our causal and conceptual state of dependence. The twin characters of *homo liber* and *sapiens* are proposed to us as two solutions to that standstill. For Spinoza, these two personalities are the only ones who can escape the bondage of passions and achieve adequate action. In this section, I will focus on *homo liber*, leaving the analysis of the *sapiens* for later. To begin such examination, we must ask: what are the decisive features that can help us identify the free person, and what are we to do to obtain such status? And most importantly, how can these characteristics help us to eliminate the structural obstacles that we have identified?

In E4p66s, *homo liber* is introduced as the one who lives according to reason. As we know from Spinoza's epistemology, reason is not incompatible with mereological individuality or with an idea of oneself as partially distinguished from the whole of Nature. It must not surprise us, then, that Spinoza does not immediately require the "free man" to identify himself with the totality of *Natura*

---

[43] It is an open debate in the literature whether the two figures of *homo liber* and *sapiens* are to be identified or distinguished, and whether they are attainable for human beings given Spinoza's overall commitment to naturalism, that is, the doctrine that no exceptions can exist in Nature. See, for example, the recent and interesting takes on this notion: Hübner, "Spinoza on Being Human and Human Perfection"; Gatens, "Spinoza's Disturbing Thesis"; Nadler, "On Spinoza's 'Free Man'"; and Soyarslan, "Two Ethical Ideals in Spinoza's *Ethics*."

naturata. Instead, *homo liber* sets his own goals, as he "complies with no one's wishes but his own and does only those things he knows to be the most important in life."[44] The capacity to match his action with his own intentions is thus the first—and perhaps the most significant—feature that characterizes the "free man." As Soyarslan has recently pointed out, this characterization is in open conflict with the ontological status of the free man as a finite mode in Spinoza's philosophy. Causal and conceptual autonomy, as we have seen in the previous section, are simply beyond the reach of finite individuals.[45] As E4p4 affirms:

> It is impossible that a man should not be a part of Nature, and that he should be able to undergo no changes except those which can be understood through his own nature alone, and of which he is the adequate cause.

This categorical statement regards the ontological nature of man as a finite being, thus limited in a causal, conceptual, and logical sense. Spinoza remarks here the essential and existential state of subjectivity (in the sense of being-subject-to-another) that inescapably characterizes all people. While the free man is surely able to delude himself, by believing that he is capable of setting his own goals and of pursuing them, the ultimate ontological tribunal sentences him to being no more than "a part of Nature," thus (at least) partially and consistently affected by external causes.

How can the free man muster the necessary "freedom" to escape such ubiquitous bondage? As several commentators have pointed out, in this context, the solution provided by Spinoza focuses on the key notion of self-reliance, or *acquiescentia in se ipso*.[46] To be

---

[44] E4p66s | G II/260/26-27.
[45] Cf. Soyarslan, "Two Ethical Ideals in Spinoza's *Ethics*," 361.
[46] The traditional translation of the Latin *acquiescentia* as "self-esteem," which figures in Curley, does not render the soothing meaning that this term has in classic literature. The structure "acquiescere + in + ablative," in particular, is used by Cicero to represent a secure feeling of comfort and complacence (cf. e.g., *Laelius seu De Amicitia*, §101;

sure, *acquiescentia* is an affect—albeit active. Thus, it is in principle coherent with Spinoza's characterization of finite modes as ultimately subject to limitation. However, this specific affect possesses unique features, which enable it to function as the gateway to a (partial) human liberation. Let us examine how Spinoza introduces *acquiescentia* in his ethological framework.

> E4p52: Self-reliance can arise from reason, and only the self-reliance which arises from reason is the greatest there can be.

> E4p52d: Self-reliance is a joy born of the fact that man considers himself and his power of acting (by E3DefAff25). But man's true power of acting, or virtue, is reason itself (by E3p3), which man considers clearly and distinctly (by E2p40 and E2p43). Therefore, self-reliance arises from reason. Next, while a man considers himself, he perceives nothing clearly and distinctly, or adequately, except those things which follow from his power of acting (by E3d2), i.e. (by E3p3), which follow from his power of understanding. And so, the greatest self-reliance there can be arises only from this reflection.

The crucial association that Spinoza emphasizes in these lines is the one between *acquiescentia* and reason. This link expresses all its strength in the demonstration of E4p52 thanks to the theoretical foundation set by E3p3, which unsurprisingly appears twice in the relatively short text of the proof. So, what does this critical proposition affirm? The text itself is brief and poignant; it reads, "the actions of the mind arise from adequate ideas alone; the passions depend on inadequate ideas alone."

Prima facie, E3p3 represents nothing more than a translation of the general paradigm of activity into the aspectual language of the attribute of thought. The power of thinking or understanding

---

Ad Atticum XII, §3; *Ad Familiares* III, §3). Cf. also Carlisle, "Spinoza's *Acquiescentia*," 310–311.

represents a quantitative assessment in the realm of thought of what the mind is capable of, or the extent to which it can conceptualize itself as the adequate cause of its own perceptions. The unhinging force of E4p52, however, is unleashed when this power of the mind is cashed out in terms of an equivalent to man's power of acting, *simpliciter*. From a technical point of view, this operation is completely legitimate for Spinoza; he had established the structural equivalence between power of acting and power of thinking long ago, through the ideas-things parallelism of E2p7. This equivalence is beautifully expressed by Soyarslan, who claims that when "we are the adequate cause of a rational idea, [this] rational idea can be clearly and distinctly perceived through our essence alone, which, in turn, means that the essence of [the] adequate idea can be defined by our essence alone."[47] The metaphysical anatomy of the "free man" as the one who can adequate his acting to his essence, then, acquires the familiar contours of the satisfaction with one's lot in life.

While the latter phrase could suggest an almost resigned tone in Spinoza's characterization of this paradigmatic figure, the realist backdrop that we have emphasized throughout this chapter should teach us otherwise. The free man acquires power over his passions and can determine his actions by refusing to overextend his perception of his own power beyond the breadth of his essence. In this quasicritical effort (in the Kantian sense), Spinoza evokes the metaphysical boundaries of human activity as the Pillars of Hercules of the mind. The freedom of the free man consists in an appropriate estimation of this activity, and in the consciousness that within such boundaries, he enjoys as much autonomy as any finite mode can achieve. As Douglas appropriately notes, once we accept these requisites, Spinoza's view of the power of human beings is far from being a defeatist one.[48] Not easy to attain, *acquiescentia in se*

---

[47] Soyarslan, "Two Ethical Ideals in Spinoza's *Ethics*," 362.
[48] Cf. Douglas, "Spinoza's Unquiet *Acquiescentia*," 8–9; and Newlands, *Reconceiving Spinoza*, 221–225.

ipso requires us to renounce abstract models of human success as delusions. By contrast, it demands that we become who we really are, aligning our self-perception to our essence.

From a metaphysical standpoint, the virtuous circle of *acquiescentia* is explained through the capacity, proper of adequate action, to increase one's power of acting. *Homo liber*, who is defined by the appropriate alignment of his activity and his essence, is minimally affected by passions, insofar as his acting spurs from an adequate idea of his own power. In the meantime, this adequate and balanced activity also gives rise to *acquiescentia*, a joyous affect that (as we have seen in the section above) accompanies the increase of power of the *homo liber*.[49] Holding this increased power, he can go back to adequately acting; only this time, with an increased power that guarantees the further reach of his activity. This cycle is potentially indefinite, in the sempiternal and durational sense that pertains to finite beings. Of course, this is only a simplified scheme, akin to the ones constructed in physics laboratory to investigate complex phenomena. Their usefulness stems from the fact that they eliminate disturbing factors that would pollute the experiment, such as (depending on the situation) friction or gravity. As for our ethological experiment, the disturbing factors bracketed here by Spinoza respond to the name of "passions." In fact, however free from passions *homo liber* might be, his essence can never grow so large and powerful as to eliminate *any* possible influence from external causes, as E4p4 reminds us. *Homo liber* is, after all, just a part of Nature.

Yet, this mereological callback reminds us that there is still one important pathway that can bring us to beatitude—the harmonization with God as *Natura naturans* and with the world as *Natura naturata*, of which we are but a part. Such harmonization constitutes the final goal of Spinoza's philosophy, as we shall

---

[49] Cf. James, *Spinoza on Learning to Live Together*, 199.

witness in the next section, where I move to examine the powerful notion of *amor Dei intellectualis*.

5.6 The Eternal Bento

In the previous section, as I was introducing the notion of *homo liber*, I mentioned how this exemplar figure finds a partial parallel in another character featured in the *Ethics*, the *sapiens* or wise person.

The adjective "wise" is likely to suggest a picture resembling an ancient mage, wearing a flowy white beard and perhaps an ample tunic. Such images, albeit picturesque, do not aid our attempt to illustrate Spinoza's conception of beatitude and wisdom as reachable by the means of our own philosophical efforts. To repel such esoteric temptations, we shall give our *sapiens* a familiar name, one likely to be heard in the streets of Amsterdam at the height of its commercial prominence in the seventeenth century. The name rings familiar throughout the quarters of the large Portuguese Jewish community. The name is Bento, and it belongs to a scrawny-looking individual who divides his time between his father's shop and a rented apartment where he attempts to study languages and philosophy. Despite his relatively young age, Bento is a wise man because he loves God. However, he does not love God as the prophets of the Old Testament loved their God, aided by their prodigious imaginations.[50] Bento loves God *intellectually*.

This is certainly a curious notion. Who ever loves with their intellect? Especially in the context of Spinoza's ethology, where love is an affect (albeit a joyous one) and the intellect is supposed to aid us in liberating ourselves from all passions, what could be the meaning of this strange alliance? This enigma has fascinated many of the readers who have taken up Spinoza's *Ethics*, given the

---

[50] Cf. *Theological-Political Treatise*, chapter 2 | G III/29/26–27.

apparent contradiction embodied by this notion. Spinoza presents this seemingly paradoxical concept in E5p32c:

> From the third kind of knowledge, there necessarily arises an intellectual love of God. For from this kind of knowledge there arises (by E5p32) joy, accompanied by the idea of God as its cause, i.e. (by E3DefAff6), love of God, not insofar as we imagine him as present (by E5p29), but insofar as we understand God to be eternal.

From a purely structural point of view, there is nothing new in what Spinoza tells us in this corollary. The object of the third kind of knowledge, according to the criteria that we have examined earlier[51] and in alignment with what Spinoza affirms in *Letter 32*, is the eternal horizon of the substance. God, insofar as he is understood to be eternal, coincides with the *Natura naturans* that causally and conceptually encompasses and grounds all being. Therefore, the love arising from the relationship between a finite intellect and this eternal aspect of substance is an affect, in the strict sense of involving a modification of the power of acting and thinking of the human mode; and it is a passion only in the even stricter sense of involving an external cause as the sufficient reason for such modification of power. Yet, this structural connection between the externality of passions and the sui generis case of intellectual love of God represents the crowbar employed by Spinoza to pry open his own system and guarantee a coherent role for this "special" affect.

In fact, the prominent position assigned to the intellectual love of God in Spinoza's system is partly explained by the way he allows for a partial remodeling of reality through the impact that gnoseological notions such as "intellect" and "intuition" can have on the metaphysical blueprint of reality. As Naaman-Zauderer beautifully puts it, since Spinoza claims that "virtue *qua* activity or

---

[51] See Section 4.2 above.

freedom consists in acting from understanding or adequate knowledge," he coherently holds that an adequate approach to virtue (i.e., freedom or autonomy) consists in "knowledge of God";[52] in particular, it consists in the third kind of knowledge that allows human beings to know all particular things through God.[53] It is on this basis that "Spinoza equates this highest level of activity and virtuousness with blessedness, salvation, and the highest form of freedom."[54] But how does this equation work? What about the intellectual love of God—an affect that should ultimately indicate dependence on all structural levels—can guarantee freedom and "salvation" for finite beings?

The answer to these pressing questions lies in Spinoza's understanding of blessedness as adequacy and can only be properly understood through a structural lens that avoids the siren-like fascination of Spinoza's suggestive writing in *Ethics* V. The closing lines of Spinoza's masterpiece outline a structural connection between blessedness, freedom, and *acquiescentia*. They affirm the distinction between the *sapiens* and the ignorant, who is not only "troubled in many ways by external causes, and unable ever to possess true peace of mind, but he also lives as if he knew neither himself, nor God, nor things; and as soon as he ceases to be acted on, he ceases to be." Presumably, then, what Spinoza intends as "blessedness" is the stability in autonomous causation. The contraposition between the *sapiens* and the ignorant acquires new meaning with the identification of the latter figure as the "acted-on," the passive. The equation between being acted on (or being subject to) and the ignorant man's very existence suggests an essential reading of this passage, in which the passivity of existence coincides with the

---

[52] Cf. E4p28: "Knowledge of God is the mind's greatest good; its greatest virtue is to know God."
[53] Cf. E5p24: "The more we understand singular things, the more we understand God"; and E5p25: "The greatest striving of the mind, and its greatest virtue is understanding things by the third kind of knowledge."
[54] Naaman-Zauderer, "Human Action and Virtue in Descartes and Spinoza," 34.

absence of an active and empowering derivation of one's actions from one's essence.

By contrast, Spinoza describes the *sapiens* by stating that "insofar as he is considered as such, [he] is hardly troubled in spirit, but being, by a certain eternal necessity, conscious of himself, and of God, and of things, he never ceases to be, but always possesses true peace of mind."[55] To understand this passage, we need to recall the definition of adequate causation as Spinoza stipulates it in E3d1. As we have seen in Section 5.1, x is an adequate cause of y if and only if y is caused by x and y is conceived through x. The joint requirements of adequate causation require self-causation and self-conception as necessary conditions, even though finite beings cannot possibly achieve either (in a complete manner) because of their limited power of acting and conceiving. How can the intellectual love of God help us overcome this ontological barrier? Spinoza's answer, in structural terms, is quite simple—and yet almost sibylline. E5p38 declares that "the more the mind understands things by the second and third kind of knowledge, the less it is acted on by affects." Thus, there is a proportionality between adequate conception of things and adequate causation (i.e., limitation of passivity). In turn, adequate conception is incrementally achieved through reason and intuition, and solidified on the affective side by the intellectual love of God.

The confusion between the affective and the structural side of the equation is highly dangerous. As we saw in the opening section of this chapter, Spinoza's understanding of affects can be reduced to a perspectival reading of causal and conceptual structures. What is it, then, that makes the mind capable of the quantic leap from passive and inadequate causation to active and adequate causation? The answer lies in the convoluted text of E5p31 and its demonstration, which deserve to be quoted extensively:

[55] E5p42s | G II/308/17–23.

The third kind of knowledge depends on the mind, as on a formal cause, insofar as the mind itself is eternal [*quatenus Mens ipsa æterna est*].

Demonstration: The mind conceives nothing under a species of eternity except insofar as it conceives its body's essence under a species of eternity i.e., except insofar as it is eternal [*nisi quatenus æterna est*]. So insofar as it is eternal, it has knowledge of God, knowledge which is necessarily adequate. And therefore, the mind, insofar as it is eternal, is capable of knowing all those things which can follow from this given knowledge of God, i.e., of knowing things by the third kind of knowledge; therefore, the mind, insofar as it is eternal, is the adequate, or formal, cause of the third kind of knowledge [*quatenus æterna est, causa est adæquata, seu formalis*].

The demonstrative arc offered by Spinoza in this proposition relies heavily on the notion of aspectual distinction that I have outlined in Chapter 2 and developed in Chapter 3, with reference to the ontological and modal understanding of eternity and duration. The human mind and the human body represent parallel ontological aspects according to the parallelist outlook established in E2p7. Moreover, the eternity of the body and the eternity of the mind assure the connection of the human mode to the necessary chain of causation that constitutes God's expression. Insofar as the human mode participates in the eternal chain of adequate horizontal causation that is *Natura naturata*, duration cannot be more than an aspect of the essence of this mode. The locution "insofar as," in this context, is a crucial term since it represents in English Spinoza's structural *quatenus*.

As I have argued in Section 5.2, the distinction between God as *Natura naturans* and God as *Natura naturata* is a distinction pertaining to the active or passive understanding of one and the same action. Once again, this thesis should not be interpreted as a claim toward the epiphenomenal nature of the distinction between *naturans* and *naturata* but rather as an affirmation of the ontological unity of the causal and conceptual network that instantiates the expression of God's essence. The revolutionary role assumed by the intellectual love of God—and by adequate knowledge in general—within Spinoza's *Ethics* offers finite modes the chance of bridging this aspectual divide by recasting their understanding of such expression. Since God and Nature are one and the same, and modes constitute a proper mereological part of Nature qua *naturata*, adequate knowledge grants the possibility of overcoming the aspectual distinction between the active and passive "sides" and thus reuniting finite modes with their infinite cause, God qua *naturans*.

The increasing nature of this collimation between the *naturans* and *naturata* aspects of divine expression—from the human point of view—is further illustrated by Spinoza's statement in E5p40 that "the more perfection each thing has, the more it acts and the less it is acted on; and conversely, the more it acts, the more perfect it is." Thus, the progressive approximation to an eternal understanding of God's unfolding causality coincides with the identification of a similarly progressive adequation of human self-causality or *acquiescentia*; the "eternal part of the mind is the intellect, <u>through which alone we are said to act</u>."[56] By contrast, the durational aspect of the mind is the imaginative aspect, which corresponds to its passive grasp of the causal pathways of God's expression. The latter aspect, as Spinoza readily admits, is the one destined to "perish," insofar as it does not belong—as a proper part—to God's self-love and self-understanding.

With this abundance of newfound knowledge regarding the *sapiens* and the intellectual love of God, let us return to our old friend Bento, who we had left wandering the streets of Amsterdam. What does it mean, for Bento, to love God intellectually? And what is the structural scaffolding that justifies such transforming love?

---

[56] E5p40c | G II/306/12–13. Emphasis is mine. That this kind of knowledge makes substantial use of structural notions is also highlighted by the text of E5p7d.

The essence of the third kind of knowledge resides in its capacity to reconnect the human mode with its ultimate cause, *Natura naturans*. The transformative value of this affective and epistemological achievement resides in the fact that it welds together the fracture represented by the divide between the two aspects of nature.[57] If Bento does indeed possess the intellectual love of God, that means that Bento has reunited his power of acting with God's power of acting, expressed through Bento's finite, yet eternal, essence. Bento has become, through his intellectual love of God, an "adequate mode," consciously assuming the mantle of proximate cause for the expression of God's causality.

In this sense, we can envision (in line with the spirit of the early modern era) the possibility of an indefinite and infinitesimal analysis of Bento's actions. Each of Bento's steps through the streets and canals of Amsterdam, each of the propositions that line up on his notebooks, each of the hairs that grows on his head or falls from it, are actions and not passions. From the affective point of view, they are greeted with love and not hate, since they stem from Bento's essence alone, understood through the eternal and necessary unfolding of the power of acting of God. The structure of expression, as we know, represents a realization of the causation and conception of God's essence. So this is the final message of the *Ethics*: the structure is finally brought to completion, in a full circle, by the eternal reconciliation of Bento's finite action and God's infinite essential determination.

---

[57] Cf. Garrett, *Nature and Necessity in Spinoza's Philosophy*, 213.

Acknowledgments

When it comes to a project that has been brewing, in different modes, for over a decade, it is always a difficult task to properly acknowledge and give thanks to all the people, colleagues and friends, who have had a positive impact on it.

First, I must be grateful to Elizabeth and Greg S. Allen, whose generous donations funded the Vanderbilt Arts and Sciences Dean's Faculty Fellowship that I received to focus on the development of the philosophical interpretation expressed in this volume, and to share my research with colleagues and other scholars around the world. I shall also thank my editor, Lucy Randall, for the passionate yet patient collaboration and support that she has provided over the years that have seen this project finally completed.

Next, I give thanks to my mentors, Gennaro Luise, Massimo Marassi, and Yitzhak Melamed, for the illuminating discussions and heartwarming encouragement that I have received from them in the course of the years. Of course, the project would never have seen the light without the indefatigable and patient help of Susan James, my doctoral supervisor, who taught me how to turn my confused and inadequate ideas into affects of joy and adequate understanding. She was an incredible mentor, not just in terms of philosophical insights, but by embodying the example any academic shall aspire to follow, as a Spinozian *free woman*.

I must also recognize the contribution of many colleagues who, over the years, have helped the crafting and carving of the concepts that have enhanced my understanding of Spinoza's metaphysics: in rigorously alphabetical order (and with apologies for my inescapable forgetfulness), I shall thank Scott Aikin, Maria Rosa Antognazza, Deborah Brown, Andrew Burnside, Clare Carlisle,

Matthew Congdon, Giuseppe D'Anna, Idit Dobbs-Weinstein, Alex Douglas, Lorenzo Fossati, Daniel Garber, Zach Gartenberg, Lenn Goodman, Karolina Hübner, Pietro Ingallina, Julie Klein, Mike LeBuffe, Noemi Magnani, Steph Marston, Vittorio Morfino, Karen Ng, Calvin Normore, Antonio Salgado Borge, Andrea Sangiacomo, Eric Schliesser, Tad Schmaltz, Lisa Shapiro, Daniel Smith, Neta Stahl, Jack Stetter, Francesco Toto, Julian Wuerth, and Jason Yonover.

The project of this book also received incommensurable help for Vanderbilt's Dean of Arts and Science, who funded a Research Studio on my work. I was able to invite incredible scholars (and friends) such as John Carriero, Michael Della Rocca, Francesca Di Poppa, and Sam Newlands, and to receive from them encouragement and feedback that went above and beyond my imagination.

To my parents, who taught me the value of hard work and relentlessness in pursuing one's goals, I give the warmest of thanks, as to my brothers, Davide and Daniele, who have been friends beyond blood for me, just like my uncle Costantino. My partner, Victoria, has supported me during the final days of editing and proofing, and I am forever thankful for her understanding and kindness. Finally, I will thank the friends who have sustained and distracted me as the work on this book became hard and rejoiced with me when it was finally ready to be delivered. This list is endless, but I'd like to particularly acknowledge Bruno, Roberto, Dario, Valeria, Chiara, Pietro, Michele, Tommaso, Jeremy, Scott, Alyssa, Lyn, Brandon, Kyle, and the whole crew at the Villager Tavern in Nashville, each of them always there for me.

Bibliography

Spinoza's Works
The Collected Works of Spinoza. 1985/2016. Translated by E. Curley. 2 vols. Princeton (NJ): Princeton University Press.
Opera. 1925. Edited by C. Gebhardt. 4 vols. Heidelberg: Carl Winter.
Tutte le Opere. 2010/2011. Edited by A. Sangiacomo. Milano: Bompiani.

Other Works
Althusser, Louis. 2012. "On Genesis." Translated by J.E. Smith. *Décalages* 1 (2): 1–4.
Althusser, Louis, Étienne Balibar, Roger Establet, Pierre Macherey and Jacques Rancière. 2016. *Reading Capital.* Translated by B. Brewster and D. Fernbach. London: Verso Books.
Antognazza, Maria Rosa. 2009. *Leibniz: An Intellectual Biography.* Cambridge (UK): Cambridge University Press.
Arola, Adam. 2007. "Under the Aspect of Eternity: Thinking Freedom in Spinoza's *Ethics*." *Tópicos* 32: 139–159.
Baugh, Bruce. 2010. "Time, Duration and Eternity in Spinoza." *Comparative and Continental Philosophy* 2 (2): 211–233.
Baxter, Donald. 2017. "Self-Differing, Aspects, and Leibniz's Law." *Noûs* 52 (4): 900–920.
Bayle, Pierre. 1991. *Historical and Critical Dictionary: Selections.* Edited by R. Popkin. Indianapolis (IN): Hackett.
Benigni, Fiormichele. 2018. *Itinerari dell'antispinozismo. Spinoza e le metafisiche cartesiane in Francia (1684–1718).* Firenze: Le Lettere.
Benjamin, Andrew. 2015. *Towards a Relational Ontology: Philosophy's Other Possibility.* Albany (NY): SUNY Press.
Bennett, Jane. 2004. "The Force of Things: Steps toward an Ecology of Matter." *Political Theory* 32 (3): 347–372.
Bennett, Jane. 2012. "Systems and Things: A Response to Graham Harman and Timothy Morton." *New Literary History* 43 (2): 225–233.
Bennett, Jonathan. 1984. *A Study of Spinoza's Ethics.* Cambridge (UK): Cambridge University Press.
Borges, Jorge Luis. 1999. *Selected Poems.* Edited by A. Coleman. New York: Viking Books.
Brandau, John. 2016. "Spinoza on Definition and Essence." PhD diss., Johns Hopkins University.

Burgersdijk, Franco. 1647. *Institutionum logicarum Libri duo.* Cambridge (UK): Roger Daniel.

Burgersdijk, Franco. 1697. *Monitio logica or, An abstract and translation of Burgersdicius his logick.* London: Richard Cumberland.

Buyse, Filip. 2014. "Corpus." In *The Bloomsbury Companion to Spinoza*, edited by W. van Bunge, H. Krop, P. Steenbakkers, and J.M.M. van de Ven. London: Bloomsbury, 190–191.

Buyse, Filip. 2017. "A New Reading of Spinoza's Letter 32 to Oldenburg: Spinoza and the Agreement between Bodies in the Universe." In *The Concept of Affectivity in Early Modern Philosophy*, edited by G. Boros, J. Szalai, and O.I Tóth. Budapest: Eötvös Loránd University, 104–123.

Carlisle, Claire. 2017. "Spinoza's *Acquiescentia*." *Journal of the History of Philosophy* 55 (2): 209–236.

Carriero, John. 1995. "On the Relationship between Mode and Substance in Spinoza's Metaphysics." *Journal of the History of Philosophy* 33 (2): 245–273.

Carriero, John. 2020. "Spinoza on the Primary Affects." In *Freedom, Action, and Motivation in Spinoza's Ethics*, edited by N. Naaman-Zauderer. London: Routledge, 82–107.

Congdon, Matthew. 2023. *Moral Articulation: On the Development of New Moral Concepts.* New York (NY): Oxford University Press.

Costa, Emanuele. 2014. "Uno Spinoza sistemico: strumenti per un'interpretazione sistemica del pensiero di Spinoza." *Rivista di Filosofia Neo-Scolastica* 106 (3): 525–535.

Costa, Emanuele. 2020. "Whole-Part Relations in Early Modern Philosophy." In *Encyclopedia of Early Modern Philosophy and the Sciences*, edited by D. Jalobeanu and C.T. Wolfe. Dordrecht: Springer, 1–8.

Costa, Emanuele. 2021. "Spinoza and Scholastic Philosophy." In *A Companion to Spinoza*, edited by Y. Melamed. London: Blackwell, 47–55.

Costa, Emanuele. 2022. "Spinoza's Metaphysics of Freedom and Its Essential Paradox." *Rivista di Filosofia Neo-Scolastica* 114 (3): 643–658.

Costa, Emanuele. 2023. "Triadic Metaphysics: Spinoza's Expression as Structural Ontology." *Journal of Early Modern Studies* 11 (2): 71–94.

Costa, Emanuele. 2023. "Spinoza and the Hybrid Distinction of Attributes." *Southern Journal of Philosophy* 61 (3): 439–456.

DeLanda, Manuel. 1997. *A Thousand Years of Nonlinear History.* Princeton (NJ): Princeton University Press.

Deleuze, Gilles. 1988. *Spinoza: Practical Philosophy.* Translated by R. Hurley. San Francisco: City Lights Books.

Deleuze, Gilles. 1990. *Expressionism in Philosophy: Spinoza.* Translated by M. Joughin. New York: Zone Books.

Della Rocca, Michael. 1993. "Spinoza's Argument for the Identity Theory." *Philosophical Review* 102 (2): 183–213.

BIBLIOGRAPHY 225

Della Rocca, Michael. 1996. *Representation and the Mind-Body Problem in Spinoza*. Oxford: Oxford University Press.
Della Rocca, Michael. 2008. *Spinoza*. London: Routledge.
Della Rocca, Michael. 2020. "Steps toward Eleaticism in Spinoza's Philosophy of Action." In *Freedom, Action, and Motivation in Spinoza's Ethics*, edited by N. Naaman-Zauderer. London: Routledge, 15–36.
Della Rocca, Michael. 2020. *The Parmenidean Ascent*. Oxford: Oxford University Press.
Deveaux, Sherry. 2003. "The Divine Essence and the Conception of God in Spinoza." *Synthese* 135 (3): 329–338.
Di Poppa, Francesca. 2006. "'God Acts from the Laws of His Nature Alone': From the *Nihil ex Nihilo* Axiom to Causation as Expression in Spinoza's Metaphysics." PhD diss., University of Pittsburgh.
Di Poppa, Francesca. 2010. "Spinoza and Process Ontology." *Southern Journal of Philosophy* 48 (3): 272–294.
Di Poppa, Francesca. 2013. "Spinoza on Causation and Power." *Southern Journal of Philosophy* 51 (3): 297–319.
Dickinson, Emily. 1924. *The Complete Poems*. Boston (MA): Little, Brown and Company.
Diodato, Roberto. 2012. *Sub specie aeternitatis. Luoghi dell'ontologia spinoziana*. Mimesis: Milano.
Douglas, Alexander. 2018. "*Quatenus* and Spinoza's Monism." *Journal of the History of Philosophy* 56 (2): 261–280.
Douglas, Alexander. 2020. "Spinoza's Unquiet *Acquiescentia*." *Proceedings of the Aristotelian Society* 120 (2): 145–163.
Driggers, Kyle. 2021. "The Unity of Substance and Attribute in Spinoza." *British Journal for the History of Philosophy* 29 (1): 45–63.
Dukić, Vladimir. "Individuation of Finite Modes in Spinoza's *Ethics*." *International Philosophical Quarterly* 57 (3): 287–303.
Durie, Robin. 2002. "Immanence and Difference: Toward a Relational Ontology." *Southern Journal of Philosophy* 40 (2): 161–189.
Esfeld, Michael, and Vincent Lam. 2011. "Ontic Structural Realism as a Metaphysics of Objects." In *Scientific Structuralism*, edited by A. Bokulich and P. Bokulich. Dordrecht: Springer, 143–159.
Friedman, Joel. 1986. "How the Finite Follows from the Infinite in Spinoza's Metaphysical System." *Synthese* 69 (3): 371–407.
Garrett, Don. 2002. "Spinoza's *Conatus* Argument." In *Spinoza: Metaphysical Themes*, edited by O. Koistinen and J. Biro. Oxford: Oxford University Press, 127–158.
Garrett, Don. 2009. "Spinoza on the Essence of the Human Body and the Part of the Mind That Is Eternal." In *The Cambridge Companion to Spinoza's Ethics*, edited by O. Koistinen. Cambridge (UK): Cambridge University Press, 284–302.

Garrett, Don. 2018. *Nature and Necessity in Spinoza's Philosophy*. Oxford: Oxford University Press.

Gartenberg, Zachary. 2017. "Spinozistic Expression." *Philosophers' Imprint* 17 (9): 1–32.

Gartenberg, Zachary. 2021. "Spinoza on Relations." In *A Companion to Spinoza*, edited by Y. Melamed. London: Blackwell, 179–188.

Gasché, Rodolphe. 1999. *Of Minimal Things: Studies on the Notion of Relation*. Stanford (CA): Stanford University Press.

Gaspari, Ilaria. 2013. "The Curious Case of the *Vermiculus*. Some Remarks on Spinoza's *Letter 32* and Spinoza's Views on Imagination and Reason." *Society and Politics* 7 (2): 77–84.

Gatens, Moira. 2009. "Spinoza's Disturbing Thesis: Power, Norms and Fiction in the *Tractatus Theologico-Politicus*." *History of Political Thought* 30 (3): 455–468.

Gilead, Amihud. 2020. *A Rose Armed with Thorns: Spinoza's Philosophy Under a Novel Lens*. Dordrecht: Springer.

Goldstein, Rebecca Newberger. 2012. "Explanatory Completeness and Spinoza's Monism." In *Spinoza on Monism*, edited by P. Goff. London: Palgrave Macmillan, 281–292.

Gorham, Geoffrey. 2013. "Spinoza on the Ideality of Time." *Idealistic Studies* 43 (1–2): 27–40.

Grey, John. 2017. "Reply to Nadler: Spinoza and the Metaphysics of Suicide." *British Journal for the History of Philosophy* 25 (2): 380–388.

Gueroult, Martial. 1969. *Spinoza I: Dieu*. Hildesheim: Georg Olms.

Hart, Alan. 1982. "Leibniz on Spinoza's Concept of Substance." *Studia Leibnitiana* 14 (1): 73–86.

Haserot, Francis. 1953. "Spinoza's Definition of Attribute." *Philosophical Review* 62 (4): 499–513.

Hegel, G.W.F. 1995. *Lectures on the History of Philosophy*. Translated by E.S. Haldane and F.H. Simson. 3 vols. Lincoln (NE): University of Nebraska Press.

Hübner, Karolina. 2014. "Spinoza on Being Human and Human Perfection." In *Essays on Spinoza's Ethical Theory*, edited by M. Kisner and A. Youpa. Oxford: Oxford University Press, 124–142.

Hübner, Karolina. 2015. "On the Significance of Formal Causes in Spinoza's Metaphysics." *Archiv für Geschichte der Philosophie* 97 (1): 196–233.

Hübner, Karolina. 2015. "Spinoza on Negation, Mind-Dependence and the Reality of the Finite." In *The Young Spinoza: A Metaphysician in the Making*, edited by Y. Melamed. Oxford: Oxford University Press, 221–237.

Huenemann, Charles. 2003. "The Necessity of Finite Modes and Geometrical Containment in Spinoza's Metaphysics." In *New Essays on the Rationalists*, edited by R.J. Gennaro and C. Huenemann. Oxford: Oxford University Press, 224–240.

Hulatt, Owen. 2018. "Structural Causality in Spinoza's *Ethics*." *European Journal of Philosophy* 27 (1): 25–39.
James, Susan. 1997. *Passion and Action: The Emotions in Seventeenth-Century Philosophy*. Oxford: Clarendon Press.
James, Susan. 2020. *Spinoza on Learning to Live Together*. Oxford: Oxford University Press.
James, Susan. 2021. "Spinoza on the Constitution of Animal Species." In *A Companion to Spinoza*, edited by Y. Melamed. London: Blackwell, 365–374.
Jarrett, Charles. 1976. "Spinoza's 'Ontological' Argument." *Canadian Journal of Philosophy* 6 (4): 685–692.
Jarrett, Charles. 1977. "Some Remarks on the 'Objective' and 'Subjective' Interpretations of the Attributes." *Inquiry: An Interdisciplinary Journal of Philosophy* 20 (1–4): 447–456.
Jarrett, Charles. 2001. "Spinoza's Distinction between Essence and Existence." *Iyyun: The Jerusalem Philosophical Quarterly* 50: 245–252.
Jonas, Hans. 1965. "Spinoza and the Theory of Organism." *Journal of the History of Philosophy* 3 (1): 43–57.
Klein, Julie. 2002. "'By Eternity I Understand': Eternity According to Spinoza." *Iyyun: The Jerusalem Philosophical Quarterly* 51: 295–324.
Klein, Julie. 2014. "'Something of It Remains': Spinoza and Gersonides on Intellectual Eternity." In *Spinoza and Jewish Philosophy*, edited by S. Nadler. Cambridge (UK): Cambridge University Press, 177–203.
Koistinen, Olli. 1998. "On the Consistency of Spinoza's Modal Theory." *Southern Journal of Philosophy* 36 (1): 61–80.
Koslicki, Kathrin. 2008. *The Structure of Objects*. Oxford: Oxford University Press.
Kulstad, Mark. 1996. "Spinoza's Demonstration of Monism: A New Line of Defense." *History of Philosophy Quarterly* 13 (3): 299–316.
Lærke, Mogens. 2016. "La grande confusione: essenze formali ed essenze attuali in Spinoza." In *Essentia actuosa. Riletture dell'Etica di Spinoza*, edited by A. Sangiacomo and F. Toto. Milan: Mimesis, 75–92.
Lærke, Mogens. 2016. "Spinoza on the Eternity of the Mind." *Dialogue* 55 (2): 265–286.
Lærke, Mogens. 2017. "Aspects of Spinoza's Theory of Essence: Formal Essence, Non-Existence, and Two Types of Actuality." In *The Actual and the Possible: Modality and Metaphysics in Modern Philosophy*, edited by M. Sinclair. Oxford: Oxford University Press, 11–44.
Lawrence, Nolan. 2020. "Descartes' Ontological Argument." In *The Stanford Encyclopedia of Philosophy*, edited by E. Zalta.
Leibniz, Gottfried Wilhelm. 1948. *Textes inédits*. Edited by G. Grua. Paris: Presses Universitaires de France.
Leibniz, Gottfried Wilhelm. 1960–1962. *Die Philosophischen Schriften*. Edited by C. Gebhardt. 7 vols. Hildesheim: Georg Olms Verlag.

Lennon, Thomas. 2005 "The Rationalist Conception of Substance." In *A Companion to Rationalism*, edited by A. Nelson. London: Blackwell, 12–30.

Lermond, Lucia. 1988. *The Form of Man: Human Essence in Spinoza's "Ethics"*. Leiden: Brill.

Lewis, Douglas. 2007. "Spinoza on Having a False Idea." *Metaphysica* 8 (1): 17–27.

Lin, Martin. 2019. *Being and Reason: An Essay on Spinoza's Metaphysics*. Oxford: Oxford University Press.

Lovejoy, Arthur. 1964. *The Great Chain of Being: A Study of the History of an Idea*. Cambridge (MA): Harvard University Press.

Maimonides, Moses. 1963. *The Guide for the Perplexed*. Translated by S. Pines. Chicago: University of Chicago Press.

Marshall, Colin. 2009. "The Mind and the Body as 'One and the Same Thing' in Spinoza." *British Journal for the History of Philosophy* 17 (5): 897–919.

Martin, Cristopher. 2008. "The Framework of Essences in Spinoza's *Ethics*." *British Journal for the History of Philosophy* 16 (3): 489–509.

Matthews Grant, W., and Mark Spencer. 2015. "Activity, Identity, and God: A Tension in Aquinas and His Interpreters." *Studia Neoaristotelica* 12 (2): 5–61.

McTaggart, John Ellis. 1908. "The Unreality of Time." *Mind* 17 (68): 457–474.

Melamed, Yitzhak. 2010. "Acosmism or Weak Individuals? Hegel, Spinoza, and the Reality of the Finite." *Journal of the History of Philosophy* 48 (1): 77–92.

Melamed, Yitzhak. 2012. "*Omnis determinatio est negatio*. Determination, Negation, and Self-Negation in Spinoza, Kant, and Hegel." In *Spinoza and German Idealism*, edited by E. Forster and Y. Melamed. Cambridge (UK): Cambridge University Press, 175–196.

Melamed, Yitzhak. 2013. *Spinoza's Metaphysics: Substance and Thought*. Oxford: Oxford University Press.

Melamed, Yitzhak. 2013. "Spinoza's Deification of Existence." *Oxford Studies in Early Modern Philosophy* 6: 75–104.

Melamed, Yitzhak. 2014. "Spinoza, Tschirnhaus et Leibniz: Qu'est un monde?." In *Spinoza/Leibniz. Rencontres, controverses, réceptions*, edited by R. Andrault and P.F. Moureau. Paris: Presses universitaires de Paris, 85–95.

Melamed, Yitzhak. 2016. "Hegel, Spinoza, and McTaggart on the Reality of Time." *Internationales Jahrbuch des Deutschen Idealismus / International Yearbook of German Idealism* 14: 211–234.

Merçon, Juliana. 2007. "Relationality and Individuality in Spinoza." *Revista Conatus: Filosofia de Spinoza* 1 (2): 51–59.

Merçon, Juliana. 2012. "La filosofía de Spinoza y el pensamiento sistémico contemporáneo." *Revista de Filosofía (Universidad Iberoamericana)* 133: 83–101.

Morfino, Vittorio. 2006. "Spinoza: An Ontology of Relation?." *Graduate Faculty Philosophy Journal* 27 (1): 103–127.

Morrison, John. 2015. "Restricting Spinoza's Causal Axiom." *The Philosophical Quarterly* 65 (258): 40–63.

Naaman-Zauderer, Noa. "Human Action and Virtue in Descartes and Spinoza." *Philosophical Explorations* 21 (1): 25–40.

Nadler, Steven. 2002. *Spinoza's Ethics: An Introduction*. Cambridge (UK): Cambridge University Press.

Nadler, Steven. 2015. "On Spinoza's 'Free Man.'" *Journal of the American Philosophical Association* 1 (1): 103–120.

Nadler, Steven. 2016. "Spinoza on Lying and Suicide." *British Journal for the History of Philosophy* 24 (2): 257–278.

Newlands, Samuel. 2007. "Spinoza's Modal Metaphysics." In *The Stanford Encyclopedia of Philosophy*, edited by E. Zalta.

Newlands, Samuel. 2010. "Another Kind of Spinozistic Monism." *Noûs* 44 (3): 469–502.

Newlands, Samuel. 2011. "Hegel's Idealist Reading of Spinoza." *Philosophy Compass* 6 (2): 100–108.

Newlands, Samuel. 2018. *Reconceiving Spinoza*. Oxford: Oxford University Press.

Nietzsche, Friedrich. *Thus Spoke Zarathustra*. Edited by A. Del Caro and R. Pippin. Cambridge (UK): Cambridge University Press.

Okrent, Nicholas. 1998. "Spinoza on the Essence, Mutability and Power of God." *Philosophy and Theology* 11 (1): 71–84.

Platt, Andrew. 2020. *One True Cause: Causal Powers, Divine Concurrence, and the Seventeenth-Century Revival of Occasionalism*. Oxford: Oxford University Press.

Primus, Kristin. 2019. "Spinoza's 'Infinite Modes' Reconsidered." *Journal of Modern Philosophy* 1 (1): 1–29.

Rice, Lee. 1985. "Spinoza, Bennett, and Teleology." *Southern Journal of Philosophy* 23 (2): 241–253.

Sangiacomo, Andrea. 2013. *L'essenza del Corpo: Spinoza e la scienza delle composizioni*. Hildesheim: Olms Verlag.

Sangiacomo, Andrea. 2015. "Fixing Descartes: Ethical Intellectualism in Spinoza's Early Writings." *Southern Journal of Philosophy* 53 (3): 338–361.

Sangiacomo, Andrea, and Ohad Nachtomy. 2018. "Spinoza's Rethinking of Activity: From the *Short Treatise* to the *Ethics*." *Southern Journal of Philosophy* 56 (1): 101–126.

Santinelli, Cristina. 2018. "*Conatus* e *corpora simplicissima*. Hobbes e Spinoza sulla natura e origine del moto." *Rivista di Filosofia* 109 (3): 383–405.

Santinelli, Cristina. 2020. "'*Assidua meditatio, propositum constantissimum*'. Il concetto di metodo nell'Epistola 37 di Spinoza a Johannes Bouwmeester, tra il *Tractatus de intellectus emendatione* e l'*Ethica*." In *Amice colende. Temi, storia e linguaggio nell'Epistolario spinoziano*, edited by M.L. De Bastiani and S. Manzi-Manzi. Milan: Mimesis, 77–96.

Schaffer, Jonathan. 2018. "Monism." In *The Stanford Encyclopedia of Philosophy*, edited by E. Zalta.

Schaffer, Jonathan. 2009. "On What Grounds What." In *Metaphysics: New Essays on the Foundations of Ontology*, edited by D. Chalmers, D. Manley, and R. Wasserman. Oxford: Oxford University Press, 347–383.

Schliesser, Eric. 2011. "Spinoza's Conatus as an Essence-Preserving, Attribute-Neutral Immanent Cause: Toward a New Interpretation of Attributes and Modes." In *Causation and Early Modern Philosophy*, edited by K. Allen and T. Stoneham. London: Routledge, 65–86.

Schliesser, Eric. 2017. "Spinoza and the Philosophy of Science: Mathematics, Motion, and Being." In *The Oxford Handbook of Spinoza*, edited by M. Della Rocca. Oxford: Oxford University Press, 155–186.

Schmaltz, Tad. 1997. "Spinoza's Mediate Infinite Mode." *Journal of the History of Philosophy* 35 (2): 199–235.

Schmaltz, Tad. 2000. "The Disappearance of Analogy in Descartes, Spinoza, and Regis." *Canadian Journal of Philosophy* 30 (1): 85–113.

Schmaltz, Tad. 2015. "Spinoza on Eternity and Duration: The 1663 Connection." In *The Young Spinoza: A Metaphysician in the Making*, edited by Y. Melamed. Oxford: Oxford University Press, 205–220.

Schmaltz, Tad. 2019. *The Metaphysics of the Material World: Suárez, Descartes, Spinoza*. Oxford: Oxford University Press.

Schneider, Daniel. 2014. "Spinoza's PSR as a Principle of Clear and Distinct Representation." *Pacific Philosophical Quarterly* 95 (1): 109–129.

Scribano, Emanuela. 1994. *L'esistenza di Dio: storia della prova ontologica da Descartes a Kant*. Bari-Roma: Laterza.

Scribano, Emanuela. 2008. *Guida Alla Lettura Dell'Etica Di Spinoza*. Roma-Bari: Laterza.

Scribano, Emanuela. 2008. "Spinoza e la scolastica sull'eternità del mondo: nota su *Cogitata Metaphysica* II, X." *Historia Philosophica* 6: 13–19.

Shein, Noa. 2009. "The False Dichotomy between Objective and Subjective Interpretations of Spinoza's Theory of Attributes." *British Journal for the History of Philosophy* 17 (3): 505–532.

Sijuwade, Joshua. 2022. "Divine Simplicity: The Aspectival Account." *European Journal for the Philosophy of Religion* 14 (1): 143–179.

Smith, Arthur David. 2014. "Spinoza, Gueroult and Substance." *Philosophy and Phenomenological Research* 88 (3): 655–688.

Soyarslan, Sanem. 2016. "The Distinction between Reason and Intuitive Knowledge in Spinoza's *Ethics*." *European Journal of Philosophy* 24 (1): 27–54.

Soyarslan, Sanem. 2019. "Two Ethical Ideals in Spinoza's *Ethics*: The Free Man and The Wise Man." *Journal of the American Philosophical Association* 5 (3): 357–370.

Soyarslan, Sanem. 2021. "Spinoza's Account of Blessedness Explored Through an Aristotelian Lens." *Dialogue: Canadian Philosophical Review/Revue canadienne de philosophie* 60 (3): 499–524.

Stern, Robert. 2006. "'Determination is negation': The Adventures of a Doctrine from Spinoza to Hegel to the British Idealists." *Hegel Bulletin* 37 (1): 29–52.

Strawser, Michael. 2011. "On the Specter of Speciesism in Spinoza." *North American Spinoza Society Monograph* 15: 2–30.

Suárez, Francisco. 2017. *Opera Omnia*. Edited by S. Castellote and M. Renemann. 27 vols. Charlottesville (VA): InteLex.

Toto, Francesco. 2014. *L'individualità dei Corpi: Percorsi nell'*Etica *di Spinoza*. Milan: Mimesis.

Toto, Francesco. 2019. "Convenienza e discrepanza. Parti e tutto nella *Lettera 32* di Baruch Spinoza." In *Morfologia del rapporto parti/tutto. Totalità e complessità nelle filosofie dell'età moderna*, edited by G. D'Anna, E. Massimilla, F. Piro, M. Sanna, and F. Toto. Milan: Mimesis, 163–190.

Trisokkas, Ioannis. 2017. "The Two-Sense Reading of Spinoza's Definition of Attribute." *British Journal for the History of Philosophy* 25 (6): 1093–1115.

Viljanen, Valtteri. 2008. "Spinoza's Essentialist Model of Causation." *Inquiry: An Interdisciplinary Journal of Philosophy* 51 (4): 412–437.

Viljanen, Valtteri. 2011. *Spinoza's Geometry of Power*. Cambridge (UK): Cambridge University Press.

Viljanen, Valtteri. 2020. "The Young Spinoza on Scepticism, Truth, and Method." *Canadian Journal of Philosophy* 50 (1): 130–142.

Wilson, Margaret. 1999. "Spinoza's Causal Axiom." In *Ideas and Mechanism: Essays on Early Modern Philosophy*. Princeton (NJ): Princeton University Press, 141–165.

Winkler, Sean. 2016. "The Conatus of the Body in Spinoza's Physics." *Society and Politics* 10 (2): 95–114.

Wolfson, Harry Austryn. 1934. *The Philosophy of Spinoza: Unfolding the Latent Processes of His Reasoning*. 2 vols. Cambridge (MA): Harvard University Press.

Yovel, Yirmiyahu. 1999. "The Third Kind of Knowledge as Alternative Salvation." In *Spinoza. Issues and directions: The Proceedings of the Chicago Spinoza Conference*, edited by P.F. Moreau and E. Curley. Leiden: Brill, 157–175.

Zylstra, Stephen. 2020. "Spinoza on Action and Immanent Causation." *Archiv für Geschichte der Philosophie* 102 (1): 29–55.

Index of Terms

For the benefit of digital users, indexed terms that span two pages (e.g., 52–53) may, on occasion, appear on only one of those pages.
Figures are indicated by an italic f following the page number.

acosmism, 163–64
action, 15, 23, 31–32, 56–58, 87–88, 189
affect, 96–97, 110–11, 189, 191–92, 204–5, 206–7
affection, 9, 10–11, 24, 35–36, 38, 39, 41, 67–68, 96–97, 142, 153–54
agreement/disagreement, 159, 160nn.26–30, 161–62, 163–67, 166n.39, 168, 169–71, 169n.47, 173, 175–76, 177–78
attribute of thought, 83, 106, 146–47

Bayle, Pierre, 193, 193n.11, 193n.13, 195–96
beatitude, 186–87, 214

Causa sui, 13, 19, 27–28, 40–46, 47, 50–51, 62–63
causality, 7–8, 12–13, 18, 26, 27–28, 39–40, 54–56, 92, 93, 97, 101–3, 105–6, 108, 109, 124, 137, 144, 149–51, 152, 161–62n.30, 162–63, 164, 185–87, 188–90, 196, 197, 200, 201–2, 205–7, 219
conatus, 32n.23, 107n.91, 142n.72, 166n.39, 176n.58, 198, 198n.21, 199–200, 201–2, 203–6
conception, 14, 15, 22–23, 24–25, 26, 29, 30, 31–32, 35–36, 36n.29, 37, 37n.30, 38–40, 38n.31, 47, 49n.45, 54–56, 55n.52, 77, 79n.32, 99, 101, 101n.76, 102–3, 106–7, 115, 120n.23, 123n.32, 128, 137, 149–50, 162n.32, 163n.33, 189–90, 192, 193, 195–96, 205–6, 214, 217, 220

distinction, aspectual, 13, 27, 45–46, 81–82, 81n.41, 83, 84–86, 86n.49, 89, 92, 93, 97, 99–100, 102–3, 104, 104n.81, 105–6, 107, 108, 109, 121, 127–29, 133, 136–37, 145–46, 160n.26, 162n.32, 165, 184, 194–97, 218

eternity, 13, 121, 127–29, 133, 146–47, 218
existence, 27–28, 45–46, 47, 58, 62–63, 89, 128–29, 146–47, 188–89, 206–7
explanation, 74, 99–100, 105–6, 108
expression, 13, 74, 85–86, 92, 97, 99–100, 103, 104–6, 108, 109, 131, 146–47, 149–50

facies totius Universi, 94–96, 179–80
finitude, 44, 89–90, 96, 98, 183–84
first kind of cognition, 155
freedom, 55–56, 57–58, 57n.59, 87–88, 208, 212–13, 215–16

god, 3, 19, 45–46, 56–57, 59, 88–89, 97, 99–100

234 INDEX OF TERMS

Hegel, Georg Wilhelm Friedrich, 3–4, 62–63, 89–90, 115n.6, 163–64

ideas, adequate, 78, 154–55
ideas, inadequate, 153, 153nn.7–8
immanence, 12–13, 27–28, 106–7, 188–89, 201–2
individual, 14–15, 27–28, 85–86, 99, 103, 104–6, 128–29, 142, 143, 144, 189–90, 193–94, 204
infinity, 91–92, 94–96
inherence, 1, 9, 11, 13, 18, 23–24, 25, 26–28, 29, 30, 31–32, 32n.23, 37, 38n.31, 39, 40, 41, 52–53, 54–56, 58–59, 93–94, 97n.70, 149–50, 185–87, 188–90, 196, 198–200, 201–2, 206–7
isomorphism, 102–3

Leibniz, Gottfried Wilhelm, 23–24
Leibniz's law, 2, 3–4, 10–11, 23–24, 24nn.10–11, 81–82, 81n.39, 122, 161–62n.30
limitation, 13, 18, 22–23, 31–32, 39–40, 45–46, 58–59, 86, 94–96, 185–87, 196, 198–200, 206–7

Malebranche, Nicolas, 8–9, 56–57
man, free, 56–57, 209–13
man, wise, 209, 214
mechanism, 45n.40, 159, 161–62n.30, 173–74
mereology, 86, 143, 168–69, 174n.55, 177–78
modes, infinite, 19, 24, 54–55, 131, 141
modes, white, 104–7, 107n.90, 109
modes of extension, 143, 146–47, 206–7

modes of thought, 99–100, 106, 114, 189, 203–4
monism, 46–53, 54, 85–86, 191
motion and rest, 140–41, 143, 144, 204

natura naturans, 58–59, 64, 188–89, 193–94, 196, 218–19
natura naturata, 12–13, 64, 193–94, 218–19
naturare, 53–55, 58–59, 188–89
necessity, 4, 56–57, 57n.59, 59

objectivism, 76–77
Oldenburg, Henry, 156–57, 159n.24, 161–62, 172

panentheism, 26–33
pantheism, 27–28
parthood, 65n.5, 174n.55
passion, 13n.17, 189–90, 191, 193–94, 196, 197, 204–6, 215
plenitude, 8–9
properties, carry-over, 85–87, 91
properties, trans-attributal, 52–53

quatenus, 79–92, 99–100, 106, 160, 160n.26, 192, 195, 218

reductionism, 7–8, 13, 32–33, 37, 39–40, 50, 189–90, 191

second kind of knowledge, 155
striving, 197, 198–200
structural pluralism, 33–40, 45–46, 49–50
structure, 7–8, 10–13, 14, 15, 17–18, 19–20, 22–23, 23n.9, 25–26, 28–29, 28n.18, 30, 31–34, 35–36, 36n.29, 37, 39–40, 41, 45–55, 58–59, 61–63, 64, 65f, 65n.5, 104–5, 109, 143, 189–90, 196, 199–200, 201–2

subjectivism, 7–8, 43, 54, 72–73, 74–75, 78

teleology, 161–62n.30, 166n.39, 180–81

third kind of knowledge, 15, 97–98, 154n.11, 154n.13, 155, 156, 157, 161n.28, 167, 168–69, 169n.47, 170, 215, 216n.53, 217, 218, 219–20

time, 82, 113–14

totality, 104n.81, 168–69, 209–10

whole, 175–78, 179–80, 182–83

Index of References

For the benefit of digital users, indexed terms that span two pages (e.g., 52–53) may, on occasion, appear on only one of those pages.

E1d1, 19, 21, 22, 23–24, 27–28, 42–43, 50–51, 117n.14
E1d2, 22–23, 23n.8, 31–32, 35, 39, 43, 43n.38, 181–82, 183–84, 183n.68, 199–200
E1d3, 23–24, 24n.11, 25–26, 29, 36n.28, 37n.30, 38, 38n.31, 39–40, 41, 44–45, 47, 52–53, 96–97, 136–37
E1d4, 25–26, 70–71, 74n.19, 76, 78
E1d5, 24, 29, 36n.28, 38, 39, 41, 52–53, 54–55, 96–97, 136–37
E1d6, 34–35, 45–46, 47, 62, 63–64, 66n.6, 70–71
E1d7, 56, 57–58
E1a1, 38, 39, 41, 96–97
E1a4, 25–26, 38, 38n.32, 39, 101n.75
E1a5, 101–2
E1a6, 77, 135
E1p1d, 10–11
E1p2, 38, 38n.31, 39
E1p3, 38, 39, 90–91, 101–2
E1p3d, 194–95
E1p4, 35–36, 35n.27
E1p4d, 78
E1p5, 35, 35n.26, 38, 39, 43, 43n.38, 48
E1p6, 37, 38, 39, 41, 47
E1p6d, 39n.33, 39n.34, 47, 50–51
E1p6c, 37, 38–39, 41, 42, 42n.36
E1p7, 42–43, 43n.38, 44
E1p7d, 43n.38
E1p8, 43, 44, 66–67, 71
E1p8S1, 44, 66–67, 71

E1p8S2, 44–45
E1p9, 45, 106n.88
E1p10, 101n.75
E1p10s, 30, 74–75, 74n.19
E1p11, 42–43, 45–46, 48, 49
E1p12, 74–75, 81n.40, 134n.55
E1p13, 74–75, 81n.40, 85–86, 94, 172–73
E1p14, 34–35, 47, 51
E1p15, 10–11, 52–53, 54–55
E1p15s, 87–88
E1p16, 59n.63, 95n.67
E1p16c1, 57n.55, 194–95
E1p17, 87
E1p17s, 122
E1p17c2, 54–55, 88n.54, 88n.55, 88n.56, 118n.16
E1p20, 129n.47
E1p22, 91, 96–97
E1p23, 91–92
E1p24, 96, 97–98
E1p25, 54–55, 96
E1p28, 96, 141–42
E1p29s, 31–32, 55, 57–58, 77
E1p30, 10–11
E1p34, 87–88, 105n.85
E1p36, 178–79, 192–93
E1app, 194n.15
E2a1, 142, 143
E2a2, 143
E2l1, 140–41, 140n.68
E2l2, 140n.68
E2l3, 140–42
E2l3d, 141

238 INDEX OF REFERENCES

E2l3c, 140n.68
E2l4, 143–44
E2l7, 141n.69, 144
E2PhysDigD, 173
E2PhysDigl4, 173–74
E2PhysDigl4d, 174n.53
E2PhysDigA2, 95n.68, 116n.10
E2PhyDigl7s, 175n.56, 175n.57, 176–77
E2P5, 71n.16
E2P6, 74n.19, 100–2, 101n.75
E2P7, 102–3, 102n.78, 139–40, 139n.67, 192, 195, 203–4, 203n.31, 211–12, 218
E2P7s, 71n.16, 74–75, 103n.79, 104, 104n.80, 105n.84, 106n.88, 134, 139n.67, 189
E2P9, 192–93
E2P11, 71n.16
E2P11c, 192–93
E2P14, 176–77, 203n.31
E2P21s, 162n.32
E2P23, 145n.80
E2P24d, 161n.28
E2P40, 211
E2P40s2, 153n.8
E2P41, 77, 135, 154n.11
E2P43, 71n.16, 211
E2P44, 135
E2P44d, 77
E2P44C1s, 115–16
E2P44C2, 126, 135
E2P44C2d, 71n.16
E2P45, 126
E2P45s, 126
E2P49s, 76n.26
E3Pref, 186n.2, 191n.7
E3P1, 192
E3d1, 187–88, 192–93, 198–99, 217
E3d2, 188–89, 190–91, 198–99, 200, 202, 211
E3P2d, 71n.16
E3P3, 195–96, 211–12

E3P4, 158–59, 158n.22, 170–71, 180n.63, 199–200, 205–6
E3P4d, 199–200
E3P5, 158–59, 170–71, 205–6
E3P5d, 158n.22
E3P6, 119–20, 197, 198–99, 198n.21
E3P7, 119–20, 197, 198
E3P8, 200n.24
E3P9s, 204
E3P11, 203–4
E3P11d, 203n.31
E3P11s, 205n.34
E3P13s, 205n.35
E318s2, 206n.37
E3P25, 207n.38
E3P26s, 207n.39
E3P56d, 71n.16
E3DefAf25, 211
E3DefAf6, 215
E4P1, 158–59
E4P2, 31–32, 31n.22, 32n.23
E4P4, 209–10, 213
E4P4d, 71n.16, 202
E4P28, 216n.52
E4P52, 211–12
E4P52d, 211
E4P66s, 209–10, 210n.44
E5P7d, 219n.56
E5P23, 132n.51, 135
E5P23s, 126
E5P24, 156, 216n.53
E5P25, 216n.53
E5P29, 133, 135, 215
E5P29d, 126, 135n.57
E5P29s, 126, 129, 133n.53
E5P31, 217
E5P31s, 76n.26
E5P32, 215
E5P32c, 214–15
E5P38, 217
E5P40, 219
E5P40c, 219n.56
E5P42s, 155n.15, 157, 217n.55